Know Your SHIPS

1999

Guide to Boats & Boatwatching on the Great Lakes & St. Lawrence Seaway

Since 1959 ~ 40 Years Afloat

© 1999 - Updated Annually

ISBN: 1-891849-01-8

Marine Publishing Co.

Box 68, Sault Ste. Marie, MI 49783

Editor & Publisher: Roger LeLievre

Listings Researchers: Philip A. Clayton, John Vournakis
Contributing Researchers: Jody Aho, Rod Burdick, Angela S. Clayton and Neil Schultheiss

Founder: Tom Manse, 1915-1994

www.knowyourships.com

On the front cover: **Seaway Queen loads grain at a Goderich, ON, elevator.** *(Rod Burdick)*

On the back cover: **Icebreaker Mackinaw leaves Grand Haven.** *(Don Geske)*

CARGO

Ships of the Inland Seas .... Inside Front Cover
Welcome Aboard 3
Vessel of the Year: **Seaway Queen** 4
Marine Milestones: The Seaway Years 6
Passages 22
Vessel Spotlight: **Canadian Transfer** 28
Great Lakes Glossary 30
Vessel Index 31
Fleet & Vessel Listings 47
Colors of the Great Lakes & Seaway
    Smokestacks 61-63
Colors of Major International Seaway
    Fleets 64-65
House Flags of Great Lakes & Seaway
    Fleets 66
Flags of Nations in the Marine Trade 67-69
Vessel Spotlight: **Alpena** 71
Vessel Spotlight: **Kaye E. Barker** 82
Vessel Spotlight: **Algosoo** 98
International Fleet Listings 105
Great Lakes & Seaway Map 126
Great Lakes Loading / Unloading Ports 127
Meanings of Boat Whistles 128
The St. Lawrence Seaway 129
The Welland Canal 130
The Soo Locks 132
Adrift on the Internet 135
Following the Fleet 135
Vessel Museums 137
Marine Museums 140

*The information contained herein was obtained from the United States
Coast Pilot (Vol. 6), the St. Lawrence Seaway Authority, the Lake Carriers
Association, Upper Lakes Group Inc., the Institute for Great Lakes
Research, Jane's Merchant Ships, the American Merchant Seaman's
Manual, the U.S. Army Corps of Engineers, the Great Lakes Log
and publications of the Great Lakes Maritime Institute, the Toronto Marine
Historical Society and the Marine Historical Society of Detroit.*

***Tug Missouri assists the LT Argosy at the Soo Locks 28 June 1998.
The Oglebay Norton is at left.*** *(Roger LeLievre)*

WELCOME ABOARD

In 1959, the St. Lawrence Seaway opened, and **"Know Your Ships"** published its first edition. Plenty has changed in those 40 years - from the number of vessels in service (more than 600 in 1959 to approximately 164 in 1999) to the size and style of the ships that pass our shores. To begin this 40th-anniversary book, marine historian Jody Aho takes a look at important events on the shipping scene during the past four decades. Appropriately, the Canadian bulk carrier **Seaway Queen** is 1999's Vessel of the Year.

You may notice this year's "Know Your Ships" is a bit heftier. We've added 16 pages and expanded our fleet coverage even further. Listings Editor Philip A. Clayton spent many hours tabulating information about international vessels - the result of his work begins on Page 105. The Vessel Spotlight feature, begun last year, also continues, with profiles of more familiar lakers. As usual, marine photographers from around the Great Lakes and Seaway system continue to superbly document the busy shipping scene from Montreal to Duluth.

A hearty "Three Long and Two Short" to all our readers who have helped us reach this maritime milestone.

- The 'Know Your Ships' staff

SEAWAY QUEEN

Vessel of the Year

SEAWAY QUEEN	
Length	713'03"
Beam	72'
Depth	37'
Built	1959
Tonnage	24,300

When the St. Lawrence Seaway opened in 1959, a new era began on the Great Lakes. To mark that event, Canada's Upper Lakes Shipping Ltd. took delivery of the appropriately-named steamer **Seaway Queen** in June 1959, the same month the St. Lawrence Seaway officially opened. Her christening ceremonies proved a memorable occasion, highlighted by a grand parade of ships led by the royal yacht, **H.M.S. Britannia**, with Queen Elizabeth and Prince Philip on board. Built at Port Weller Drydocks, the Seaway Queen cost more than $7 million. At 713.03 feet in length, she was 36 feet longer than her near sister, **Frank A. Sherman**, built the year before.

The Seaway Queen has a capacity of 24,300 tons of bulk cargo and can also move more than 828,000 bushels of wheat. Powered by a Inglis turbine steam engine with 7,500 horsepower, she runs at 15.5 knots fully loaded, with a daily fuel consumption of about 58 tons of Bunker "C" fuel oil. She is the oldest Canadian straight decker on the lakes, and the third oldest (only the self-unloaders **Cuyahoga**, built in 1943, and **James Norris**, of 1952, have more seniority) laker in Canadian lake service.

The Seaway Queen has spent much of her career in the grain run from the head of the lakes to the Seaway, although she has also brought cargos of ore and coal to the Dofasco Steel Mill in Hamilton, ON. She delivered the 100 millionth ton of iron ore to Dofasco 20 December 1988, a milestone achieved after a six-year lay-up during the 1980s recession.

In recent years, due to high fuel consumption and small size, many of her sister vessels, including the Frank A. Sherman, have gone to the scrapyard or been converted to self-unloaders, but the Seaway Queen carries on, used now as a late-season grain boat. In 1997, Seaway Queen received a major

refit at Port Weller Drydocks, which should guarantee her operation well into the next century. The selection of Seaway Queen as Vessel of the Year honors not only the anniversary of that waterway but salutes a class of handsome vessels whose numbers are rapidly disappearing from the Inland Seas.

Seaway Queen ties at Port Colborne for fuel.

A grain-laden Seaway Queen in the Rock Cut, October, 1995. (Bob Campbell)

MARINE MILESTONES

Seaway
The Years

In honor of the 40th anniversary of the opening of the St. Lawrence Seaway and the 40th edition of this book, marine historian Jody Aho offers this look back at the past four decades in Great Lakes history.

1959

The bulk freighter **Seaway Queen** enters service for Upper Lakes Shipping Ltd. 20 June. The Canadian vessel honors both the new St. Lawrence Seaway, which opens 26 June, and the fact that this vessel is the largest Canadian vessel on the Great Lakes. She is literally a queen of the Seaway.

1960

A long-time favorite of boatwatchers, **Edward L. Ryerson**, begins service on 4 August for Inland Steel.

Great Lakes Engineering Works ceases operations with the completion of **Arthur B. Homer**. This sistership to the **Edmund Fitzgerald** sails on 20 April.

1961

Many new vessels begin Great Lakes service from unlikely sources. Several World War II T-2 and T-3 tankers are converted into lakers, ▶

With the opening of the St. Lawrence Seaway in 1959, scores of small canallers such as the Keystate, shown in the Eisenhower Lock, were rendered immediately obsolete.

(St. Lawrence Seaway Authority)

Stewart J. Cort, the Great Lakes' first 1,000-footer. Each of the 13 such vessels built replaced three of the standard-sized 600-footers that had been the mainstay of the lakes trade since the turn of the century. (Roger LeLievre)

including the **Leon Falk Jr., Paul H. Carnahan, Pioneer Challenger** and **Walter A. Sterling**. On the Canadian side, the **Hilda Marjanne** and **Northern Venture** are similar converts.

The 25,000 ton mark is broken for the first time, when the Canadian bulk freighter **Red Wing** sets a cargo record of 25,004 tons of iron ore.

1962

The saltie **Montrose** sinks on 30 July after a collision in the Detroit River.

1963

An idea ahead of its time transforms the Wilson Marine Transit Company bulk freighter **Horace S. Wilkinson** to a barge. Renamed **Wiltranco**, the vessel is shortened 15 feet and has a notch cut in its stern for a tug. The experiment is not considered a success.

Three members of Canada Steamship Lines' "Bay" class of straight-deckers, the **Baie St. Paul**, the **Black Bay**, and the **Murray Bay**, enter service. They become favorites for many boatwatchers. ▶

Leon Falk Jr., one of several former ocean tankers adapted for Great Lakes service in the early 1960s. (Tom Manse)

The 730-foot Leecliffe Hall sank in 1964 after a collision. (Tom Manse)

Cason J. Callaway takes part in winter navigation experiments at the Soo Locks. She was one of the first of the '50's-built bulkers lengthened in the '70s and converted to self-unloaders in the '80s. (Tom Manse)

1964

The three-year-old Canadian bulk freighter **Leecliffe Hall** sinks on 5 September after a collision with the Greek ocean vessel **Apollonia**. This is the first loss of a maximum-sized Seaway bulk carrier.

Algoma Central Railway's first new bulk freighter of the Seaway era is built. **Sir Denys Lowson** is comparatively small at 605 feet, but she marks the beginning of a nearly 20-year program of new construction for the fleet. The Lowson sits idle at Thunder Bay in 1999 as the **Vandoc**.

1965

The first new American vessel in four years, the cement carrier **J.A.W. Iglehart**, sails on 26 May. Following the trend of the American fleets in the 1960s, she is another converted ocean tanker.

The limestone carrier **Cedarville** sinks on 7 May following a collision with the ocean vessel **Topdalsfjord** not far from the Mackinac Bridge. Ten of her crew are lost.

1966

Edmund Fitzgerald becomes the first Great Lakes vessel to surpass the 26,000 ton mark for an iron ore cargo.

The ocean vessel **Nordmeer** is wrecked not far from Thunder Bay Island in Lake Huron during an early November storm. The vessel is stranded on the rocks and is later abandoned, but a small portion of the hulk remains visible to this day. On 29 November, the **Daniel J. Morrell** - one of the Great Lakes' first 600-footers - sinks in a storm on Lake Huron. All but one of the Morrell's 29-man crew is lost.

1967

This year marks the end of two eras. Regular passenger service disappears from the lakes as the historic **South American** is retired in October. Also, the era of steam propulsion in new construction ends when the **Feux-Follets** (now **Canadian Leader**) begins service on 12 October. She is the last new laker built with a steam engine.

1968

The new Poe Lock is opened by the **Philip R. Clarke**, although it is not formally dedicated until June 1969.

1969

Edmund Fitzgerald sets her final Great Lakes cargo record with a load of 27,402 tons loaded at Silver Bay on 10 August.

The last new straight decker built with a pilothouse forward, the **Ottercliffe Hall** (now **Canadian Trader**), is built. There are other vessels built in later years with the pilothouse forward, but they are self-unloaders. Coincidentally, 1969 marks the 100th anniversary of this traditional laker design first used in the **R. J. Hackett**.

Reiss Steamship Company is absorbed by the **American Steamship Company**, ending the presence of a historic Great Lakes fleet. ▶

The overnight passenger steamer South American (top) sailed her last in 1967.

The St. Lawrence Seaway allowed oceangoing vessels access to ports deep in the U.S. heartland (left).

(Marine Publishing Co. Collection)

1970

The last Great Lakes iron ore record set by a vessel other than a 1,000-footer is set by the **Arthur B. Homer**.

One of the oldest and smallest Canadian straight-deck, dry bulk vessels, the **Ontadoc**, is retired at the end of the year. This 67-year-old laker was the last of many similar-sized 436-foot bulk freighters that entered service just after the turn of the century.

1971

Some familiar names disappear from the Great Lakes at the end of the year. The **Wilson Marine Transit Company** and the **Republic Steel Corporation** are absorbed by other fleets.

Roger Blough is nearly destroyed by an explosion and fire at the American Shipbuilding Company yard in Lorain, OH on 24 June. The incident delays the vessel's entry into service until the following June.

1972

Stewart J. Cort sails as the Great Lakes' first 1,000-footer on 1 May. Her maiden cargo of 49,343 tons surpasses the previous record by more than 20,000 tons.

A trend of major reconstruction to keep smaller vessels competitive begins with the lengthening of the **Charles M. Beeghly** from 710 feet to 806 feet. Many other American vessels undergo similar modification throughout the decade.

1973

The last two new vessels built for the Kinsman Marine Transit Company, **William R. Roesch** and the **Paul Thayer**, enter service.

Presque Isle begins her career on 16 December as the lakes' second 1,000-footer. This unique, integrated tug-barge unit is predicted to become the trend in shipbuilding, although no other rigidly connected units are constructed. It is another idea somewhat ahead of its time, given the proliferation of tug-barge conversions in the 1990s.

1974

The first AAA class vessels undergo lengthening. By the end of the year the **Philip R. Clarke**, **Cason J. Callaway** and **Armco** have new 120-foot midsections added.

Year-round navigation attempts begin over the winter of 1974-75. U.S. Steel is the primary fleet participating in the experiment.

The last new vessel with a pilothouse forward, **Algosoo**, enters service on 4 December.

1975

The bulk carrier **Edmund Fitzgerald** goes down in eastern Lake Superior on 10 November with her entire crew of 29.

1976

The **Superior Midwest Energy Terminal** opens in June. Shipments of ▶

Buckeye, typical of many older vessels converted to self-unloaders in the early 1980s, passes Algocape at the Soo Locks 27 May 1998. (Roger LeLievre)

low-sulfur coal on the Great Lakes have increased each year since, and the cargo now accounts for approximately 40 percent of the total annual cargo shipped through Duluth-Superior.

The new 1,000-footer **James R. Barker** becomes the largest vessel on the Great Lakes.

Vessels of U.S. Steel's Great Lakes Fleet and other companies are painted in Bicentennial colors for the year.

1977

The year is an active one in U.S. and Canadian shipyards. **Belle River** (now **Walter J. McCarthy Jr.**) and **Mesabi Miner** enter service on the U.S. side, while the **Algolake**, **Louis R. Desmarais** and **Jean Parisien** are christened on the Canadian side. Also, the **Lake Nipigon**, **Cartiercliffe Hall** and **Montcliffe Hall** are converted for Great Lakes use.

The "140" class of Coast Guard harbor tug makes its presence felt on the Great Lakes when the **Katmai Bay** arrives from the Tacoma Boat Building Company in Tacoma, WA.

1979

Edwin H. Gott sails on her maiden voyage on 16 February, marking the earliest (or latest) maiden voyage for any laker. The Gott is also the most powerful vessel on the Great Lakes, with 19,500 horsepower.

Cartiercliffe Hall is severely damaged by fire on 5 June while downbound on Lake Superior. Six crewmembers die in the blaze.

The Cleveland-Cliffs bulk freighter **Frontenac** is wrecked at Silver Bay 22 November after running aground attempting to enter the harbor in a storm. She is later refloated, but is eventually determined to be a total loss and sent to the scrapyard.

The year is the busiest year on record for the Great Lakes, with more than 215 million tons of cargo handled.

1980

The Great Lakes shipping industry enters a recession, and many vessels sail their last. Cleveland-Cliffs is especially hard hit after losing an important Republic Steel contract, and U.S. Steel sends several vessels into final lay-up, including **John Hulst** and **Ralph H. Watson**.

1981

William J. DeLancey (now **Paul R. Tregurtha**) sails on 10 May, becoming the largest vessel on the Great Lakes. (As of April 1999, this vessel has held that honor longer than any other in Great Lakes history.)

The last new U.S. Great Lakes vessel, other than tug/barge combinations or conversions, enters service on 30 May. The **Columbia Star** not only holds this honor, but she is also the final new 1,000-footer built.

1982

Shipments of iron ore on the Great Lakes reach their lowest levels since the Great Depression. Many Great Lakes fleets have vessels laid up, including several of the 1,000-footers.　　　　　▶

Paterson, the last major vessel built on the lakes, holds several cargo records. (Terry W.F. Heyns)

Champlain, Ashland and Thomas Wilson ... all obsolete lakers withdrawn from service during the 1980s recession. *(Jim Hoffman)*

1983

Despite the downturn in iron ore shipping, the Duluth, Missabe and Iron Range Railway converts part of ore dock #6 in West Duluth into a new shiploader to accommodate the 1,000-footers. **Columbia Star** is one of the regular visitors to that dock that year.

1984

The **Cleveland-Cliffs Steamship Company** ceases operations in October. Its final two operating vessels, **Walter A. Sterling** and **Edward B. Greene**, are sold to the Ford Motor Company. With the acquisition of the Cleveland-Cliffs vessels, **Ford Motor Company** retires two favorites of many boatwatchers, primarily because they are not self-unloaders. Hence, **William Clay Ford** (i) and **Benson Ford** (ii) sail their last.

1985

The last new Canadian bulk freight vessel built from the keel up, the **Paterson**, enters service on 28 June. She is also the last new vessel built at Collingwood Shipyards.

1986

The record for the largest cargo in a single trip aboard a Great Lakes vessel is set in November when the **Lewis Wilson Foy** (now **Oglebay Norton**) carries a cargo of 72,351 gross tons of taconite pellets from Escanaba to Burns Harbor.

1987

The Great Lakes shipping industry comes out of its downturn. **Courtney Burton** and **Roger Blough** are among the vessels that had been in long-term lay-up that return to service.

▶

The 1,000-foot Oglebay Norton at Oak Ridge Point on the St. Mary's River 4 October 1998. (Phillip A. Clayton)

U.S. Steel sends several more of its straight-deck bulk freighters to scrap, including **Ralph H. Watson** and **Enders M. Voorhees**.

The **Hall Corporation of Canada** (Halco) ends operation after the 1987 season. The vessels are split up among several Canadian fleets.

1988

Kinsman Lines purchases the largest bulk freighter it has ever owned, the **Ernest R. Breech**, from Ford Motor Company. She is renamed **Kinsman Independent**. Meanwhile, **Ford Motor Co.** ceases its fleet operations at the end of the year. The remaining vessels are sold early in 1989 to an Interlake Steamship subsidiary called **Lakes Shipping Company**.

1989

A new expedition to the wreckage of the **Edmund Fitzgerald** takes some clearer video and finds the open port side pilothouse door, but still does not provide an answer as to the cause of the vessel's loss.

The Coast Guard buoy tender **Mesquite** is wrecked off the Keweenaw Peninsula in Lake Superior on 5 December. Her hull is later sunk for use by recreational divers.

1990

The USS Great Lakes Fleet receives new colors. The majority of the hull is painted red, and black and gray stripes are added at the bow. The circular U.S. Steel logo is removed from the stack. This marks the first time that the former Bradley Fleet vessels are painted red.

The tanker **Jupiter** explodes in Bay City, MI, on 16 September as it is unloading gasoline. All but one of the crewmembers survive, although the vessel burns for the next two days and is a complete loss.

Some familiar vessels receive new names during 1990. **Belle River** and the **William J. DeLancey** are renamed **Walter J. McCarthy Jr.** and **Paul R. Tregurtha**, respectively, while the **T.R. McLagan** makes her debut in the sharp color scheme of P. & H. Shipping as **Oakglen**.

The tug-barge combination experiment is re-introduced to the Great Lakes when the **Joseph H. Thompson** is converted to a self-unloading barge. A tug named **Joseph H. Thompson Jr.** is built to push the barge. Contrary to other experiments from years past, the unit proves successful, and other vessels have similar conversions.

1991

Alpena makes its maiden voyage in June after conversion from the ore carrier **Leon Fraser** to a self-unloading cement carrier.

Bethlehem Steel Corporation cuts its Great Lakes fleet in half by selling the **Lewis Wilson Foy** and the **Sparrows Point** to the Oglebay Norton Company. The vessels are re-christened **Oglebay Norton** and **Buckeye**.

1992

Carferry service resumes on Lake Michigan after the **Badger** is sold to new owners, the Lake Michigan Carferry Co.

▶

Ford Motor Co.'s Benson Ford (i) last sailed in 1981, and was scrapped in 1986. (Tom Manse)

1993

The **Misener** fleet folds at the end of the year, with its vessels split up between Algoma Central and ULS Corporation. Canada Steamship Lines also ends operation of its straight-deckers, and they are also sold to the same two Canadian fleets.

The future of straight-deckers does not appear bright on the American side of the Lakes, as the **J. L. Mauthe** sails for the last time as a straight-decker and the last under her own power.

1994

The **Edward L. Ryerson** is laid up in late January after sailing steadily since 1988. This vessel faces an uncertain future and lengthy lay-up for the second time in 10 years, but she re-enters service in 1997.

After the shuffling of Canadian straight-deckers, many vessels sail their last. One example is the **Simcoe**, which is renamed **Algostream**, and operates under that name for only one season.

S. T. Crapo is converted to oil-fired boilers after the 1994 season, leaving the carferry **Badger** as the only remaining coal-fired vessel on the lakes.

1995

Mail boat service turns 100 years old in 1995. The **J. W. Westcott II** serves vessels in the Detroit River with mail, newspapers and other items.

J. Burton Ayers returns to active duty after being sold to Black Creek Shipping Company. She is renamed **Cuyahoga**.

1996

A new tug-barge combination, the **Jacklyn M.** / **Integrity**, enters service for the LaFarge Corporation

1997

Overnight passenger service returns with the German-owned **c. Columbus**. The vessel's arrival is celebrated at its stops around the Great Lakes.

J. L. Mauthe is converted to a self-unloading tug-barge combination in Sturgeon Bay. The vessel re-enters service early in 1998 under a name from Interlake Steamship Company's past - **Pathfinder**.

1998

Amid much speculation about potential activity, the **E.M. Ford** celebrates her 100th year on the Great Lakes. Unfortunately, the vessel does not see activity during this milestone year.

The **Imperial Oil Company** sells its remaining tankers to Algoma Central Marine, marking this company's first venture into the tanker business.

Canadian Transfer enters service in August, built by combining the forward end of the **Hamilton Transfer** and the stern of the **Canadian Explorer**.

- Jody Aho

(Jody Aho, a resident of Duluth and a former Great Lakes sailor, is author of the book "William A. Irvin: Queen of the Silver Stackers.")

Canadian Transfer ties at Saginaw 5 September 1998. (Roger LeLievre)

PASSAGES

Changes in the shipping scene since our last edition

Fleets & Vessels

Lake vessels braved an unusually intense fall storm 10-13 November, one compared by forecasters to the gale that sank the **Edmund Fitzgerald** exactly 23 years earlier. Most vessels sought shelter before the blow began; wind gusts up to 92 mph were reported, and seas ran as high as 15-20 feet in some areas.

Following the acquisition in 1998 of Inland Steel Co. by Netherlands-based Ispat International, Ispat sold its three Inland Steel lakers to the newly-created Central Marine Logistics, Inc. The move was made in order to comply with the Jones Act, which mandates that cargo carried between U.S. ports be carried in U.S.-flag, U.S.-built and U.S.-crewed vessels. The **Wilfred Sykes** and **Joseph L. Block** continue to carry taconite to Indiana Harbor, much as they have in the past, however the classic straight-decker **Edward L. Ryerson** will most likely remain laid-up in 1999. A new stack marking was unveiled during spring fit-out. Meanwhile, the **Adam E. Cornelius**, chartered to Inland since 1994, returns to American Steamship colors this season, and that fleet's veteran **John J. Boland** will not fit out in 1999.

In March 1998, the Texas-based cement manufacturer Southdown Inc. acquired Medusa Corp., and with it Medusa's two-boat fleet, the 1906-vintage steamer **Medusa Challenger** and barge **Medusa Conquest**.

Stinson shows her new colors.

The 1,000-footer **George A. Stinson**, in year two of a charter by the American Steamship Co., received ASC colors in early June. The Stinson is busy hauling taconite for National Steel Co., and so bears a large red "N" painted on her bow.

In what must be an advertising first, Canada Steamship Lines' motor vessel **Atlantic Erie** was repainted in late 1998 with her owners' address on the World Wide Web, www.csl.ca, painted on both sides. The floating billboard measures 125 feet long by 7-feet high.

At the start of the 1998 shipping season, Algoma Central Marine entered the tanker trade on the Great Lakes by forming **Algoma Tankers Ltd.** and assuming ownership of Imperial Oil Ltd.'s five vessels. As it enters the 1999 ▶

Newly-converted self-unloader Algowest loading coal at the CSX #4 dock in Toledo during 1998. (Jim Hoffman)

season, Algoma Tankers has expanded its fleet again by purchsing the three vessels operated by EnerChem Transport Inc., **Enerchem Catayst, Enerchem Trader** and **Enerchem Refiner**. Renames are likely. In addition, Algoma Tankers now owns a 25 percent interest in Cleveland Tankers Inc.

Petrolia Desgagnes is the name chosen for the 1975-built tanker acquired from saltwater interests during the spring of 1998 by Groupe Desgagnes' Petro-Nav affiliate.

Interlake's former steamer **J.L. Mauthe**, converted to a self-unloading barge at Bay Shipbuilding during the winter of 1997-'98 and renamed **Pathfinder**, made her debut in the Great Lakes stone trade in April 1998, pushed by the tug **Joyce L. Van Enkevort**. The new tug **Dorothy Ann**, built at Bay Ship during 1998, is expected to take over the Pathfinder in 1999. Meanwhile, a 740-foot self-unloading barge is under construction at Halter Marine Group of Gulfport, MS, to be paired with Joyce Van Enkevort upon delivery in 2000. The barge, to be operated by the Van Enkevort interests in Escanaba, MI, will be named **Great Lakes Trader**.

Casualties

ULS Group's bulk carrier **Canadian Leader** suffered steering gear failure 21 August 1998 and ran hard aground in a boulder field on the Crab Island Shoal near Drummond Island in the lower St. Mary's River. Boatwatchers breathed a sigh of relief when the veteran steamer was immediately repaired and put back in service.

Algoma Central Marine's **Algolake** grounded at Nanticoke, ON, 14 October 1998. After some of her cargo was removed, she was refloated and repaired.

Records

Since its opening in 1976, the **Midwest Energy Terminal** in Superior has shipped more than 200-million tons of low-sulfur Western coal. The dock broke the 200-million-ton mark 8 November 1998 when it loaded 16,017 tons aboard the **Joseph H. Thompson**. The Thompson was the 4,068th vessel to load at the terminal, which has the highest loading rate on the lakes.

Construction
Conversions
Scrappings

Canada Steamship Lines has embarked on a three-year modernization program that will see a trio of its older self-unloaders rebuilt from the engine room forward at Port Weller Drydocks in St. Catharines, ON. The $100-million project began this past winter with the forebody replacement of the 1972-built **J.W. McGiffin**. The new sections are of a design that takes advantage of increased size allowances on the St. Lawrence Seaway. Hence, the length of the three ships will increase to 740 feet from 730 feet. The breadth increases to 78 feet, up from 75 feet. The ships will also feature the latest in cargo-handling systems. The procedure is expected to add up to 25 years of service life to each ship. Work on the McGiffin is set for completion in time for the 1999 shipping season. Two other CSL vessels, **H.M. Griffith** and **Jean Parisien**, are ▶

Steamer E.M. Ford spent its 100th anniversary as a storage hull in Saginaw. Here she fights spring ice in the Mackinac Straits, December 1989. (Eric Treece)

slated for forebody replacement in 1999 and 2000. The company also holds options to improve two more ships in 2002 and 2003; these may be **Louis R. Desmarais** and **Tadoussac**.

Algoma Central Marine's self-unloader **Agawa Canyon** received a $5.3-million mid-life refit at Port Weller Drydocks during the winter of 1998-99.

The hybrid Upper Lakes Group motor vessel **Canadian Transfer** was re-commissioned in a ceremony 4 August 1998 at Port Weller Dry Docks (see Vessel Spotlight on Page 28).

Black Creek Shipping will repower the 1943-vintage steamer **Cuyahoga** during the winter of 1999-2000, using diesel engines salvaged from the laker **Nicolet**, which was scrapped in 1997. The Cuyahoga's current Lentz-Poppet steam engine is the last of its kind in service on the lakes.

The Algoma Central Marine motor vessel **Algowest** was re-dedicated in a ceremony 10 July 1998 at Port Weller Dry Docks. The $20-million conversion to a self-unloader was completed during the previous eight months.

Christening was held 18 June 1998 for the new barge **Pere Marquette 41**, the former Lake Michigan carferry **City of Midland 41**, which had been laid-up for a number of years. She is operated by the **Pere Marquette Shipping Company** and pushed by the tug **Undaunted**.

The U.S. Coast Guard Icebreaker **Mackinaw** received a new coat of red hull paint in early June 1998, replacing the gleaming white paintwork that had been its trademark since she was built in 1944. The new color is designed to make the vessel show up better in ice and snow.

Lay-up Log

Thanks to a strong economy, most U.S. flag vessels saw service in 1998, with the exception of the grain boat **Kinsman Enterprise**, held in reserve in Buffalo, and the cement carrier **S.T. Crapo**, which remains in lay-up with the **Lewis G. Harriman** at Green Bay. The veteran cement boat **E.M. Ford**, which marked its centennial in 1998, continues as a storage hull at Saginaw, while her former fleetmate, **J.B. Ford**, does the same near Chicago. Rumors continue about a possible self-unloader conversion for Interlake's 806-foot steamer **John Sherwin**, idle at Superior, WI, since 1981. The long lay-up continues for the former passenger liner **Aquarama**, still rusting away at a Lackawanna, NY, dock. The same goes for the historic Detroit River passenger steamers **Ste. Claire** and **Columbia**, deteriorating at Detroit. Time may be running out in Escanaba, MI, for the worn-out hull of the 1927-built steamer **L.E. Block**, which has been sitting there since 1981. The carferry **Viking** still remains in limbo at Erie, PA, with no plans for a return to service.

On the Canadian side, most of the fleet was out and running in time for the fall grain rush. Exceptions include Paterson's **Comeaudoc**, laid up at Montreal, plus the **Vandoc** and **Quedoc**, in long-term storage at Thunder Bay. In addition, Canada Steamship Lines' self-unloader **Tarantau** remains at the wall in Toronto, her future uncertain, while the fleet's former **Saguenay** is still involved in an environmental project at Thunder Bay, ON.

Former ocean tanker Petrolia Desgagnes near Montreal in early 1998 on her first trip into the Seaway system. (Rene Beauchamp)

CANADIAN TRANSFER

Vessel Spotlight

Two ships became one in 1998 with the christening 4 August at Port Weller Drydocks of the motor vessel **Canadian Transfer**. The new unit came from joining the engine room portion of the **Canadian Explorer**, a 730-foot straight deck bulk carrier, and the **Hamilton Transfer**, a 620-foot self-unloading vessel. The cargo hold, wheelhouse and self-unloading system of the Hamilton Transfer were retained and new, 24-foot section was built to wed the two ships. Canadian Transfer, which emerged from the shipyard at 650 feet in length, is owned by the ULS Corp. and chartered to Seaway Self Unloaders.

This is the first time a bulker and a self-unloader have been joined to create a new vessel. The Canadian Explorer herself was a combination of two other hulls. She was created in 1983 when the stern of the former package freighter **Cabot** was mated with the forebody of the steamer **Northern Venture** (itself a 1961 project that used the engine portion of the World War 2 tanker **Edenfield**). The Cabot had been rendered obsolete by the growth in container traffic, while the Northern Venture was hampered by high fuel consumption and that era's soaring fuel costs.

The Hamilton Transfer began life as the 1943-built, Maritime Class bulk carrier **J.H. Hillman Jr.** for the Wilson Marine Transit fleet. In 1974 she was sold to the Columbia Transportation Co. and renamed **Crispin Oglebay**.

J.H. Hillman Jr. in Wilson Marine colors.

Converted to a self unloader, the Crispin Oglebay sailed until May, 1991, when she was declared surplus tonnage. Sold to Upper Lakes Group in 1995, she was renamed Hamilton Transfer and taken to Hamilton, ON, for use as a temporary cargo transfer station at Dofasco Inc. Although the vessel's hull and unloading gear were in excellent shape, the original 2,500 hp triple-expansion steam engine made the Hamilton Transfer unsuitable for use as a powered vessel. (The Canadian Explorer's diesel powerplant, built in 1965, offered 6,100 hp.)

The Transfer's first season was not without incident. On 8 September 1998, the vessel's rudder was damaged at Saginaw and she had to be towed to Thunder Bay for repairs that took nearly two months. In late December, she again sustained rudder damage while backing in the Rouge River and had to undergo further repairs during the winter of 1999.

Canadian Transfer upbound in the Detroit River 22 August 1998. (Todd Davidson)

GREAT LAKES GLOSSARY

AAA CLASS - New vessel design popular on the Great Lakes in the early 1950s. **Arthur M. Anderson** is one example.

AFT - Toward the back, or stern, of a ship.

AHEAD - Forward.

AMIDSHIPS - The middle point of a vessel, referring to either length or width.

ARTICULATED TUG-BARGE (or ATB) - Tug-barge combination. The two vessels are mechanically linked in one axis, but with the tug free to move, or articulate, on another axis. **Jacklyn M/Integrity** is one example.

BACKHAUL - The practice of carrying a revenue-producing cargo (rather than ballast) on a return trip from hauling a primary cargo.

BARGE - Vessel with no engine, either pushed or pulled by a tug.

BEAM - The width of a vessel measured at the widest point.

BILGE - The lowest part of a hold or compartment, generally where the rounded side of a ship curves from the keel to the vertical sides.

BOOMER - Great Lakes slang for self-unloader.

BOW - The front of a vessel.

BOWTHRUSTER - Propeller mounted transversely in a vessel's bow under the waterline to assist in moving sideways. A sternthruster may also be installed.

BRIDGE - The platform above the main deck from which a ship is steered or navigated. Also **PILOTHOUSE** or **WHEELHOUSE.**

BULKHEAD - A wall or partition that separates rooms, holds or tanks within the hull of a ship.

BULWARK - The part of the ship that extends fore and aft above the main deck to form a rail.

DEADWEIGHT TONNAGE - The actual carrying capacity of a vessel, equal to the difference between the light displacement tonnage and the heavy displacement tonnage, expressed in long tons (2,240 pounds or 1,016.1 kg).

DISPLACEMENT TONNAGE - The actual weight of the vessel and everything aboard her, measured in long tons. The displacement is equal to the weight of the water displaced by the vessel. Displacement tonnage may be qualified as light, indicating the weight of the vessel without cargo, fuels, stores; or heavy, indicating the weight of the vessel loaded with cargo, fuel and stores.

DRAFT - The depth of water a ship needs to float. Also the distance from keel to waterline.

FIT-OUT - The process of preparing a vessel for service after a period of inactivity.

FOOTER - Slang for 1,000-foot vessel.

FORECASTLE - (FOHK s'l) Area at the forward part of the ship and beneath the main cabins, often used for crew's quarters or storage.

FOREPEAK - The space below the forecastle.

FORWARD - Toward the front of an object on a ship.

FREEBOARD - The distance from the waterline to the main deck.

GROSS TONNAGE - The internal space of a vessel, measured in units of 100 cubic feet (2.83 cubic cubic meters) = a gross ton.

HATCH - An opening in the deck through which cargo is lowered or raised. A hatch is closed by securing a hatch cover over it.

HOLD - The space below decks where cargo is stored.

HULL - The body of a ship, not including its superstructure, masts or machinery.

INBOARD - Toward the center of the ship.

INTEGRATED TUG-BARGE (or ITB) - Tug-barge combination in which the tug is rigidly mated to the barge. **Presque Isle** is one example.

JONES ACT - U.S. law that requires cargos moved between American ports to be carried by U.S. flag, U.S. built and U.S.-crewed vessels.

KEEL - A ship's steel backbone. It runs along the lowest part of the hull.

LAID UP - Out of service. Also: at the wall.

MARITIME CLASS - Style of lake vessel built during World War 2 as part of the nation's war effort. The **Richard Reiss** is one example.

NET REGISTERED TONNAGE - The internal capacity of a vessel available for carrying cargo. It does not include the space occupied by boilers, engines, shaft alleys, chain lockers, officers' and crew's quarters. Net registered tonnage is usually referred to as registered tonnage or net tonnage and is used to figure taxes, tolls and port charges.

PELLETS - See TACONITE.

PORT - The left side of the ship facing the bow.

RIVER-CLASS SELF-UNLOADER - Group of vessels built in the '70s to service smaller ports and negotiate narrow rivers such as Cleveland's Cuyahoga. **Charles E. Wilson** is one example.

SELF-UNLOADER - Vessel able to discharge its own cargo using a system of conveyor belts and a moveable boom.

STARBOARD - The right side of the ship facing forward.

STEM - The extreme forward end of the bow.

STEMWINDER - A vessel with all cabins aft.

STERN - The back of the ship.

STRAIGHT-DECKER - A non-self-unloading vessel. **Edward L. Ryerson** is one example.

TACONITE - Processed, pelletized iron ore. Easy to load and unload, this is the primary method of shipping ore on the lakes and Seaway.

TRACTOR TUG - Newer style of highly maneuverable tug propelled by either a z-drive (located at the stern) or cycloidal system (mounted amidships under the center of the hull).

Vessel Index

Elton Hoyt 2nd, Edwin H. Gott in the St. Mary's River. (Roger LeLievre)

Vessel Name / Fleet Number	Vessel Name / Fleet Number	Vessel Name / Fleet Number
A	Algoeast A-4	Anangel Prosperity IA-9
	Algofax A-4	Anangel Sky IA-9
A-390 ....A-10	Algogulf {1} A-4	Anangel Spirit IA-9
A-397 ....A-10	Algogulf {2} A-4/S-4	Anangel Triumph IA-9
A-410 ....A-10	Algoisle A-4/S-4	Anangel Victory IA-9
Aburg C-10	Algolake A-4/S-5	Anangel Wisdom IA-9
Acacia U-4	Algomah A-14	Anastasia IE-8
ACBL 1613 ....D-14	Algomarine A-4/S-5	Anax IP-14
ACBL 1614 ....D-14	Algonorth A-4/S-4	Anchor Bay G-17
Adanac................P-11	Algonova A-4	Anderson, Arthur M. U-17
Admiral Ushakov IM-13	Algontario A-4/S-4	Andre H. T-17
Adrienne B. K-5	Algoport A-4/S-5	Andrea Marie I D-3
Advent C-5	Algorail {2} A-4/S-5	Andrealon IH-2
Adventure IP-4	Algoriver A-4/S-4	Andrew J..............E-4
Aegean Sea IA-3	Algosar A-4	Andrie, Barbara A-10
Agamemnon IA-15	Algoscotia A-4	Andrie, Candice A-10
Agawa Canyon A-4/S-5	Algosea A-4	Andrie, Clara A-10
Aggie C I-1	Algosoo {2} A-4/S-5	Andrie, Karen {1} B-3
Aghia Marina IA-7	Algosound A-4/S-4	Andrie, Karen {2} A-10
Agiodektini IZ-1	Algosteel {2} A-4/S-5	Andrie, Mari Beth A-10
Agios Georgios IC-6	Algoville A-4/S-5	Anemi IP-14
Agoming T-7	Algoway {2} A-4/S-5	Anemone IP-14
Aird, John B. A-4/S-5	Algowest A-4/S-5	Anezina IG-5
Akebono Star IC-7	Algowood A-4/S-5	Anglian Lady P-11
Akmi IN-1	Alice E. E-6	Angus, D. J. G-13
Akti IZ-1	Alidon IH-2	Anita Dee T-3
Aktis IL-3	Alka IS-23	Anita Dee II T-3
Al Aliyu IH-11	Alkyon II-2	Anita I IH-2
Al Baky IH-11	Allegra IS-6	Anja C IC-3
Al Battal S-22	Allied Chemical No. 12 .....A-5	Ann Arbor No. 6 ....C-29
Al Hafizu IH-11	Allvag IB-10	Ann Arbor No. 7 ....C-29
Alabama {2} G-20	Allvang IB-10	Anna IP-13
Alam Jaya IP-1	Alpena {2} I-4	Anna John IM-11
Alam Karang IP-1	Alpha IS-17	Antalina IT-2
Alam Kembong IP-1	Al-Sayb-7 ....S-22	Antares IA-8
Alam Kerisi IP-1	Alsterstern IR-5	Anthony IB-8
Alam Pari IP-1	Alsydon IH-2	Anthos IA-11
Alam Sejahtera IP-1	Altnes ID-9	Antiquarian G-19
Alam Sempurna IP-1	Ambassador U-15	Anvantage M-17
Alam Senang IP-1	Amber Mae R-6	Apache D-5
Alam Tabah IP-1	Ambridge 528 ....M-9	Apex Chicago A-11
Alam Talang IP-1	Ambridge 529 ....M-9	APJ Anand IS-31
Alam Tangkas IP-1	America {3} G-20	APJ Angad IS-31
Alam Tegas IP-1	American Girl G-9	APJ Anjli IS-31
Alam Teguh IP-1	American Gulf V A-9	APJ Karan IS-31
Alam Teladan IP-1	American Mariner A-9	APJ Priti IS-31
Alam Tenega IP-1	American Republic A-9	APJ Sushma IS-31
Alam Tenggiri IP-1	American Viking A-10	Apollo C IS-8
Alam Tenteram IP-1	Amherst Islander {2} O-4	Appledore T-1
Alamdar, A. IH-11	Amherstburg I-8	Aptmariner IC-11
Alaska G-20	Amilla IA-9	Aquarama E-7
Albatros II-2	Amitie IG-2	Aquatique IA-8
Albert B. M-17	Amoco I-4	Arabella IA-15
Albert C I-1	Amoco Great Lakes C-26	Arabian Express ID-1
Alcona R-6	Amoco Indiana S-17	Arctic F-3
Aldebaran IA-8	Amoco Michigan C-26	Arctic Kalvik F-3
Alecto IC-2	An Qing Jiang IC-11	Arctic Trader S-9
Alexander, William Sir C-5	An Ze Jiang IC-11	Arctic Viking C-1
Alexandria IP-5	Anangel Ares IA-9	Ardal IN-11
Alexandria IZ-1	Anangel Endeavor IA-9	Argonaut IS-21
Alexandria Belle U-1	Anangel Fidelity IA-9	Argut IF-4
Alexis IT-8	Anangel Honesty IA-9	Ariake Star IC-7
Alexis-Simard A-3	Anangel Honour IA-9	Ariel J-1
Algobay A-4/S-5	Anangel Hope IA-9	Arion IW-1
Algocape {1} P-1	Anangel Horizon IA-9	Arizona G-20
Algocape {2} A-4/S-4	Anangel Liberty IA-9	Arkansas {2} G-20
Algocen {2} A-4/S-4	Anangel Might IA-9	Arktis Atlantic IE-2
Algodart A-4		

Vessel Name / Fleet Number	Vessel Name / Fleet Number	Vessel Name / Fleet Number
Arktis Blue IE-2	Aurora Borealis C-25	Biograd IS-16
Arktis Breeze IE-2	Aurora Gold IA-18	Biscayne Bay U-4
Arktis Carrier IE-2	Aurora Jade IA-18	Bison IS-19
Arktis Crystal IE-2	Aurora Topaz IA-18	Bittern C-5
Arktis Dream IE-2	Avdeevka IA-19	Bizerte IC-10
Arktis Fantasy IE-2	Avenger P-11	Black Bay U-15
Arktis Fighter IE-2	Avenger IV P-11	Black Carrier M-17
Arktis Future IE-2	Avondale K-5	Black, Martha L. C-5
Arktis Grace IE-2	Ayers, J. Burton B-13	Blackie B. H-7
Arktis Hope IE-2	Aynur Kalkavan IA-5	Blanco, C. F-3
Arktis Hunter IE-2	Ayse Ana IA-5	Block, Emil H. Major ...Page 139
Arktis Light IE-2		Block, Joseph L. C-11
Arktis Meridian IE-2		Block, L. E. B-3
Arktis Morning IE-2	**B**	Blough, Roger U-17
Arktis Ocean IE-2		Blue Bay IS-12
Arktis Orion IE-2	Badger {2} L-1	Blue Breeze IS-12
Arktis Pearl IE-2	Bagotville C-6	Blue Heron U-11
Arktis Pioneer IE-2	Baker, M. H. III C-3	Blue Lagoon IS-12
Arktis Pride IE-2	Baker, Melvin H. II {2} C-3	Blue Marine IS-12
Arktis River IE-2	Balaban 1 ....IE-4	Blue Moon IS-12
Arktis Sea IE-2	Baldy B. S-6	Blue Topaz IH-2
Arktis Sirius IE-2	Balkan IN-6	Boardman, John W. S-23
Arktis Sky IE-2	Baltia IO-4	Bob Lo Islander I-9
Arktis Spring IE-2	Baltic Confidence IV-6	Bogun, Ivan IM-13
Arktis Star IE-2	Baltic Trader IH-8	Bois, Beau C-5
Arktis Sun IE-2	Bantry Bay G-2	Bol IS-23
Arktis Trader IE-2	Barbara Ann {1} A-6	Boland, John J. {3} A-9
Arktis Venture IE-2	Barbara H IB-13	Bolder IA-8
Arktis Vision IE-2	Barbara Rita A-10	Bondarchuk, Tonya IM-13
Armco O-3	Barbarossa IM-7	Bonesey B. K-5
Arosette IC-4	Barge 252 ....M-17	Bontegracht IS-22
Artaki IA-12	Barker, James R. I-6	Boskovic, Ruder IA-17
Arundel B-3	Barker, Kaye E. I-6	Botany Trader IB-9
Asher, Chas R-3	Barnes, Richard J. E-13	Botany Trojan IB-9
Asher, John R. R-3	Barry J K-6	Bounty V-5
Asher, Stephen M. R-3	Basse-Cote L-10	Bowen, Dana T. P-11
Aslan-1 ....IA-14	Bataafgracht IS-22	Boyd, David G-19
Astra Lift IC-4	Baugh, Joe Jr. P-11	Boye, Andreas IH-9
Astrea IF-5	Bayfield ....Page 140	Boye, Anne IH-9
Astron IP-4	Bayship B-6	Boye, Birthe IH-9
ATA-230 ....S-6	BD 1 ....G-2	Boye, Elisabeth IH-9
ATC 610 ....M-17	Beam Beginner G-14	Boye, Hermann C. IH-9
Atkinson, Arthur K. C-29	Beaver A-14	Boye, Sine IH-9
ATL 2301 ....I-8	Beaver U-7	Boyer, Willis B. .....Page 138
ATL 2302 ....I-8	Beaver D. M-17	Bramble U-4
ATL 2401 ....I-8	Beaver Islander B-8	Brandon E. C-30
ATL 2402 ....I-8	Beavercliffe Hall N-1	Bray, James M. U-3
Atlantic Cedar I-8	Becky E. E-6	Breech, Ernest R. G-15
Atlantic Erie C-3	Bee Jay G-4	Bremon IB-1
Atlantic Fir {2} I-8	Beeghly, Charles M. I-6	Brenda L. F-5
Atlantic Freighter M-8	Belle River A-9	Bribir IC-12
Atlantic Hemlock I-8	Beluga IL-3	Bristol Bay U-4
Atlantic Hickory C-3	Bergen Bay IB-4	Brochu F-3
Atlantic Huron {1} C-3	Bergen Sea IB-4	Brooknes A-4
Atlantic Huron {2} C-3	Bergon IB-1	Broompark ID-2
Atlantic Oak I-8	Bert, Donald M-2	Brown, Colon C-3
Atlantic Poplar I-8	Bethlake No. 1 ....G-2	Brunto IJ-8
Atlantic Spruce {2} I-8	Betsiamites L-10	Buccaneer W-1
Atlantic Superior C-3	Betty D. D-14	Buckeye {3} O-3
Atlantic Teak I-8	Bge 6704 ....S-21	Buckley K-5
Atlantic Trader A-4	Bickersgracht IS-22	Buckthorn U-4
Atlantis Joy IA-16	Bickerton C-5	Buffalo U-3
Atlantis Spirit IA-16	Bide-A-Wee {3} S-16	Buffalo {3} A-9
Atomic M-17	Bigane, Jos. F. B-11	Bunyan, Paul U-3
Audacious IP-14	Bigorange XVI S-22	Burns Harbor {1} O-3
Auriga IA-8	Bilice IS-16	Burns Harbor {2} B-10
Aurora IO-2	Billie M. M-17	Burro M-7
	Billmaier, D. L. U-3	

Vessel Name / Fleet Number	Vessel Name / Fleet Number	Vessel Name / Fleet Number
Burton, Courtney O-3	Carroll Jean A-6	Clyde, William G. U-17
Busch, Gregory J. B-19	Cartier, Jacques C-34	CMBT Ensign ID-5
Busse, Fred A. C-16	Cartiercliffe Hall A-4	Coastal Cruiser T-7
Butterfield A-10	Cartierdoc {2} N-1	Coastal Delegate I-4
Buzet IC-12	Cassidy, R. G. G-14	Cobia . . . . .Page 138
	Catherine IA-19	Cod . . . . .Page 138
	Catherine-Legardeur S-14	Cohen, Wilfred M. P-11
C	Cavalier M-17	Colinette M-17
c. Columbus IH-4	Cavalier des Mers C-32	Collins, E. C. I-4
C.T.C. No.1 . . . . .S-17	Cavalier Grand Fleuve C-32	Colombe, J. E. U-7
C-11 . . . . .K-4	Cavalier Maxim C-32	Colorado G-20
Cabo San Lucas C-3	Cavalier Royal C-32	Columbia {2} S-25
Cabot U-15	Cay IN-2	Columbia Star O-3
Cadillac {5} S-24	Celebrezze, Anthony J. C-21	Comeaudoc N-1
Calcite II U-17	Celine M IM-10	Commuter N-4
California G-20	Cemba D-4	Compaen IA-8
Callaway, Cason J. U-17	Chada Naree IG-4	Concorde IS-15
Canada Marquis F-3	Challenge G-18	Concordia IO-4
Canadian C-11	Challenger {1} S-23	Condarrell M-17
Canadian Ambassador U-15	Challenger {2} H-4	Confederation {2} N-6
Canadian Century U-15/S-5	Challenger {3} D-14	Coniscliffe Hall {2} P-2
Canadian Empress S-19	Champion {1} C-12	Conny IS-6
Canadian Enterprise . . .U-15/S-5	Champion {3} D-14	Consensus Atlantic F-3
Canadian Explorer U-15/S-4	Charlevoix {1} C-13	Consensus Manitou ID-4
Canadian Leader U-15/S-4	Chebucto C-5	Constructor D-11
Canadian Mariner U-15/S-4	Cheetah IV-1	Cooper, Flo P-5
Canadian Miner U-15/S-4	Chembulk Fortitude IM-2	Cooper, J. W. C-31
Canadian Navigator . . .U-15/S-4	Chembulk Singapore IM-2	Cooper, Wyn M-17
Canadian Olympic U-15/S-5	Cherokee L-2	Coral IS-25
Canadian Pioneer U-15	Cherokee {1} E-6	Corithian Trader IT-1
Canadian Progress U-15/S-5	Cherokee {2} B-2	Cornelius, Adam E. {3} C-3
Canadian Prospector . . .U-15/S-5	Cheryl C IC-3	Cornelius, Adam E. {4} A-9
Canadian Provider U-15/S-4	Chicago II C-14	Corner Brook IB-1
Canadian Ranger U-15/S-4	Chicago Peace I-1	Cornett, J. A. H-6
Canadian Trader U-15/S-4	Chicago's First Lady M-20	Cornwallis, Edward C-5
Canadian Transfer U-15/S-5	Chi-Cheemaun O-8	Corsair A-14
Canadian Transport {2} .U-15/S-5	Chief Shingwauk L-12	Cort, Stewart J. B-10
Canadian Venture U-15/S-4	Chief Wawatam P-11	Cotter, Edwin M. B-18
Canadian Voyager U-15/S-4	Chimo U-15	Coulby, Harry {2} G-15
Canmar Sea Eagle S-22	Chios Harmony IH-5	Coulet, Louis J. P-2
Canmar Shuttle S-22	Chippewa {6} A-14	Cove Isle C-5
Cantankerous E-11	Chippewa {7} G-20	Crapo, S. T. I-4
Cap Aux Meules C-5	Chippewa {8} G-8	Credo IR-1
Cape Hurd C-5	Chisholm, Alex D. S-17	Creed, Frederick G. C-5
Cape Kennedy IC-1	Chiwawa I-6	Crio IO-4
Capetan Michalis IU-2	Chris Ann H-7	Croaker . . . . .Page 138
Capricorn IC-7	Christiaan IA-8	Crow E-6
Capt. Roy B-16	Cisco U-5	CSL Atlas C-3
Capt. Shepler S-10	City of Algonac D-1	CSL Cabo C-3
Captain Barnaby L-2	City of Flint 32 . . . . .M-14	CSL Innovator C-3
Captain George F-6	City of Midland 41 . . . . .U-3	CSL Trailblazer C-3
Captain Ioannis S. L-10	City of Milwaukee . . . . .Page 138	CSL Trillium I M-17
Carey, Emmet J. O-7	Clarke, Philip R. U-17	Csokonai IH-12
Cargo Carrier #1 . . . . .M-17	Clarkson Carrier S-22	CTCO 2505 . . . . .P-11
Cargo Carrier #2 . . . . .M-17	Claudia I IH-2	Cumella C-5
Cargo Master M-17	Clifford, A.E. S-13	Curly B. L-2
Caribbean Express I ID-1	Clinton C-23	Cushing, John F. U-14
Caribou M-8	Clipper Adventurer C-24	Cuyahoga B-13
Caribou Isle C-5	Clipper Amaryllis IP-14	Cvijeta Zuzoric IA-17
Carl M. C-11	Clipper Amethyst IP-14	Cygnus C-5
Carleton, George N. G-14	Clipper Antares IP-14	Cygnus IS-14
Carmencita IG-6	Clipper Aquamarine IS-3	
Caro IO-4	Clipper Eagle IP-7	
Carol Ann K-6	Clipper Falcon IP-7	**D**
Carol Lake P-1	Clipper Majestic ID-8	Daan IA-8
Carola I IH-2	Cloud Chaser H-10	Dakota E-6
Carolyn Jo M-17	Clyde M-9	Daldean B-15
		Dali IR-4

Vessel Name / Fleet Number	Vessel Name / Fleet Number	Vessel Name / Fleet Number
Dalmig D-2	Duc d' Orleans D-13	Equity IM-2
Daniel E. E-6	Duchess V M-17	Erie West M-17
Daniella IJ-12	Duden IS-20	Erikousa Wave IT-2
Danielson, Dennis IN-3	Dufresne M-58 . . . . .M-17	Escort S-6
Danielson, Ulla IN-3	Duga T-17	Escort II B-3
Darrell, William H-8	Duluth B-12	Escort Protector M-17
Darya Kamal IC-8	Duluth U-3	Escorte M-17
Darya Ma IC-8	Durocher, Ray D-14	Eskimo T-14
Dauntless M-18	Durrington IS-26	Espoir IM-2
Daviken F-3		Ethel E. E-6
Davitaja IA-10	**E**	Etoile IO-2
Dawnlight C-10	E-63 . . . . .D-12	Euroreefer IG-2
Dawson B. M-17	Eagle Island A-12	Evangeline ID-7
DC 710 . . . . .D-12	Eagle Quick IP-14	Everest, D. C. M-17
Dean, Americo D-6	Eber IS-20	Evimeria IA-9
Dean, Annie M. D-6	Eclipse N-3	Evmar IN-1
Dean, Wayne D-6	Ecosse G-16	Eyrarbakki W-2
Debbie Lyn M-2	Edda IH-8	
Defiance A-8	Edelweiss I E-3	**F**
DeLancey, William J. I-6	Edelweiss II E-3	Fairchild U-3
Delaware {4} G-20	Edith J. E-4	Fairlift IJ-12
Demeterton U-15	Edna G. . . . . .Page 138	Fairload IJ-12
Denise E. E-6	Eemshorn IA-8	Fairmast IJ-12
Derek E. E-6	Eighth Sea S-21	Faith B-12
Des Groseilliers C-5	Eileen C I-1	Faith Star IH-7
des Jarnins, Alphonse S-14	Ek-Sky T-14	Falcon Carrier IJ-1
Des Plaines C-2	El Jem IC-10	Falcon, G. W. L-2
Deschenes, Jos S-14	El Kef IC-10	Famille DuFour F-1
Desgagnes, Amelia T-14	Elbestern R-1	Famille DuFour II F-1
Desgagnes, Anna T-14	Eleanor R. C-8	Farquharson, A. G. A-4
Desgagnes, Catherine T-14	Elena G IP-12	Fastov IM-13
Desgagnes, Cecelia T-14	Elikon IH-6	Fatezh IA-19
Desgagnes, Jacques T-14	Elina IC-2	Federal Aalesund F-3
Desgagnes, Mathilda T-14	Elisabeth G IA-8	Federal Agno F-3
Desgagnes, Melissa T-14	Elizabeth C IC-3	Federal Asahi F-3
Desgagnes, Petrolia T-14	Ellie IB-13	Federal Baffin F-3
Desgagnes, Stella G-14	Elliot, James R. P-9	Federal Bergen F-3
Desgagnes, Thalassa T-14	Elm ID-5	Federal Calliope F-3
Desmarais, Louis R. C-3	Elmglen {2} L-10	Federal Calumet {2} F-3
Detroit {1} N-5	Emerald Empress N-4	Federal Danube F-3
Diamant IA-8	Emerald Isle {1} D-9	Federal Dora F-3
Diamond Belle D-9	Emerald Isle {2} B-8	Federal Franklin F-3
Diamond Jack D-9	Emerald Star R-1	Federal Fraser F-3
Diamond Queen D-9	Emerald Wave IB-11	Federal Fuji F-3
Diamond Star R-1	Emery, John R. E-12	Federal Maas {1} F-3
Dilmuan Shearwater ID-6	Emilie K IA-1	Federal Maas {2} F-3
Dilmun Fulmar ID-6	Emily C IC-3	Federal MacKenzie F-3
Dilmun Tern ID-6	Empire Sandy E-8	Federal Matane F-3
Dinara IS-16	Empress E-10	Federal Oslo F-3
Doan Transport A-4	Empress II E-10	Federal Ottawa F-3
Dobrush IA-19	Empress III E-10	Federal Pioneer T-14
Docegulf IV-3	Empress of Canada E-9	Federal Polaris F-3
Dolgorukiy, Yuriy IM-13	Ems Ore N-1	Federal Rhine {2} F-3
Donald Mac G-14	Emsstern R-1	Federal Richelieu F-3
Donaustern IR-5	Enchanter IS-22	Federal Saguenay {1} F-3
Don-De-Dieu A-4	Encounter IM-2	Federal Saguenay {2} F-3
Donner, William H. U-16	Encouragement IG-2	Federal Schelde {2} F-3
Donskoy, Dmitriy IM-13	Endeavor N-4	Federal St. Laurent {1} F-3
Dorothy Sue I-6	EnerChem Catalyst A-4	Federal St. Laurent {2} F-3
Douglas, Edwin T. L-10	EnerChem Refiner A-4	Federal St. Louis F-3
Dover M-2	EnerChem Trader A-4	Federal Sumida F-3
Dover Light C-3	English River C-3	Federal Thames F-3
Drnis IS-16	Enterprise 2000 . . . . .G-3	Federal Vibeke F-3
Drummond Islander E-2	Enterprise I IG-2	Federal Vigra F-3
Drummond Islander II M-1	Entity IM-2	Felicity S-10
Drummond Islander III E-2	Epos IG-2	Felix-Antoine-Savard S-14
Duc d' Orleans D-13		

Vessel Name / Fleet Number	Vessel Name / Fleet Number	Vessel Name / Fleet Number
Ferbec C-3	Giacinta IS-6	Green Lily IN-10
Fetish ID-7	Gibralter C-23	Green Rose IN-10
Feux - Follets U-15	Gillen, Edward E. III E-4	Green Tulip IN-10
Finlith IJ-10	Gitana IA-8	Green Violet IN-10
Finnfighter IF-5	Gladys Bea A-10	Green Winter IG-6
Finnmaster IF-5	Glen Shore L-3	Greene, Edward B. I-6
Finnpine IF-5	Glenada T-7	Greenland Saga IA-1
Finnsnes ID-9	Glenbrook M-17	Greenstone U-7
Flinders, Matthew Captain . .M-13	Glenevis M-17	Greenwood, Irene C-19
Flo-Mac M-17	Glenmont J-5	Greta C IC-3
Florida G-20	Glenora O-4	Greta V M-17
Fonnes ID-9	GLMA Barge G-17	Gretchen B. L-13
Ford, Benson {3} I-6	Glory Star IH-7	Grey Fox U-8
Ford, E. M. I-4	Glossbrenner, A. S. A-4	Grey, Earl C-5
Ford, J. B. I-4	Goki P-11	Griffith, H. M. C-3
Ford, William Clay {2} I-6	Gold Bond Conveyor C-3	Griffon C-5
Forney U-3	Gold Bond Trailblazer C-3	Grobnik IC-12
Fort Dearborn C-17	Golden Fumi ID-10	Grue Des Iles S-14
Fort Hoskins M-17	Golden Georgia ID-10	Gulfoil O-3
Fort Saint-Jean II C-36	Golden Laker IJ-6	Gull Isle C-5
Fort William C-3	Golden Shield IT-6	Gunay-A ID-3
Fortuna IO-4	Golden Sky IC-7	Gur Maiden IJ-7
Fossnes IJ-8	Golden Sun IC-7	Gur Master IJ-7
Fourth Coast D-5	Golden Venture IE-8	Gustav Sule IE-6
Fox, Terry C-5	Gonio IM-3	
Foy, Lewis Wilson O-3	Goodtime I G-11	**H**
Fradiavolo IM-7	Goodtime III G-12	Habib IC-10
France, John A. {2} A-4	Gorthon, Ada IB-1	Haci Hilmi Bey IB-5
Frankcliffe Hall {2} C-3	Gorthon, Alida IB-1	Haci Hilmi II IB-5
Frantz, Joseph H. O-3	Gorthon, Carl T-14	Hagieni IN-7
Fraser . . . . .Page 138	Gorthon, Ingrid IB-1	Hai Wang Xing C-3
Fraser, Leon I-4	Gorthon, Ivan IB-1	Haida . . . . .Page 138
Fraser, Simon C-5	Gorthon, Joh. IB-1	Haight IS-17
Frederick, Owen M. U-3	Gorthon, Lovisa IB-1	Halifax C-3
Freja Nordic IF-7	Gorthon, Margit IB-1	Halton C-6
Freja Scandic IF-7	Gorthon, Maria IB-1	Hamilton U-15
Friendship P-10	Gorthon, Ragna IB-1	Hamilton Energy U-15
Frines ID-9	Gorthon, Stig IB-1	Hamilton Transfer U-15
Frontenac {5} C-3	Gorthon, Viola IB-1	Hammond Bay L-11
Frontenac II O-4	Gosforth T-14	Hammond Bay U-3
Fuji Star IC-7	Gotia IO-4	Handy Andy M-17
Fujisan Maru IG-4	Gott, Edwin H. U-17	Handy Boy M-17
Fullnes ID-9	Gouin, Lomer S-14	Handymariner IC-11
Furunes IJ-8	Goviken F-3	Hanlan, Ned . . . . .Page 142
	Gozde-B IB-12	Hanlan, Ned II T-11
G	Grampa Woo A-12	Hannah 1801 . . . . .H-4
G.L.B. No. 1 . . . . .P-11	Grampa Woo III L-4	Hannah 1802 . . . . .H-4
G.L.B. No. 2 . . . . .P-11	Grand Island {2} P-3	Hannah 2801 . . . . .H-4
G.T.B. No. 1 . . . . .G-2	Grande Baie A-3	Hannah 2901 . . . . .H-4
Gaillard, D. D. Col. . . . .Page 139	Grande Caribe A-7	Hannah 2902 . . . . .H-4
Gajah Borneo IJ-12	Grande Hermine U-15	Hannah 2903 . . . . .H-4
Galactica 001 . . . . .G-3	Grande Mariner A-7	Hannah 3601 . . . . .H-4
Galassia IS-14	Grande Prince A-7	Hannah 5101 . . . . .H-4
Gale, Betty H-4	Grande Ronde U-15	Hannah, Daryl C. {2} H-4
Gardiner, David K. U-15	Grant Carrier F-3	Hannah, Donald C. H-4
Garnes ID-9	Grant, R. F. T-17	Hannah, Hannah D. H-4
Gemini A-4	Grayling U-5	Hannah, James A. H-4
Gemini IS-14	Grazia IS-6	Hannah, Kristin Lee H-4
Gemini IS-17	Great Laker IB-11	Hannah, Mark H-4
General Blazhevich IA-19	Great Lakes {2} C-26	Hannah, Mary E. H-4
General Cabal IJ-8	Great Lakes Trader V-4	Hannah, Mary Page {1} S-6
Genmar 252 . . . . .M-17	Grecia, Stena M-8	Hannah, Mary Page {2} H-4
George L. IC-6	Green Bay G-20	Hannah, Peggy D. H-4
Georgian Queen A-13	Green Flake IG-6	Hannah, Susan W. S-17
Georgian Storm S-27	Green Freesia IN-10	Hanne Mette IN-11
Gercon #1 . . . . .L-10	Green Frost IN-10	Happy Rover IS-22
Gerda Vesta IN-11	Green Ice IN-10	Harbor Builder E-4

American Mariner meets Medusa Conquest 25 October 1998 in the Welland Canal. (Roger LeLievre)

Vessel Name / Fleet Number	Vessel Name / Fleet Number	Vessel Name / Fleet Number
Harbor Master R-6	Iberian Express ID-1	Island Duchess U-1
Harriman, Lewis G. S-23	Ida IB-6	Island Empress V-3
Harris, James L-2	Ida M. R-2	Island Express A-14
Hart, J. L. C-5	Ida M. II R-2	Island Gem S-1
Harvey U-3	Idaho G-20	Island Princess O-6
Havelstern IR-5	Iglehart, J. A. W. I-4	Island Queen {1} P-8
Hays, Sarah A-10	Ihsan IP-6	Island Queen {2} M-3
Heleen C IC-3	Ikan Selar IP-1	Island Queen {3} C-32
Helene S-8	Ikan Selayang IP-1	Island Queen III K-7
Helle Stevns IN-11	Ikan Sepat IP-1	Island Queen V {3} T-19
Hellenic Confidence IM-1	Ikan Tamban IP-1	Island Skipper S-1
Hennepin I I-1	Ikan Tanda IP-1	Island Sky S-1
Henry T. L-9	Ile Des Barques C-5	Island Star K-7
Henry, Alexander . . . . .Page 138	Ile Saint-Ours C-5	Island Wanderer U-1
Henry, John L-2	Illinois {2} G-20	Islander {1} C-16
Henson, Elish K. Major .Page 139	Illinois {3} L-2	Islander {2} R-5
Hero IO-4	Imbeau, Armand S-14	Islander {3} M-21
Hiawatha {1} S-13	Imperial Acadia A-4	Isle Rouge C-5
Hiawatha {2} S-16	Imperial Bedford A-4	Isle Royale Queen III T-4
Hichens, Mary C-5	Imperial Dartmouth A-4	Istrian Express ID-1
Hickory Coll I-4	Imperial Kingston P-11	Italian Express ID-1
Highway 16 . . . . .W-6	Imperial Lachine {2} I-2	Ithaki IS-7
Hilal II IH-10	Imperial Sarnia {2} U-15	ITM No. 1 . . . . .S-17
Hill Annex U-17	Imperial St. Clair A-4	Ivi IC-9
Hill, Louis W. . . . . .Page 140	Imperial St. Lawrence {2} . . .A-4	
Hillman, J. H. Jr. U-15	Incat 046 . . . . .N-6	
Hoey, Carolyn G-2	Indian Express ID-1	**J**
Hoey, Patricia {2} G-2	Indian Maiden B-9	J. G. II M-7
Hoey, Susan {1} G-2	Indiana G-20	Jacklyn M. A-10
Hoey, Susan {2} H-7	Indiana Harbor A-9	Jackman, Henry Capt. . . .A-4/S-5
Hogan, Joseph J. J-2	Industrial Advantage IC-4	Jackson, Charles E. N-5
Holck-Larsen F-3	Industrial Faith IA-1	Jackson, Herbert C. I-6
Holiday S-16	Industrial Hope IP-14	Jackson, W. G. G-13
Holiday Island N-6	Industrial Spirit IP-14	Jade Star R-1
Holly Ann H-7	Industrial Transport A-4	Jadestern R-1
Holmes, Edwin F. I-4	Infra IB-9	Jadran C-9
Holmon IB-2	Inglis, William T-12	Jaguar II C-25
Hope I IS-23	Ingram, E. Bronson S-22	Jamica W-1
Hope (The) S-10	Inland Seas I-5	Jan Meeder II-1
Horizon Montreal S-9	Innisfree C-17	Jarco 1402 . . . . .R-6
Horth, Alcide C. U-9	Integrity A-10	Jarmac 42 . . . . .S-22
Houghton B-12	Inviken F-3	Jason M-11
Howe Islander (The) H-9	Ionian Express ID-1	Jeannie IT-9
Howe Point C-5	Iowa G-20	Jelsa IS-23
Hoyt, Elton 2nd {2} I-6	Ira IC-9	Jenclipper IH-1
Hoyt, Elton II {1} S-17	Irene IC-2	Jenny D ID-7
Hreljin IC-12	Irene IF-2	Jenny T. II J-6
Hudson C-5	Iroquois {1} I-7	Jenolin IG-1
Hui Fu IC-11	Iroquois {2} G-20	Jet Express P-12
Hull 28 . . . . .T-14	Iroquois {3} L-2	Jet Express II P-12
Hull No. 3 . . . . .S-17	Irvin, William A. . . . . . .Page 139	Jhulelal IT-3
Humber Arm IB-1	Irving Arctic I-8	Jiggs L-5
Humbolt Current IS-16	Irving Beech I-8	Jiimaan O-8
Hun Jiang IC-11	Irving Birch I-8	Jing Hong Hai IC-11
Huron U-3	Irving Canada I-8	Jo Adler IJ-9
Huron {5} A-14	Irving Dolphin I-8	Jo Aspen IJ-9
Huron Belle L-6	Irving Elm I-8	Jo Calluna IJ-9
Huron Lady B-14	Irving Eskimo I-8	Jo Ebony IJ-9
Huron Maid L-6	Irving Juniper I-8	Jo Elm IJ-9
Hutchinson, Charles L. {3} .G-15	Irving Maple I-8	Jo Hassel IH-3
Hydra IS-17	Irving Miami C-3	Jo Hegg IJ-9
	Irving Pine I-8	Jo Maple IJ-9
I	Irving Tamarack I-8	Jo Palm IJ-9
I.V. No. 9 . . . . .V-1	Irving Timber I-8	Jodie D ID-7
I.V. No.10 . . . . .V-1	Isarstern IR-5	John Joseph A-10
I.V. No.14 . . . . .V-1	Island Belle I K-7	John, Robert G-14
Ian Mac M-2	Island Clipper {2} V-5	Johnson L-5
		Johnson II L-5

Vessel Name / Fleet Number		
Johnson, Charles W.	P-11	
Johnson, F. A.	G-14	
Johnson, Martin E.	P-11	
Johnson, Rueben	F-5	
Joliet {3}	S-24	
Jollity	IC-11	
Jubilee Queen	T-13	
Juleen I	C-31	
Julia	IG-1	
Julie Dee	K-6	
Julio	J-8	
Jumbo Challenger	IJ-12	
Jumbo Spirit	IJ-12	
Juniata	Page 139	
Juris Avots	IL-1	

K

Kadinger, David J. Jr.	K-1
Kadinger, Jason A.	K-1
Kadinger, Ruffy J.	K-1
Kaho	U-5
Kairos	IS-23
Kairouan	IC-10
Kalisti	IT-9
Kalliopi L.	IC-6
Kalvik	F-3
Kamenitza	IN-6
Kamilla	IR-3
Kamingoak, Peter	M-17
Kaner 1	A-2
Kansas	G-20
Kapitan Alekseyev	IN-12
Kapitan Bochek	IM-13
Kapitan Chukhchin	IM-13
Kapitan Georgi Georgiev	IN-6
Kapitan Glazachev	IN-12
Kapitan Kudley	IM-13
Kapitan Milovzorov	IF-4
Kapitan Rudnev	IM-12
Kapitan Zamyatin	IN-12
Kapitonas A. Lucka	IL-4
Kapitonas Andzejauskas	IL-4
Kapitonas Chromcov	IL-4
Kapitonas Daugela	IL-4
Kapitonas Daugirdas	IL-4
Kapitonas Domeika	IL-4
Kapitonas Kaminskas	IL-4
Kapitonas Marcinkus	IL-4
Kapitonas Serafinas	IL-4
Kapitonas Sevcenko	IL-4
Kapitonas Stulpinas	IL-4
Karen D	ID-7
Karlobag	IC-12
Kasla	IA-6
Kasteelborg	IW-1
Kate B.	M-17
Kate N. L.	U-15
Kathrin	IP-12
Kathy Lynn	R-6
Katie Ann	H-7
Katmai Bay	U-4
Kavo Alexandros	IG-3
Kavo Flora	IG-3
Kavo Mangalia	IG-3
Kavo Sidero	IG-3
Kavo Yerakas	IG-3

Kaw	G-2
Kawartha Voyager	O-5
Kaye, Rochelle	R-6
Kayla Marie	K-3
Keewatin	Page 139
Keizerborg	IW-1
Kelley Islander	N-4
Kellstone 1	K-4
Kemira	IF-5
Kendora, Wally	F-5
Kenosha	U-3
Kent Atlantic	I-8
Kent Carrier	I-8
Kent Forest	IR-4
Kent Transport	I-8
Kent Voyageur	I-8
Kentucky {2}	G-20
Keta Lagoon	IB-7
Keta V	V-1
Kevser Gunes	IP-6
Kianda	ID-9
Kihu	IN-8
Kings Pointer	L-1
Kinsman Enterprise {2}	G-15
Kinsman Independent {3}	G-15
Kirby D	ID-7
Klazina C	IC-3
Knutsen, Ellen	IK-1
Knutsen, Helene	IK-1
Knutsen, Hilda	IK-1
Knutsen, Pascale	IK-1
Knutsen, Sidsel	IK-1
Knutsen, Synnove	IK-1
Knutsen, Torill	IK-1
Knutsen, Turid	IK-1
Kobasic, Erika	B-3
Kobuleti	IM-3
Komsomolets Adzharii	IA-19
Komsomolets Armenii	IA-19
Komsomolets Moldavii	IA-19
Komsomolets Rossii	IA-19
Konigsberg	M-17
Koningsborg	IW-1
Koper, Danis	IS-28
Kraljica Mira	IS-23
Kramatorsk	IA-19
Krissa	IG-2
Kristen D.	P-6
Krk	IC-12
Kroonborg	IW-1
Krystal K.	L-1
Kupa	IC-12
Kupari	IA-17
Kutuzov, Mikhail	IM-13
Kwan Siu	IM-2
Kydonia	IM-5
Kyes, Roger M.	A-9
Kyzikos	IM-5

L

L.S.C. 236	G-2
La Prairie	S-20
La Rabida	IE-5
La Salle {4}	S-24
Lac Como	M-17
Lac Erie	M-17

Lac Manitoba	M-17
Lac St-Francois	L-10
Lac Vancouver	M-17
Ladler	C-20
Lady Belle II	O-6
Lady Elda	S-17
Lady Emily	IS-30
Lady Franklin	C-1
Lady Hamilton	F-3
Lake Carling	F-3
Lake Champlain	F-3
Lake Charles	F-3
Lake Erie	F-3
Lake Guardian	U-6
Lake Manitoba	A-4
Lake Michigan	F-3
Lake Nipigon	A-4
Lake Ontario	F-3
Lake Runner	S-7
Lake Shidaka	F-3
Lake Superior	F-3
Lake Superior	Page 139
Lake Tahoe	B-5
Lake Wabush	A-4
Laketon {2}	A-4
Lamda	IG-5
Langton, J. G.	T-11
Lansdowne	S-18
Laola	IF-1
Lapad	IA-17
Lapish, Art	L-2
Lapointe, Ernest	Page 139
Larson, Wells	F-5
Latania	IN-11
Laud, Sam	A-9
Laura Lynn	H-7
Laurentian	U-10
Laurina Neeltje	IA-8
Lawrencecliffe Hall {2}	U-15
Le Bateau-Mouche	L-8
Le Brave	A-4
Le Chene No. 1	A-4
Le Draveur	C-34
Le Roy Brooks	C-10
Le Survenant III	C-33
Le Vent	M-17
Ledastern	IR-5
Ledenice	IC-12
Lee, Nancy	L-11
Lehigh {3}	G-10
Leitch, Gordon C. {2}	U-15/S-4
Lemeshev, Sergey	IN-13
Lemoyne {2}	U-15
Lette Lill	IH-9
LeVoyageur	S-16
Lida	IJ-5
Lido	T-14
Lime Island	V-2
Limestone Clipper	S-2
Limnos	C-5
Linda Beth	S-13
Link Star	IG-1
Linnhurst	F-2
Lis Weber	IH-9
Lisa E.	E-6
Liscomb, Charles F.	M-11
Lita	IB-6

Vessel Name / Fleet Number	Vessel Name / Fleet Number	Vessel Name / Fleet Number
Little Rock ....Page 139	Mackinaw U-4	Marine Angel U-14
Little Toot R-4	Mackinaw City M-1	Marine Courier S-7
Livanov, Boris IN-13	Madeline M-3	Marine Robin U-16
Lois T. N-2	Madzy IR-1	Marine Star E-7
Lok Maheshwari IT-3	Maersk Manila IP-6	Marine Trader A-2
Lok Pragati IT-3	Magnetic F-4	Marinik G IP-12
Lok Prakash IT-3	Maid of the Mist M-4	Marinor IB-9
Lok Pratap IT-3	Maid of the Mist III M-4	Mariposa Belle M-13
Lok Pratima IT-3	Maid of the Mist IV M-4	Marjan I IS-23
Lok Prem IT-3	Maid of the Mist V M-4	Marjanne, Hilda U-15
Lok Rajeshwari IT-3	Maid of the Mist VI M-4	Marjolaine II C-35
Longobarda IM-7	Maid of the Mist VII M-4	Mark C IC-3
Looiersgracht IS-22	Maine {1} G-20	Marka L. IC-6
Losinj IC-12	Maisonneuve S-15	Markborg IW-1
Louisbourg C-5	Majestic Star {2} B-1	Market, Wm. M-21
Louisiana G-20	Makeevka IA-19	Marlyn S-12
Louis-Joliet C-32	Malabar T-16	Marquette O-3
Loutre Consol T-14	Malden P-11	Marquette {5} S-24
Lowell D. D-1	Malene IA-1	Marquette {6} C-17
Lowson, Sir Denys N-1	Malinska F-3	Martin, Andrew A10
LT Argosy F-3	Mallard IN-4	Martin, Argue M-17
LT Odyssey F-3	Malyovitza IN-6	Martin, Paul Hon. C-3
LT-5 ....Page 139	Mana IG-2	Mary C I-1
LT-280 ....H-4	Mangal Desai F-3	Mary C IC-3
LT-815 ....H-4	Manila Angus IC-13	Maryland {2} G-20
LT-821 ....H-4	Manitou {1} T-16	Marysville G-2
Lucien L. S-14	Manitou {2} M-5	Massachusetts G-20
Lucien-Paquin T-15	Manitou Isle M-6	Matador VI K-2
Luckyman IT-11	Manitoulin {5} C-3	Mather, William G. {2} .Page 139
Luedtke, Alan K. L-13	Manitowoc M-14	Matthew C-5
Luedtke, Chris E. L-13	Manitowoc U-3	Mauthe, J. L. I-6
Luedtke, Erich R. L-13	Manitowoc U-4	MBT 10 ....M-22
Luedtke, Karl E. L-13	Manjoya IE-5	MBT 20 ....M-22
Luedtke, Kurt L-13	Mantadoc {2} N-1	MBT 33 ....M-22
Luedtke, Paul L. L-13	Maple ....Page 139	McAllister 132 ....A-1
Luna Verde IP-11	Maple ID-5	McAllister 252 ....M-17
Lunni IN-8	Maple City T-11	McAllister No. 3 ....L-10
Lynx IV-1	Maple Grove O-1	McAllister No. 50 ....L-10
Lyra IN-2	Maplecliffe Hall U-15	McAllister, Cathy L-10
	Mapleglen {2} P-1	McAllister, Daniel .....Page 139
M	Marcey M-7	McAsphalt 401 ....M-16
M. Melody IJ-7	Marcoux, Camille S-14	McBride, Sam T-12
M.I.L. Venture M-17	Margaret Ann H-7	McCarthy, Walter J. Jr. A-9
M/V Happy Dolphin T-3	Margaret M. H-4	McCauley U-3
M/V Montreal C-32	Maria Angelicoussi IA-9	McCombs, Judge H-2
Macassa Bay M-17	Maria G. L. IC-6	McGiffin, J. W. C-3
Mackenzie, Wm. Lyon T-10	Mariana IS-29	McGrath, James E. U-15
Mackinac Express A-14	Marie-Clarisse F-1	McKee Sons U-14
Mackinac Islander D-9	Marilis T. IT-2	McKeil, Doug {2} M-17
		McKeil, Evans M-17
		McKeil, Florence M-17
		McKeil, Jarrett M-17
		McKeil, Wyatt M-17
		McKellar, John O. {2} L-10
		McKeller P-11
		McLagan, T. R. P-1
		McLane ....Page 140
		McLean, John P-11
		McWatters, J. N. {2} A-4
		Meagan Beth D-14
		Mecta Sea F-3
		Med Transporter IS-20
		Medill, Joseph {2} C-15
		Medusa Challenger S-17
		Medusa Conquest S-17
		Mekhanik Aniskin IA-19
		Melkki IN-8

Vessel Name / Fleet Number	Vessel Name / Fleet Number	Vessel Name / Fleet Number
Menasha {2} M-19	Mississippi G-20	Nea Elpis IF-2
Menier Consol T-9	Missouri {1} G-20	Nea Tyhi IF-2
Menominee IJ-8	Missouri {2} G-20	Neah Bay U-4
Mentor IA-16	Misty IL-2	Nebhana IC-10
Mervine II C-20	Mitsa IE-8	Nebraska G-20
Merweborg IW-1	Mljet IA-17	Necat A ID-3
Mesabi Miner I-6	Mobile Bay U-4	Neebish Islander C-22
Meta IO-4	Mobiloil I-6	Neebish Islander II E-2
Metauro IM-7	MOBRO 2000 . . . . .D-14	Needier, Alfred C-5
Meteor . . . . .Page 139	MOBRO 2001 . . . . .D-14	Nelvana U-15
Metis C-3	MOBRO 2005 . . . . .D-14	Nelvana {1} G-1
Metz Beirut IM-10	Moby Dick S-6	Nememcha IS-18
Metz Belgica IM-10	Moezelborg IW-1	Neptune H-11
Metz Italia IM-10	Mohawk D-9	Neptune III D-6
Metz, Carl IM-10	Montana G-20	Neshanic O-3
Metz, Pablo IM-10	Montcliffe Hall N-1	Nevskiy, Aleksandr IM-13
Metz, Pauline IM-10	Montmagny C-5	New Hampshire {2} G-20
Metz, Peter IM-10	Montrealais U-15/S-4	New Jersey G-20
Michigan U-3	Montrealer U-15	New Mexico {1} G-20
Michigan {9} G-20	Moon Trader IT-10	New Mexico {2} H-7
Michigan {10} C-26	Moor Laker IV-4	New York G-20
Middle Channel C-12	Moore, Olive M. U-14	New York News {3} G-14
Middletown O-3	Moran, Edmond J. A-10	Newberry, Jerry M-17
Midstate I S-3	Morgan K-5	Newbrunswicker U-15
Midstate II S-3	Morgenstond IA-8	Newfield, Jane P-11
Milanos IE-5	Morraborg IW-1	Niagara . . . . .Page 139
Milin Kamak IN-6	Morton Salt 74 . . . . .M-23	Niagara Clipper B-17
Millenium Condor F-3	Moscenice IC-12	Niagara Prince A-7
Millenium Eagle F-3	Motovun IC-12	Nichevo II M-3
Millenium Falcon F-3	Mott, Charlie U-7	Nicola D ID-7
Millenium Hawk F-3	Moulares IC-10	Nicole S. M-10
Millenium Osprey F-3	Mountain Blossom L-7	Nicolet U-3
Miller, William M. B-4	Mr. Micky H-1	Nicolet {2} S-24
Milroy, Phil F-5	Mrs. C. C-31	Nimet IP-6
Milwaukee Clipper . . . .Page 139	Munksund IB-1	Nindawayma O-8
Mimer IG-1	Munson, John G. {2} U-17	Nipissing {2} M-24
Mina Cebi IC-5	Munteborg IW-1	Nitinat Carrier I-8
Miners Castle P-3	Murray Bay {2} N-1	Njord IA-8
Ming Talent IE-7	Murray Bay {3} U-15	No. 25 . . . . .H-4
Mini Lace IC-6	Murray R. F-5	No. 26 . . . . .H-4
Mini Star IG-1	Musinskiy, Vasiliy IN-12	No. 28 . . . . .H-4
Miniforest IG-1	Muskegon {1} H-4	No. 29 {1} M-9
Minka C IC-3	Muskegon {2} K-6	No. 29 {2} H-4
Minnesota {1} G-20	Musky II U-5	No. 49 . . . . .L-2
Miseford N-2	Musselborg IW-1	Noble, Robert W-2
Misener, Peter U-15	MV 77 . . . . .M-17	Nokomis S-16
Misener, Ralph U-15		Nomadic Patria IG-6
Misener, Scott {4} A-4		Nomadic Pollux IG-6
Mishe-Mokwa M-6	**N**	Nomadic Princess IG-6
Miska IA-8	Nadro Clipper N-2	Nomadic Princess IN-10
Miss Brockville U-13	Nancy Ann M-11	Noor IS-12
Miss Brockville IV U-13	Nancy Anne D-14	Norcove IB-1
Miss Brockville V U-13	Nanook L-10	Nordic Blossom L-7
Miss Brockville VI U-13	Nanticoke C-3	Nordic Moor IP-2
Miss Brockville VII U-13	Nantucket Clipper C-24	Nordik Express T-14
Miss Brockville VIII U-13	Narragansett IB-3	Nordik Passeur T-14
Miss Buffalo B-17	Nash . . . . .Page 139	Nordon IB-1
Miss Buffalo II B-17	Natacha C IC-3	Nordstrand IC-3
Miss Edna K-6	Nathan S. M-10	Norgoma . . . . .Page 140
Miss Ivy Lea II I-10	Naugatuck S-6	Norisle . . . . .Page 140
Miss Ivy Lea III I-10	Nautica Queen J-3	Norma B. F-4
Miss Kingston II C-32	Navajo {1} H-7	Normac P-9
Miss Midland P-7	Navajo {2} E-6	Norman Star ID-7
Miss Montreal C-36	Navcomar #1 . . . . .L-10	Norris, James U-15/S-5
Miss Munising S-11	Navicula C-5	North Carolina {2} G-20
Miss Olympia C-32	Navigo IR-1	North Channel C-12
Miss Superior P-3	Nea Doxa IF-2	North Dakota G-20

Vessel Name / Fleet Number	Vessel Name / Fleet Number	Vessel Name / Fleet Number
Northern Spirit I M-13	Ongiara T-12	Perelik IN-6
Northwestern {2} G-17	Ontadoc {2} T-14	Performance S-21
Norton, David Z. {3} O-3	Ontamich B-15	Periandros IS-10
Nouvelle-Orleans C-32	Opatija IC-12	Perseus IC-7
Novikov, Nikolay IN-12	Ophelia IF-3	Pete, C. West N-2
NST Challenge IN-14	Opilio C-5	Petite Forte S-22
Nyanza IS-9	Oregon {1} E-6	Petka F-3
	Oregon {2} G-20	Petrel V T-2
O	ORG 5503 ....P-11	Phaethon IL-3
O' Toole, Donald K-5	ORG 6502 ....P-11	Pharos IS-23
Oak ID-5	Orinoco T-14	Philippine Express ID-1
Oak Grove O-1	Oriole M-13	Phoenician Trader U-2
Oakglen {2} P-1	Orsula F-3	Phoenix M IE-3
Oatka A-2	Osborne, F. M. {2} O-7	Pia II-1
Obod IP-9	Oshawa C-11	Pictured Rocks P-3
Ocean Abys L-10	Osprey P-11	Pinta II-1
Ocean Alpha L-10	Ostfriesland B-5	Pintail C-7
Ocean Bird IJ-4	Ostfriesland, S. A. B-5	Pioneer U-15
Ocean Bravo L-10	Ostria I II-2	Pioneer {3} S-17
Ocean Charlie L-10	Ottawa {2} A-14	Pioneer Challenger O-3
Ocean Echo II L-10	Ottercliffe Hall U-15	Pioneer Princess T-13
Ocean Foxtrot L-10	Outer Island E-5	Pioneer Queen T-13
Ocean Golf L-10		Pioneerland M-9
Ocean Grace IG-2	**P**	Pionier II-1
Ocean Hauler M-17	P. S. Barge No. 1 ....L-10	Pionir IC-12
Ocean Hauler 10 ....M-17	P.M.L. 357 ....P-11	Pira IB-5
Ocean Hercule L-10	P.M.L. 2501 ....P-11	Pirat II-1
Ocean Intrepide L-10	P.M.L. Alton P-11	Pirol II-1
Ocean Jupiter L-10	P.M.L. Salvager P-11	Pistis IA-9
Ocean Lake IG-2	Pacific Standard M-17	Plitvice IA-17
Ocean Leader IU-1	Pacific Star IM-2	Po Siu IM-2
Ocean Priti IC-11	Paj U-3	Point Carroll E-1
Ocean Venture A-9	Palladino, Frank Jr. K-4	Point Chebucto E-1
Ochimos IL-3	Paloma I II-1	Point Halifax E-1
Oderstern IR-5	Pamela II-1	Point Vibert E-1
Odranes IP-8	Pan Amoco I-4	Point Vigour E-1
Odyssey II O-2	Pan Hope IP-3	Point Vim E-1
Offshore Supplier M-17	Pan Noble IP-3	Pointe Aux Basques E-1
Oglebay, Crispin {2} U-15	Pan Voyager IP-3	Pointe Comeau E-1
Oglebay, Earl W. O-3	Pandalus III C-5	Pointe Sept-Iles E-1
Oglebay, Norton O-3	Pantazis L. IC-6	Polana H-3
Ohio {3} G-20	Pany R IJ-3	Polydefkis IS-10
Oil Queen G-9	Parisien, Jean C-3	Polykratis IS-10
Ojibway {1} U-17	Parizeau C-5	Pomorze Zachodnie IP-8
Ojibway {2} L-2	Parkgracht IS-22	Pontokratis IM-9
OKA No. 12 ....L-10	Partington U-15	Pontoporos IM-9
Oklahoma G-20	Partridge Island C-5	Poolgracht IS-22
Okoltchitza IN-6	Paterson {2} N-1	Port City Princess P-8
Old Fox IM-10	Pathfinder {3} I-6	Port Mechins V-1
Old Mission K-5	Pathum Navee IU-3	Portside Belle D-11
Oldendorff, Anna IE-1	Patria II-1	Poseidon II-1
Oldendorff, Bernhard C-3	Patria IO-4	Pozharskiy, Dmitriy IM-13
Oldendorff, Christopher C-3	Patriot II-2	Prabhu Daya IT-7
Oldendorff, Erna IE-1	Patronicola, Calliroe IO-3	Prairie Harvest C-3
Oldendorff, Helena IE-1	Paul E. No. 1 ....M-17	Prairieland M-9
Oldendorff, Regina IE-1	Paula M. C-6	Praxitelis IS-10
Oldendorff, Rixta IE-1	PBI L-2	Premiere II-1
Olga IB-6	Pearkes, George R. C-5	Presque Isle {1} I-4
Olympic Melody IO-3	Peckinpaugh, Day E-12	Presque Isle {2} U-17
Olympic Mentor IO-3	Pelagos IC-7	Pride of Michigan U-8
Olympic Merit IO-3	Pelee Islander O-8	Primosten IS-16
Olympic Miracle IO-3	Peninsula G-14	Princess J-6
Omis IS-23	Pennsylvania {3} G-20	Princess No. 1 ....J-6
Omni Sorel L-10	Peonia IS-6	Princess of Acadia N-6
Omni St-Laurent L-10	Pere Marquette 10 ....M-14	Princess Wenonah B-4
Omni-Atlas L-10	Pere Marquette 12 ....M-17	Progress N-2
Omni-Richelieu L-10	Pere Marquette 41 ....L-1	Project Americas IS-22

42

Vessel Name / Fleet Number	Vessel Name / Fleet Number	Vessel Name / Fleet Number
Project Arabia IS-22	Rhea IF-6	Sand Pebble D-5
Project Europa IS-22	Rheinstern IR-5	Sandpiper H-5
Project Orient IS-22	Rhine Ore N-1	Sapanca IS-20
Proof Gallant IJ-9	Rhode Island G-20	Saskatchewan Pioneer F-3
Proussa IM-5	Richelieu {3} A-4	Saturn {4} A-4
Provence II-1	Richter, C. G. W-2	Sault au Couchon M-17
Provider S-13	Rickey, James W. D-11	Sauniere A-4
Provmar Terminal U-15	Ridgeway, Benjamin K-4	Sava IC-12
Provmar Terminal II U-15	Rijeka IC-12	Savard, Joseph S-14
Provo Wallis C-5	Rio Orinoco T-14	Saxon Star ID-7
Prvic IS-16	Risley, Samuel C-5	Says S-22
Purcell, Robert A-10	Risnes ID-9	Scan Polaris IS-5
Purnell, Frank {1} S-17	Rivershell {4} S-9	Scandrett, Fred T-11
Purves, John A-10	Riza Sonay IB-5	Scarab ID-7
Purvis, W. I. Scott P-11	Roanoke {2} M-14	Schemn, H. R. I-4
Purvis, W. J. Ivan P-11	Robert H. T-17	Schlaeger, Victor L. C-15
Put-In-Bay {2} S-10	Robert W. T-7	Schoonmaker, James M. Col.
Put-In-Bay {3} M-21	Robert, Joseph X. G-10	................Page 138
	Robin E. E-6	Schwartz, H. J. U-3
Q	Robinson Bay S-21	Scotsman S-22
Quebecois U-15/S-4	Rockefeller, Frank .....Page 139	Scully, V. W. A-4
Quedoc {3} N-1	Rocket P-11	Sea Barge One C-3
Queen IE-8	Roen, John III S-6	Sea Eagle S-22
Queen City {2} H-3	Roesch, William R. O-3	Sea Eagle IB-11
Queen of Andersonville W-5	Rollnes ID-9	Sea Eagle II S-22
Queng #1 ....L-10	Roman, Stephen B. C-3	Sea Flower IA-1
Quinte Loyalist (The) O-4	Rong Cheng IC-11	Sea Fox II S-2
Quo-Vadis IA-8	Rong Jiang IC-11	Sea Hound M-17
	Rosalee D. T-7	Sea Maid IF-1
R	Rosali IR-7	Sea Pearl IA-1
R. & L. No. 1 ....G-16	Rose Islands IV-5	Sea Queen II A-12
R.C. L. No. 1 ....C-6	Rosemary M-13	Sea Rose IA-1
Rab IC-12	Rossel Current IS-16	Sea Wolf C-2
Racine U-3	Royalton {2} U-15	Seadaniel IC-11
Radisson {1} S-14	Rubin Eagle IN-9	Seaflight I C-25
Radisson {2} S-24	Rubin Falcon IN-9	Seaflight II C-25
Radisson, Pierre C-5	Rubin Hawk IN-9	Seaglory ID-11
Radnoti IH-12	Rubin Stork IA-13	Seal VII I-8
Rafnes ID-9	Rugia IO-4	Sealion VII I-8
Railship I IF-5	Ruhr Ore A-4	Seapearl II IN-4
Ramsoy, Jon A-4	Ryerson, Edward L. C-11	Searanger II IT-4
Randolph, Curtis D-8		Seaway Queen U-15/S-4
Ranger III U-7	**S**	Sedoy IA-4
Rankki IN-8	S' Hib IC-10	Segwun M-24
Rantum IT-5	S.M.T.B. No. 7 ....M-17	Selemat, Kota B-5
Rapid Cities G-14	Sac Flix IE-5	Selkirk Settler F-3
Ratana Sopa IE-2	Sac Huelva IE-5	Selvick, Bonnie G. S-6
Raymond, Jean M-17	Sac Malaga IE-5	Selvick, Carla Anne S-6
Razboieni IN-7	Sachem E-6	Selvick, John M. S-6
Razin, Stepan IM-13	Sackville ....Page 140	Selvick, Sharon M. S-6
RC1 ....R-6	Sacre Bleu S-10	Selvick, William C. S-6
RC2 ....R-6	Sadan Kaptanoglu IG-7	Seneca B-12
Rebecca Lynn A-10	Sagittarius IS-14	Senneville A-4
Red Crown S-17	Saguenay {2} P-4	Sentosa IG-5
Redestos IM-5	Sajo IH-12	Serenade IM-8
Reiss ....Page 139	Salty Dog No. 1 ....M-17	Serendipity Princess P-7
Reiss, Richard E-12	Salvage Monarch L-10	Sevilla Wave IT-2
Reiss, Richard J. E-13	Salvage Scow No. 1 ......L-10	Shamrock {1} J-7
Relief R-6	Sammi Aurora IP-3	Shannon G-2
Rennie, Thomas T-12	Sammi Herald IP-3	Shannon 66-5 ....T-6
Repulse Bay IA-2	Samrat Ajaya IS-2	Shark C-5
Reserve O-3	Samrat Rucaka IS-2	Shark VII I-8
Resolute D-7	Samrat Vijaya IS-2	Sheila P. P-11
Rest, William T-11	Samson II D-14	Shelter Bay U-3
Retriever M-12	San Juan C-4	Shenango II I-6
Reuben, Lee H-4	San Marino IR-2	Sherwin, John {2} I-6
		Shipka IN-6

Wilfred Sykes enters port at Grand Haven, MI, 22 July 1998. (Dave Swian)

Vessel Name / Fleet Number		Vessel Name / Fleet Number		Vessel Name / Fleet Number	
Shirley Irene	K-3	Spring Ocean	IP-10	Susak	IC-12
Shirley Joy	L-2	Spring Ocean	IS-13	Susan E.	E-6
Shoreline II	S-12	Spring Trader	IS-13	Susan K	IA-1
Showboat Royal Grace	M-13	Sprint Runner	S-7	Susan Michelle	D-3
Sideracrux	IS-14	Spuds	R-3	Susanin, Ivan	IM-13
Sidercastor	IS-14	Spume	C-5	Sverdlov, Jakov	IM-12
Siderpollux	IS-14	St. Clair {2}	M-17	Sykes, Wilfred	C-11
Sillery	M-17	St. Clair {3}	A-9		
Silver Isle	A-4	St. George	IS-24	**T**	
Silversides	Page 140	St. John, J. S.	E-12	T. A. Adventurer	IE-1
Silvia	IP-12	St. Joseph	G-14	T. A. Discoverer	IE-1
Simard, Edouard	A-4	St. Laurent, Louis	C-5	T. A. Explorer	IE-1
Simard, J. Edouard	A-4	St. Lawrence Navigator	U-15	T. A. Voyager	IE-1
Simcoe	C-5	St. Lawrence Prospector	U-15	Tabarka	IC-10
Simons, Roger R.	Page 139	St. Martin	IS-24	Tadoussac {2}	C-3
Simonsen	U-3	St. Mary's Cement	S-23	Tandem	C-32
Simpson, Shawn Miss	M-17	St. Mary's Cement II	S-22	Tarantau	C-3
Sioux {1}	L-2	St. Mary's Cement III	S-22	Tartan Sea	T-14
Sioux {2}	E-6	St. Thomas	IS-24	Tatiana L.	IC-6
Sirri	IN-8	Stahl, Roger	G-2	Tawas Bay	U-3
Siscowet	U-5	Stalvang	IB-10	Taylor, Myron C.	U-17
Skelly, James E.	U-14	Stamon	IS-1	Tecam Sea	F-3
Skradin	IS-16	State of Haryana	IT-3	Techno St-Laurent	T-2
Skyline Princess	M-20	STC 2004	B-19	Techno Venture	M-17
Skyline Queen	M-20	Ste. Claire	S-26	Tecumseh {2}	G-14
Slano	IA-17	Ste. Marie I	E-6	Tecumseh II	P-11
Slapy	IC-14	Ste. Marie II	E-6	Telesis	P-2
Slavonija	IC-12	Steelcliffe Hall	N-1	Temple Bar	A-4
Sloan, George A.	U-17	Steelton {3}	S-17	Tennessee	G-20
Slovenija	IC-12	Stefanos	IS-29	Tenyu	ID-10
Smallwood, Joseph & Clara	M-8	Steinvang	IB-10	Terry S.	N-2
Smith, Edward V. Capt.	C-3	Stella	IB-13	Tevfik Kaptan I	IM-6
Smith, F. C. G.	C-5	Stella Borealis	C-25	Texaco Brave {2}	A-4
Smith, H. A.	H-6	Stellamare	IJ-12	Texaco Chief {2}	A-4
Smith, L. L. Jr.	U-12	Stellanova	IJ-12	Texas	G-20
Snowrose	IS-4	Stellaprima	IJ-12	Thayer, Paul	O-3
Snyder, William P.	S-17	Sterling, Walter A.	I-6	Thompson, Joseph H.	U-16
Solin	IS-23	Stevns Bulk	IN-11	Thompson, Joseph H. Jr.	U-16
Solta	IS-23	Stevns Pearl	IN-11	Thompson, Maxine	F-5
Soo River Belle	W-4	Stevns Sea	IN-11	Thor 1	C-19
Soodoc {2}	T-14	Stevns Trader	IN-11	Thor Scan	IS-22
Sooneck	II-1	Stevnsland	IS-27	Thorhild	IO-1
Sora	C-5	Still Watch	T-5	Thornburg	IO-1
Sotka	IN-8	Stinson, George A.	A-9	Thorndale	IO-1
South Bass	M-21	Stolt Alliance	S-28	Thornhill	U-15
South Channel	C-12	Stolt Aspiration	S-28	Thorold {4}	T-14
South Islands	IN-5	Stolt Kent	S-28	Thorscape	C-19
South Park	Page 139	Stolt Taurus	S-28	Thorswave	C-19
South Shore	B-8	Stormont	M-17	Thorunn	IO-1
South Trader	IT-10	Storon	IB-1	Thousand Islander	G-5
Spar Garnet	F-3	Straits Express	A-14	Thousand Islander II	G-5
Spar Jade	F-3	Straits of Mackinac (The)	C-28	Thousand Islander III	G-5
Spar Opal	F-3	Straits of Mackinac II	A-14	Thousand Islander IV	G-5
Sparrows Point	O-3	Strange Attractor	IO-2	Thousand Islander V	G-5
Spartan [42] {2}	L-1	Strelkov, Petr	IN-12	Thunder Bay	E-2
Spear	IV-2	Sugar Islander	E-2	Thunder Bay	F-3
Speer, Edgar B.	U-17	Sugar Islander II	E-2	Tiira	IN-8
Spence, John	M-17	Sullivans (The)	Page 140	Tim Buck	IN-4
Spencer, Sarah	C-3	Sumy	IA-19	Timberland	M-9
Spindrift	C-5	Sundew	U-4	Timmy B.	S-6
Spiridon, A. M.	IS-12	Sunny Blossom	L-7	Timmy L.	S-6
Spiridon, S. M.	IS-12	Sunrise	IS-25	Timofeyev, Vladimir	IJ-11
Spirit of Rochester	G-7	Sunrise I	S-7	Tina C	IC-3
Spirit Trader	IT-10	Sunrise II	S-7	Titan Scan	IS-22
Split	IS-23	Sunrise V	S-7	Tobermory	C-5
Spray	C-5	Sunrise VI	S-7	Todd L.	F-5
Spring Laker	IP-10	Superior {3}	G-20		

Vessel Name / Fleet Number	Vessel Name / Fleet Number	Vessel Name / Fleet Number
Tofton IB-1	Valley Camp {2} ......Page 140	Welland D-3
Tokachi Star IC-7	Valour T-8	Wellington Kent {2} I-8
Toledo M-17	Vamand Wave IT-2	Wendella Clipper W-5
Tomacelli, Caterina IM-7	Van Enkevort, Joyce L. V-4	Wendella Limited W-5
Tommy B. C-2	Van, Joe D-14	Wendella Sunliner W-5
Tommy Ray D-5	Vandoc {2} N-1	Wenonah S-13
Tonawanda R-6	Vanessa C IC-3	Weserstern IR-5
Tonawanda U-3	Vechtborg IW-1	West Shore {2} M-15
Toni D. M-17	Vectis Falcon IC-3	West Wind J-4
Topaz IS-24	Vectis Isle IC-3	Westcott, J. W. II J-2
Tor Belgia IB-1	Veerseborg IW-1	Westfort C-5
Tor Flandria IB-1	Vega IA-8	Weston IB-1
Tor Scandia IB-1	Vekua IA-4	Whitby C-11
Torontonian M-13	Velasco S-22	White, Fred R. Jr. O-3
Torres, Robert L. A-10	Velebit IC-12	White, H. Lee {2} A-9
Toubro, Soren F-3	Velikiy, Pyotr IM-13	Whitefish Bay U-3
Townsend, Paul H. I-4	Vento Del Golfo IC-4	William C I-1
Tozeur IC-10	Verendrye D-10	Willis, Emma G-2
Tracy C-5	Verge, Bert N-2	Willowglen G-10
Tradewind Express IB-9	Vermont G-20	Wilmac M-17
Transit C-32	Versluis, James J. C-18	Wilson, Charles E. A-9
Travestern IR-5	Vesting IA-8	Windmill Point T-11
Tregurtha, Lee A. I-6	Victoria A-13	Windoc {2} N-1
Tregurtha, Paul R. I-6	Vigsnes ID-9	Windsor {2} M-14
Trenton {1} E-13	Viking {2} C-29	Winnebago J-8
Trias IT-9	Vikingbank IA-8	Winnipeg {2} A-4
Trident Mariner IM-4	Vikla IN-8	Winter Star IH-7
Triena IS-11	Viljandi IE-6	Wisconsin {4} G-20
Triglav IC-12	Ville Marie T-5	Wislanes IP-8
Trillium T-12	Ville Marie II C-32	Wolf River G-14
Trinidad {2} W-1	Villmont No. 2 ....U-9	Wolfe Islander III O-4
Trinity C-2	Vinland Saga IA-1	Wolverine M-1
Triton {1} E-6	Vios IA-8	Wolverine {4} O-3
Triton {2} S-23	Virginia K-4	World Star IH-7
Trois Rivieres S-14	Virginia {2} G-20	Wyoming G-20
Tropic Confidence IM-1	Vista King V-3	
True North of Toronto G-18	Vista Star V-3	
Trump Casino T-18	Vlieborg IW-1	**Y**
Truskavets T-14	Vlistborg IW-1	Ya Latif IH-11
Tuhobic IC-12	VM/S Hercules S-20	Ya Rab IH-11
Tupper C-5	VM/S Iroquois S-20	Ya Samadu IH-11
Twolan, W. N. A-1	VM/S Massinouve S-20	Yankcanuck {2} P-11
	Volta River IB-7	Yankee Clipper V-5
	Voorneborg IW-1	Yankee Lady G-21
U	Vortice M-17	Yankee Lady II G-21
U-505 ....Page 140	Voyager W-2	Yavuz Sultan Selim IB-12
U-727 ....P-11	Voyageur V-6	Yetter, B. M-11
Uikku IN-8	Voyageur II S-13	Yick Hua IC-11
Ulloa IP-1	Vysotskiy, Vladimir IN-13	Yorktown Clipper C-24
Ulmo IA-8		
Ulusoy, Suat IP-6		**Z**
Uncle Sam II U-1	**W**	Zafer Tomba IM-6
Uncle Sam Jr. U-1	Wagenborg, Egbert IW-1	Zarnesti IN-7
Uncle Sam VII U-1	Walpole Islander D-1	Ziemia Chelminska IP-8
Undaunted L-1	Wana Naree IG-4	Ziemia Cieszynska F-3
Ungava Transport U-15	Wanda III M-24	Ziemia Gnieznienska IP-8
Unilifter T-15	Wartanes IP-8	Ziemia Gornoslaska F-3
United IP-1	Washington U-3	Ziemia Lodzka F-3
Upper Canada B-7	Washington {1} G-20	Ziemia Suwalska IP-8
Utviken F-3	Washington {2} W-2	Ziemia Tarnowska IP-8
Uznadze IA-4	Washington Rainbow II IJ-2	Ziemia Zamojska IP-8
	Waterways 1 ....W-3	Zlarin IS-16
	Wave Runner S-7	Zuiderzee IA-8
V	Wayward Princess E-8	Zulfikar IH-11
Vac N-2	Weber, Camilla IH-9	Zuljenah IH-11
Vachon F-3	Weir, Ernest T. O-3	
Vakhtangov IA-4	Welcome {2} G-20	
Valga IE-6	Welcome (The) S-10	

Fleet & Vessel Listings

Emerald Star discharges petroleum products at a Sault Ste. Marie, ON dock 10 October 1998. (Roger LeLievre)

U.S. & CANADIAN FLEETS

Listed after each vessel (only 35 feet or longer are included) in order are; Type of Vessel, Year Built, Type of Engine, Cargo Capacity (at mid-summer draft in long tons) or Gross Tonnage* (tanker capacities are listed in barrels), Overall Length, Breadth and Depth or Draft*. The figures given are as accurate as possible and are given for informational purposes only. Vessels and owners are listed alphabetically as per American Bureau of Shipping and Lloyd's Register of Shipping format. Former names of vessels and years of operation under former names appear beneath the vessel's name.

For convenience, the following abbreviations have been used.

TYPE OF VESSEL

AC	Auto Carrier	GA	Gambling Casino	RR	Roll On/Roll Off
BC	Bulk Carrier	GC	General Cargo	RT	Refueling Tanker
BK	Bulk Carrier/Tanker	GL	Gate Lifter	RV	Research Vessel
BT	Buoy Tender	GU	Grain Self Unloader	SB	Supply Boat
CC	Cement Carrier	HY	Hydrofoil	SC	Sand Carrier
CF	Car Ferry	IB	Ice Breaker	SR	Search & Rescue
CLG	Guided Missile Cruiser	KO	Corvette	SS	Submarine
CS	Crane Ship	LS	Lightship	SU	Self Unloader
DB	Deck Barge	LT	Lighthouse Tender	SV	Survey Vessel
DD	Destroyer	MB	Mail Boat	TB	Tug Boat
DR	Dredge	MS	Mine Sweeper	TF	Train Ferry
DS	Dump Scow	PA	Passenger Vessel	TK	Tanker
DV	Drilling Vessel	PB	Pilot Boat	TT	Tractor Tug Boat
ES	Excursion Ship	PC	Passenger Catamaran	TV	Training Vessel
EV	Env. Response Ship	PF	Passenger Ferry	WM	Med. Endurance Cutter
FB	Fire Boat	PK	Package Freighter	2B	Brigantine
FD	Floating Dry Dock	PT	Patrol Torpedo Boat	2S	2 Masted Schooner
FF	Frigate			3S	3 Masted Schooner

PROPULSION

B	Barge	L	Steam - Quad Exp. Double Compound Engine "Lentz Poppet"
D	Diesel	Q	Steam - Quad Exp. Compound Engine
V	Batteries	R	Steam - Triple Exp. Compound Engine
W	Sailing Vessel	S	Steam - Skinner "Unaflow" Engine
		T	Steam - Turbine
		U	Steam - Uniflow Engine - "Skinner" Design

Fleet No. & Name Vessel Name	Type of Vessel	Year Built	Type of Engine	Cargo Cap. or Gross*	Overal Length	Breadth	Depth or Draft*
A-1 — A. B. M. MARINE, THUNDER BAY, ON							
McAllister 132	DB	1954	B	7,000	343' 00"	63' 00"	19' 00"
(Powell No. 1 '54 - '61, Alberni Carrier '61 - '77, Genmar 132 '77 - '79)							
W. N. Twolan	TB	1962	D	299*	106' 00"	29' 05"	15' 00"
A-2 — ACME MARINE SERVICE, KNIFE RIVER, MN							
Kaner 1	SB	1950	D	38*	55' 00"	15' 00"	7' 01"
Marine Trader	SB	1939	D	60*	65' 00"	15' 00"	7' 06"
Oatka	TB	1934	D	10*	40' 00"	10' 00"	4' 06"
A-3 — ALCAN ALUMINUM LTD., PORT ALFRED, PQ							
Alexis-Simard	TT	1980	D	286*	92' 00"	34' 00"	13' 07"
Grande Baie	TT	1973	D	194*	86' 06"	30' 00"	12' 00"

Fleet No. & Name / Vessel Name	Type of Vessel	Year Built	Type of Engine	Cargo Cap. or Gross*	Overal Length	Breadth	Depth or Draft*
A-4 — ALGOMA CENTRAL CORP., SAULT STE. MARIE, ON							
ALGOMA CENTRAL MARINE GROUP - A DIVISION OF ALGOMA CENTRAL CORP.							
Agawa Canyon	SU	1970	D	23,400	647' 00"	72' 00"	40' 00"
Algobay	SU	1978	D	34,900	730' 00"	75' 10"	46' 06"
(Algobay '78 - '94, Atlantic Trader '94 - '97)							
Algocape {2}	BC	1967	D	29,950	730' 00"	75' 00"	39' 08"
(Richelieu {3} '67 - '94)							
Algocen {2}	BC	1968	D	28,400	730' 00"	75' 00"	39' 08"
Algogulf {2}	BC	1961	T	26,950	730' 00"	75' 00"	39' 00"
(J. N. McWatters {2} '61 - '91, Scott Misener {4} '91 - '94)							
Algoisle	BC	1963	D	26,700	730' 00"	75' 00"	39' 03"
(Silver Isle '63 - '94)							
Algolake	SU	1977	D	32,150	730' 00"	75' 00"	46' 06"
Algomarine	SU	1968	D	27,000	730' 00"	75' 00"	39' 08"
(Lake Manitoba '68 - '87)							
Algonorth	BC	1971	D	28,000	729' 09"	75' 02"	42' 11"
(Temple Bar '71 - '77, Lake Nipigon '77 - '84, Laketon {2} '84 - '86, Lake Nipigon '86 - '87)							
Algontario	BC	1960	D	29,100	730' 00"	75' 09"	40' 02"
(Ruhr Ore '60 - '76, Cartiercliffe Hall '76 - '88, Winnipeg {2} '88 - '94)							
Algoport	SU	1979	D	32,000	658' 00"	75' 10"	46' 06"
Algorail {2}	SU	1968	D	23,750	640' 05"	72' 03"	40' 00"
Algoriver	BC	1960	T	26,800	722' 06"	75' 00"	39' 00"
(John A. France {2} '60 - '94)							
Algosoo {2}	SU	1974	D	31,300	730' 00"	75' 00"	44' 06"
Algosound	BC	1965	T	27,700	730' 00"	75' 00"	39' 00"
(Don-De-Dieu '65 - '67, V. W. Scully '67 - '87)							
Algosteel {2}	SU	1966	D	27,000	730' 00"	75' 00"	39' 08"
(A. S. Glossbrenner '66 - '87, Algogulf {1} '87 - '90)							
Algoville	SU	1967	D	31,250	730' 00"	78' 00"	39' 08"
(Senneville '67 - '94)							
Algoway {2}	SU	1972	D	24,000	650' 00"	72' 00"	40' 00"
Algowest	SU	1982	D	32,000	730' 00"	75' 10"	42' 00"
Algowood	SU	1981	D	31,750	730' 00"	75' 10"	46' 06"
Capt. Henry Jackman	SU	1981	D	30,550	730' 00"	75' 10"	42' 00"
(Lake Wabush '81 - '87)							
John B. Aird	SU	1983	D	31,300	730' 00"	75' 10"	46' 06"
ALGOMA TANKERS LTD. - A DIVISION OF ALGOMA CENTRAL CORP.							
Algodart	RT	1970	D	15,265	205' 06"	40' 00"	16' 00"
(Imperial Dartmouth '70 - '98)							
Algoeast	TK	1977	D	77,999	431' 05"	65' 07"	35' 05"
(Texaco Brave {2} '77 - '86, Le Brave '86 - '97, Imperial St. Lawrence {2} '97 - '97)							
Algofax	TK	1969	D	117,602	485' 05"	70' 02"	33' 03"
(Imperial Bedford '69 - '97)							
Algonova	TK	1969	D	53,002	400' 06"	54' 02"	26' 05"
(Texaco Chief {2} '69 - '87, A. G. Farquharson '87 - '98)							
Algosar	TK	1974	D	105,645	435' 00"	74' 00"	32' 00"
(Imperial St. Clair '74 - '97)							
Algoscotia	TK	1966	D	82,222	440' 00"	60' 00"	31' 00"
(Imperial Acadia '66 - '97)							
EnerChem Catalyst	TK	1972	D	84,097	431' 00"	62' 04"	34' 05"
(Jon Ramsoy '72 - '74, Doan Transport '74 - '86)							
EnerChem Refiner	TK	1969	D	69,327	391' 00"	55' 00"	27' 06"
(Industrial Transport '69 - '86)							
EnerChem Trader	TK	1961	D	64,581	430' 07"	52' 00"	28' 00"
(J. Edouard Simard '61 - '67, Edouard Simard '67 - '82, Le Chene No. 1 '82 - '97)							
CLEVELAND TANKERS (1991), INC. - CHARTERED BY ALGOMA TANKERS LTD.							
Gemini	TK	1978	D	73,000	432' 06"	65' 00"	29' 04"
Saturn {4}	TK	1974	D	45,000	384' 01"	54' 06"	25' 00"
SOCIETE QUEBECOISE D' EXPLORATION MINIERE - CHARTERER							
Sauniere	SU	1970	D	23,900	642' 10"	74' 10"	42' 00"
(Bulknes '70 - '70, Brooknes '70 - '76, Algosea '76 - '82)							
A-5 — ALLIED SIGNAL, INC., DETROIT, MI							
Allied Chemical No. 12	TK	1969	B	1,545	200' 01"	35' 01"	8' 06"*
A-6 — ALLOUEZ MARINE SUPPLY, SUPERIOR, WI							
Barbara Ann {1}	SB	1948	D	5*	38' 00"	10' 00"	3' 00"

Fleet No. & Name Vessel Name	Type of Vessel	Year Built	Type of Engine	Cargo Cap. or Gross*	Overal Length	Breadth	Depth or Draft*
Carroll Jean	SB		D	5*	38' 00"	10' 00"	3' 00"

A-7 — AMERICAN CANADIAN CARIBBEAN LINE, INC., WARREN, RI

Grande Caribe	PA	1998	D	99*	182' 00"	39' 00"	9' 08"
Grande Mariner	PA	1998	D	99*	182' 00"	39' 00"	9' 08"
Grande Prince	PA	1997	D	99*	182' 00"	39' 00"	9' 08"
Niagara Prince	PA	1994	D	687*	174' 00"	40' 00"	14' 00"

A-8 — AMERICAN MARINE CONSTRUCTION, BENTON HARBOR, MI

AMC 100	DB	1979	B	2,273	200' 00"	52' 00"	14' 00"
AMC 200	DB	1979	B	2,273	200' 00"	36' 00"	11' 08"
Defiance	TB	1966	D	26*	44' 08"	18' 00"	6' 00

A-9 — AMERICAN STEAMSHIP CO., WILLIAMSVILLE, NY

Adam E. Cornelius {4}	SU	1973	D	28,200	680' 00"	78' 00"	42' 00"
(Roger M. Kyes '73 - '89)							
American Gulf V	BC	1981	B	33,700	550' 00"	78' 00"	50' 00"
American Mariner	SU	1980	D	37,200	730' 00"	78' 00"	45' 00"
American Republic	SU	1981	D	24,800	634' 10"	68' 00"	40' 00"
Buffalo {3}	SU	1978	D	23,800	634' 10"	68' 00"	40' 00"
Charles E. Wilson	SU	1973	D	33,800	680' 00"	78' 00"	45' 00"
H. Lee White {2}	SU	1974	D	35,200	704' 00"	78' 00"	45' 00"
Indiana Harbor	SU	1979	D	78,850	1,000' 00"	105' 00"	56' 00"
John J. Boland {3}	SU	1953	T	20,200	639' 03"	72' 00"	36' 00"
Ocean Venture	TB		D				
Sam Laud	SU	1975	D	23,800	634' 10"	68' 00"	40' 00"
St. Clair {3}	SU	1976	D	44,000	770' 00"	92' 00"	52' 00"
Walter J. McCarthy Jr.	SU	1977	D	78,850	1,000' 00"	105' 00"	56' 00"
(Belle River '77 - '90)							

STINSON, INC. - MANAGED BY AMERICAN STEAMSHIP CO.

George A. Stinson	SU	1978	D	59,700	1,004' 00"	105' 00"	50' 00"

A-10 — ANDRIE, INC., MUSKEGON, MI

A-390	TK	1982	B	39,000	310' 00"	60' 00"	19' 03"
A-397	TK	1962	B	39,700	270' 00"	60' 00"	25' 00"
A-410	TK	1955	B	41,000	335' 00"	54' 00"	26' 06"
Barbara Andrie	TB	1940	D	298*	121' 10"	29' 06"	16' 00"
(Edmond J. Moran '40 - '76)							
Barbara Rita	TB	1981	D	15*	36' 00"	14' 00"	6' 00"
Candice Andrie	CS	1958	B	1,000	150' 00"	52' 00"	10' 00"
Clara Andrie	DR	1930	B	1,000	110' 00"	30' 00"	6' 10"
John Joseph	TB	1993	D	15*	40' 00"	14' 00"	5' 00"
John Purves	TB	1919	D	436*	150' 00"	27' 07"	16' 00"
(Butterfield '19 - '42, U.S. Army Butterfield [LT-145] '42 - '45, Butterfield '45 - '57)							
Karen Andrie {2}	TB	1965	D	433*	120' 00"	31' 06"	16' 00"
(Sarah Hays '65 - '93)							
Mari Beth Andrie	TB	1961	D	147*	87' 00"	24' 00"	11' 06"
(Gladys Bea '61 - '73, American Viking '73 - '83)							
Rebecca Lynn	TB	1964	D	433*	120' 00"	31' 08"	18' 09"
(Kathrine Clewis '64 - '96)							
Robert Purcell	TB	1952	D	28*	45' 00"	12' 06"	7' 09"

LAFARGE CORP. - MANAGED BY ANDRIE, INC.

Integrity	CC	1996	B	14,000	460' 00"	70' 00"	37' 00"
Jacklyn M.	TB	1976	D	198*	140' 02"	40' 01"	22' 03"
(Andrew Martin '76 - '90, Robert L. Torres '90 - '94)							
(Integrity/Jacklyn M. overall dimensions together)					543' 00"	70' 00"	37' 00"

A-11 — APEX OIL CO., GRANITE CITY, IL

Apex Chicago	TK	1981	B	35,000	288' 00"	60' 00"	19' 00"

A-12 — APOSTLE ISLAND CRUISE SERVICE, BAYFIELD, WI

Eagle Island	ES	1976	D	12*	42' 00"	14' 00"	3' 06"
(Grampa Woo '93 - '96)							
Sea Queen II	ES	1971	D	12*	42' 00"	14' 00"	2' 07"

A-13 — ARGEE CRUISES, INC., PENETANGUISHENE, ON

Georgian Queen	ES	1918	D	249*	119' 00"	36' 00"	16' 06"
(Victoria '18 - '18, Murray Stewart '18 - '48, David Richard '48 - '79)							

Fleet No. & Name Vessel Name	Type of Vessel	Year Built	Type of Engine	Cargo Cap. or Gross*	Overall Length	Breadth	Depth or Draft*
A-14 — ARNOLD TRANSIT CO., MACKINAC ISLAND, MI							
Algomah	PK	1961	D	125	93' 00"	31' 00"	8' 00"
Beaver	CF	1952	D	87*	61' 02"	30' 02"	8' 00"
Chippewa {6}	PK	1962	D	125	93' 00"	31' 00"	8' 00"
Corsair	CF	1955	D	98*	94' 06"	33' 00"	8' 06"
Huron {5}	PK	1955	D	80	91' 06"	25' 00"	10' 01"
Island Express	PC	1988	D	90*	82' 07"	28' 06"	8' 05"
Mackinac Express	PC	1987	D	90*	82' 07"	28' 06"	8' 05"
Ottawa {2}	PK	1959	D	125	93' 00"	31' 00"	8' 00"
Straits Express	PC	1995	D	99*	101' 00"	29' 11"	6' 08"
Straits of Mackinac II	PF	1969	D	89*	89' 11"	27' 00"	8' 08"
B-1 — BARDEN DEVELOPMENT, GARY, IN							
Majestic Star {2}	GA	1997	D	12,805*			
B-2 — BARGE TRANSPORTATION, INC., DETROIT, MI							
Cherokee {2}	DB	1943	B	1,200	155' 00"	50' 00"	13' 06"
B-3 — BASIC TOWING, INC., ESCANABA, MI							
Erika Kobasic	TB	1939	D	226*	110' 00"	26' 05"	15' 01"
(USCG Arundel [WYT/WYTM-90] '39 - '84, Karen Andrie {1} '84 - '90)							
Escort II	TB	1969	D	26*	50' 00"	13' 00"	7' 00"
L. E. Block	BC	1927	T	15,900	621' 00"	64' 00"	33' 00"
(Last operated 31 October, 1981 — Currently laid up in Escanaba, MI.)							
B-4 — BAY CITY BOAT LINE, LLC, BAY CITY, MI							
Princess Wenonah	ES	1954	D	96*	64' 09"	32' 09"	9' 09"
(William M. Miller '54 - '98)							
B-5 — BAY OCEAN MANAGEMENT, INC., ENGLEWOOD CLIFFS, NJ							
Kota Selemat	GC	1978	D	17,800	524' 09"	75' 02"	41' 10"
Lake Tahoe	BC	1974	D	23,720	607' 04"	75' 00"	46' 05"
B-6 — BAY SHIPBUILDING CO., STURGEON BAY, WI							
Bayship	TB	1943	D	19*	45' 00"	12' 06"	6' 00"
B-7 — BEAUSOLEIL FIRST NATION, CHRISTIAN ISLAND, ON							
Upper Canada	CF	1949	D	165*	143' 00"	36' 00"	11' 00"
B-8 — BEAVER ISLAND BOAT CO., CHARLEVOIX, MI							
Beaver Islander	CF	1963	D	95*	96' 03"	9' 09"	9' 09"
Emerald Isle {2}	CF	1997	D	95*	130' 00"	38' 08"	12' 00"
South Shore	CF	1945	D	67*	64' 10"	24' 00"	9' 06"
B-9 — BERNARD McCUE, CHRISTIAN ISLAND, ON							
Indian Maiden	PF	1987	D	128*	74' 00"	23' 00"	8' 00"
B-10 — BETHLEHEM STEEL CORP., CHESTERTON, IN							
Burns Harbor {2}	SU	1980	D	78,850	1,000' 00"	105' 00"	56' 00"
Stewart J. Cort	SU	1972	D	58,000	1,000' 00"	105' 00"	49' 00"
B-11 — BIGANE VESSEL FUELING CO. OF CHICAGO, CHICAGO, IL							
Jos. F. Bigane	RT	1973	D	7,500	140' 00"	40' 00"	14' 00"
B-12 — BILLINGTON CONTRACTING, INC., DULUTH, MN							
Duluth	DR	1962	B	401*	106' 00"	36' 00"	8' 04"
Faith	CS	1906	B	705*	120' 00"	38' 00"	10' 02"
Houghton	TB	1944	D	21*	45' 00"	13' 00"	6' 00"
Seneca	TB	1939	D	152*	90' 02"	22' 00"	9' 00"
(General '39 - '39, Raymond Card '39 - '40, Keshena '40 - '47, Mary L. McAllister '47 - '81)							
B-13 — BLACK CREEK SHIPPING CO. LTD., PORT DOVER, ON							
Cuyahoga	SU	1943	L	15,675	620' 00"	60' 00"	35' 00"
(J. Burton Ayers '43 - '95)							
B-14 — BLUE WATER EXCURSIONS, INC., FORT GRATIOT, MI							
Huron Lady	ES	1961	D	55*	65' 00"	17' 00"	5' 00"
(Falcon '61 - '65, Bucky '65 - '68, Holiday '68 - '72, Speedy IV '72 - '74, Capt. Bill Van '74 - '76, Pilot 76 - '77, Capt. Eddie B. '77 - '94)							
B-15 — BLUE WATER FERRY LTD., SOMBRA, ON							
Daldean	CF	1951	D	145*	75' 00"	35' 00"	7' 00"
Ontamich	CF	1939	D	55*	65' 00"	28' 10"	8' 06"
(Harsens Island '39 - '73)							

Barge Pathfinder, formerly the steamer J.L. Mauthe, was paired in 1998 with the tug Joyce L. Van Enkevort. (Roger LeLievre)

Algoma Tankers' newly-acquired Algonova is the former A.G. Farquharson. (Roger LeLievre)

Fleet No. & Name Vessel Name	Type of Vessel	Year Built	Type of Engine	Cargo Cap. or Gross*	Overal Length	Breadth	Depth or Draft*
B-16 — BRIAN UTILITIES SERVICES, INC., MUSKEGON, MI							
Capt. Roy	TB	1987	D	27*	42' 06"	12' 08"	6' 06"
B-17 — BUFFALO CHARTERS, INC., BUFFALO, NY							
Miss Buffalo	ES	1964	D	88*	64' 10"	23' 05"	7' 04"
(Miss Muskoka {1} '64 - '69, Miss Niagara '69 - '72)							
Miss Buffalo II	ES	1972	D	88*	86' 00"	24' 00"	6' 00"
Niagara Clipper	ES	1983	D	65*	112' 00"	29' 00"	6' 06"*
B-18 — BUFFALO DEPT. OF PUBLIC WORKS, BUFFALO, NY							
Edwin M. Cotter	FB	1900	D	208*	118' 00"	24' 00"	11' 06"
(W. S. Grattan '00 - '53, Firefighter '53 - '54)							
B-19 — BUSCH MARINE, INC., CARROLLTON, MI							
Gregory J. Busch	TB	1919	D	299*	151' 00"	28' 00"	16' 09"
(Humaconna '19 - '77)							
STC 2004	DB	1986	B	2,364	240' 00"	50' 00"	9' 05"
C-1 — C. A. CROSBIE SHIPPING LTD., MONTREAL, PQ							
Arctic Viking	GC	1967	D	1,265	244' 06"	41' 03"	21' 11"
(Baltic Viking '67 - '81)							
Lady Franklin	GC	1970	D	3,627	339' 04"	51' 10"	27' 11"
(Baltic Valiant '70 - '81)							
C-2 — CALUMET RIVER FLEETING, INC., WHITING, IN							
Des Plaines	TB	1956	D	175*	98' 00"	28' 00"	8' 04"*
Sea Wolf	TB	1954	D	95*	72' 00"	22' 00"	7' 00"*
Tommy B.	TB	1962	D	43*	45' 00"	11' 10"	4' 11"*
Trinity	TB	1939	D	51*	45' 00"	12' 10"	5' 07"*
C-3 — CANADA STEAMSHIP LINES, INC., MONTREAL, PQ							
Atlantic Erie	SU	1985	D	38,200	736' 06"	75' 10"	50' 00"
(Hon. Paul Martin '85 - '88)							
Atlantic Huron {2}	SU	1984	D	34,600	736' 06"	75' 10"	46' 06"
(Prairie Harvest '84 - '89, Atlantic Huron {2} '89 - '94, Melvin H. Baker II {2} '94 - '97)							
Ferbec	BC	1966	D	56,887	732' 06"	104' 02"	57' 09"
(Fugaku Maru '65 - '77)							
Frontenac {5}	SU	1968	D	27,500	729' 07"	75' 03"	39' 08"
Halifax	SU	1963	T	30,100	730' 00"	75' 00"	39' 03"
(Frankcliffe Hall {2} '63 - '88)							
H. M. Griffith	SU	1973	D	31,250	730' 00"	75' 00"	46' 06"
Jean Parisien	SU	1977	D	33,000	730' 00"	75' 00"	46' 06"
J. W. McGiffin	SU	1972	D	33,100	740' 00"	78' 00"	46' 06"
Louis R. Desmarais	SU	1977	D	33,000	730' 00"	75' 00"	46' 06"
Manitoulin {5}	SU	1966	D	28,100	730' 00"	75' 00"	41' 00"
Nanticoke	SU	1980	D	35,100	730' 00"	75' 08"	46' 06"
Tadoussac {2}	SU	1969	D	29,700	730' 00"	75' 03"	42' 00"
Tarantau	SU	1965	T	27,600	730' 00"	75' 00"	46' 06"
(Last operated 23 December, 1996 — 5 year survey expired April, 1999.)							
(Currently laid up in Toronto, ON.)							
CSL INTERNATIONAL, INC. - A DIVISION OF CANADA STEAMSHIP LINES, INC.							
CSL Atlas	SU	1990	D	67,308	746' 01"	105' 02"	63' 00"
CSL Cabo	SU	1971	D	31,364	596' 02"	84' 04"	49' 10"
(Bockenheim '71 - '80, Cabo San Lucas '80 - '95)							
CSL Trailblazer	SU	1978	D	26,608	583' 11"	85' 02"	46' 03"
([Main Cargo Section] Colon Brown '74 - '75, Gold Bond Conveyor '75 - '78)							
([Completed Vessel] Gold Bond Trailblazer '78 - '98)							
M. H. Baker III	SU	1982	D	38,900	730' 00"	75' 10"	50' 00"
(Atlantic Superior '82 - '97)							
EGON OLDENDORFF LTD. - PARTNERSHIP WITH CSL INTERNATIONAL, INC.							
Bernhard Oldendorff	SU	1991	D	77,548	803' 10"	105' 08"	60' 00"
(Yeoman Burn '91 - '94)							
Christopher Oldendorff	SU	1982	D	62,732	747' 02"	106' 00"	63' 00"
(Pacific Peace '82 - '86, Atlantic Huron {1} '86 - '88, CSL Innovator '88 - '93)							
Hai Wang Xing	SU	1995	D	37,532	612' 02"	95' 02"	43' 04"
PETROLEUM TOWING - A DIVISION OF CANADA STEAMSHIP LINES, INC.							
Dover Light	TK	1968	B	7,870	146' 05"	50' 00"	13' 07"
(Jackson Purchase '68 - '83, Eliza S-1877 '83 - '86)							
(5 year survey expired April, 1995 — Currently laid up in Port Dover, ON.)							

Fleet No. & Name Vessel Name	Type of Vessel	Year Built	Type of Engine	Cargo Cap. or Gross*	Overal Length	Breadth	Depth or Draft*
ESSROC CANADA, INC. - MANAGED BY CANADA STEAMSHIP LINES, INC.							
Stephen B. Roman	CC	1965	D	7,600	488' 09"	56' 00"	35' 06"
(Fort William '65 - '83)							
Metis	CC	1956	B	5,800	331' 00"	43' 09"	26' 00"
(Last operated 19 August, 1993.)							
(Currently in use as a cement storage barge in Windsor, ON.)							
LAFARGE CANADA, INC. - MANAGED BY CANADA STEAMSHIP LINES, INC.							
English River	CC	1961	D	7,450	404' 03"	60' 00"	36' 06"
GREAT LAKES TRANSPORT LTD.							
CHARTERED BY CANADA STEAMSHIP LINES, INC.							
Sarah Spencer	SU	1959	B	23,200	611" 03"	72' 00"	40' 00"
(Adam E. Cornelius {3} '59 - '89, Capt. Edward V. Smith '89 - '91, Sea Barge One '91 - '96)							
ATLANTIC TOWING LTD. - CHARTERED BY GREAT LAKES TRANSPORT LTD.							
Atlantic Hickory	TB	1973	D	886*	153' 06"	38' 10"	22' 00"
(Irving Miami '73 - '95)							
C-4 — CANADA WEST INDIES MOLASSES CO. LTD., MISSISSAUGA, ON							
San Juan	TK	1962	B	913*	195' 00"	35' 00"	12' 06"
(5 year survey expired April, 1998 — Currently laid up in Hamilton, ON.)							
C-5 — CANADIAN COAST GUARD, OTTAWA, ON							
CENTRAL AND ARCTIC REGION							
Advent	RV	1972	D	72*	77' 01"	18' 05"	5' 03"*
Bittern	SR	1982	D	21*	40' 08"	13' 06"	4' 04"
Cape Hurd	SR	1982	D	55*	70' 10"	18' 00"	8' 09"
Caribou Isle	BT	1985	D	92*	75' 06"	19' 08"	7' 04"
Cove Isle	BT	1980	D	92*	65' 07"	19' 08"	7' 04"
Griffon	IB	1970	D	2,212*	234' 00"	49' 00"	21' 06"
Gull Isle	BT	1980	D	80*	65' 07"	19' 08"	7' 04"
Limnos	RV	1968	D	460*	147' 00"	32' 00"	12' 00"
Samuel Risley	IB	1985	D	1,988*	228' 09"	47' 01"	21' 09"
Shark	RV	1971	D	30*	52' 06"	14' 09"	7' 03"
Simcoe	BT	1962	D	961*	179' 01"	38' 00"	15' 06"
Sora	SR	1982	D	21*	41' 00"	14' 01"	4' 04"
Spray	SR	1994	D	42*	51' 09"	17' 00"	8' 02"
Spume	SR	1994	D	42*	51' 09"	17' 00"	8' 02"
Tobermory	SR	1973	D	17*	44' 02"	12' 06"	6' 07"
Westfort	SR	1973	D	22*	44' 02"	12' 08"	5' 11"
LAURENTIAN REGION							
Des Groseilliers	IB	1983	D	5,910*	322' 07"	64' 00"	35' 06"
F. C. G. Smith	SV	1985	D	439*	114' 02"	45' 11"	11' 02"
Frederick G. Creed	SV	1988	D	151*	66' 11"	32' 00"	11' 10"
George R. Pearkes	IB	1986	D	3,809	272' 04"	53' 02"	25' 02"
Ile Des Barques	BT	1985	D	92*	75' 06"	19' 08"	7' 04"
Ile Saint-Ours	BT	1986	D	92*	75' 06"	19' 08"	7' 05"
Isle Rouge	SR	1980	D	57*	70' 10"	18' 01"	5' 03"*
Louisbourg	RV	1977	D	295*	124' 00"	26' 11"	11' 06"
Martha L. Black	IB	1986	D	3,818*	272' 04"	53' 02"	25' 02"
Montmagny	BT	1963	D	328*	110' 04"	28' 00"	7' 00"*
Pierre Radisson	IB	1978	D	5,910*	322' 00"	62' 10"	35' 06"
Tracy	BT	1968	D	963*	181' 01"	38' 00"	16' 00"
MARITIMES REGION							
Alfred Needier	RV	1982	D	959*	165' 09"	36' 09"	22' 01"
Bickerton	SR	1989	D	32*	53' 04"	17' 00"	4' 11"*
Chebucto	RV	1966	D	751*	179' 02"	30' 10"	27' 02"
Cap Aux Meules	SR	1982	D	32*	51' 09"	17' 00"	4' 01"
Cumella	RV	1983	D	80*	76' 01"	16' 09"	11' 02"
Cygnus	RV	1982	D	1,211*	205' 01"	40' 00"	15' 05"
Earl Grey	IB	1986	D	1,971*	230' 00"	46' 02"	22' 01"
Edward Cornwallis	IB	1986	D	3,727*	272' 04"	53' 02"	24' 06"
Howe Point	RV	1983	D	11*	42' 00"	12' 10"	5' 11"*
Hudson	RV	1963	D	3,740*	296' 07"	50' 06"	32' 10"
J. L. Hart	RV	1974	D	90*	65' 00"	20' 00"	12' 02"
Louis St. Laurent	IB	1969	D	10,908*	392' 06"	80' 00"	53' 06"
Mary Hichens	SR	1985	D	1,684*	210' 00"	45' 03"	22' 07"
(Beau Bois '85 - '89)							
Matthew	RV	1990	D	857*	165' 00"	34' 05"	16' 05"

Fleet No. & Name Vessel Name	Type of Vessel	Year Built	Type of Engine	Cargo Cap. or Gross*	Overal Length	Breadth	Depth or Draft*
Navicula	RV	1968	D	80*	65' 00"	19' 00"	10' 06"*
Opilio	RV	1989	D	74*	55' 01"	20' 04"	9' 10"*
Pandalus III	RV	1986	D	28*	42' 00"	14' 09"	5' 11"*
Parizeau	RV	1967	D	1,328*	211' 07"	40' 00"	21' 00"
Partridge Island	BT	1985	D	92*	75' 06"	19' 08"	4' 05"*
Provo Wallis	BT	1969	D	1,313*	209' 03"	42' 08"	16' 07"
Simon Fraser	BT	1960	D	1,353*	204' 06"	42' 00"	18' 03"
Sir William Alexander	IB	1986	D	3,550*	272' 06"	45' 00"	17' 06"
Spindrift	SR	1992	D	42*	51' 09"	17' 00"	8' 02"
Terry Fox	IB	1983	D	4,234*	288' 09"	58' 06"	29' 08"
Tupper	BT	1959	D	1,353*	204' 06"	42' 00"	18' 03"

C-6 — CANADIAN DREDGE & DOCK, INC., DON MILLS, ON

Bagotville	TB	1964	D	65*	65' 00"	18' 06"	10' 00"
Halton	TB	1942	D	15*	42' 09"	14' 00"	7' 06"
Paula M.	TB	1959	D	12*	46' 06"	16' 01"	4' 10"
R.C. L. No. 1	TB	1958	D	20*	42' 09"	14' 03"	5' 09"

C-7 — CANADIAN FOREST NAVIGATION CO. LTD., MONTREAL, PQ

Pintail	BC	1983	D	28,035	647' 08"	75' 10"	46' 11"

C-8 — CAPT. JOE BOAT SERVICE, CHICAGO, IL

Eleanor R.	ES	1988	D	75*	90' 00"	22' 00"	4' 06"*

C-9 — CAPTAIN NORMAC'S RIVERBOAT INN LTD., TORONTO, ON

Jadran	BC	1957	D	2,520*	295' 06"	42' 08"	24' 08"

(Former Jadranska Plovidba vessel which last operated in 1975.)
(Currently in use as a floating restaurant in Toronto, ON.)

C-10 — CAROL N. BAKER, PENETANGUISHENE, ON

Dawnlight	TB	1891	D	64*	75' 00"	24' 00"	12' 00"

(Le Roy Brooks 1891 - '25, Henry Stokes '25 - '54, Aburg '54 - '81)

C-11 — CENTRAL MARINE LOGISTICS, INC., HIGHLAND, IN

Edward L. Ryerson	BC	1980	T	27,500	730' 00"	76' 00"	30' 00"
Joseph L. Block	SU	1976	D	37,200	728' 00"	78' 00"	45' 00"
Wilfred Sykes	SU	1949	T	21,500	678' 00"	70' 00"	37' 00"

C-12 — CHAMPION'S AUTO FERRY, INC., ALGONAC, MI

Champion {1}	CF	1941	D	65*	65' 00"	29' 00"	8' 06"
Middle Channel	CF	1997	D	97*	79' 00"	31' 00"	8' 03"
North Channel	CF	1967	D	67*	75' 00"	30' 00"	8' 00"
South Channel	CF	1973	D	94*	79' 00"	31' 00"	8' 03"

C-13 — CHARLEVOIX COUNTY ROAD COMMISSION, BOYNE CITY, MI

Charlevoix {1}	CF	1926	D	43*	50' 00"	32' 00"	3' 09"

C-14 — CHICAGO CRUISES, INC., CHICAGO, IL

Chicago II	ES	1983	D	42*	123' 03"	28' 06"	7' 00"

(Star of Sanford '83 - '86, Star of Charlevoix {1} '86 - '87, Star of Toronto '87 - '87, Star of Chicago II '87 - '94)

C-15 — CHICAGO FIRE DEPT., CHICAGO, IL

Joseph Medill {2}	FB	1949	D	350*	92' 06"	24' 00"	11' 00"
Victor L. Schlaegar	FB	1949	D	350*	92' 06"	24' 00"	11' 00"

C-16 — CHICAGO FIREBOAT CRUISE CO., CHICAGO, IL

Fred A. Busse	FB	1937	D	209*	92' 00"	23' 00"	8' 00"
Islander {1}	ES	1946	D	39*	53' 04"	21' 00"	5' 05"

C-17 — CHICAGO FROM THE LAKE LTD., CHICAGO, IL

Fort Dearborn	ES	1985	D	72*	64' 10"	22' 00"	7' 04"
Innisfree	ES	1953	D	34*	61' 08"	16' 00"	4' 06"
Marquette {6}	ES	1957	D	29*	50' 07"	15' 00"	4' 00"

C-18 — CHICAGO WATER PUMPING STATION, CHICAGO, IL

James J. Versluis	TB	1957	D	126*	83' 00"	22' 00"	11' 02"

C-19 — CHRISTENSEN CANADIAN AFRICAN LINES, MONTREAL, PQ

Thor 1	GC	1978	D	20,075	541' 08"	75' 02"	48' 03"
Thorscape	GC	1977	D	20,075	541' 08"	75' 02"	48' 03"
Thorswave	GC	1982	D	21,894	549' 03"	75' 02"	46' 00"

(Irene Greenwood '83 - '89, Marbonita '89 - '95, Thorswave '95 - '96, Stella K. '96 - '97)

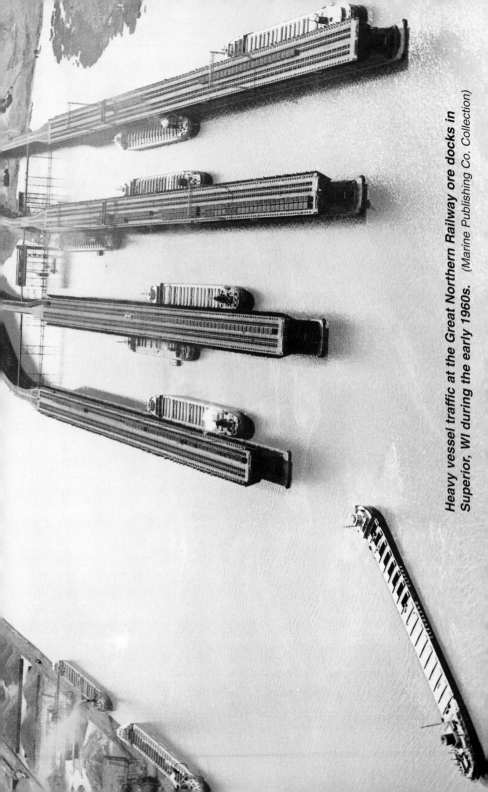

Heavy vessel traffic at the Great Northern Railway ore docks in Superior, WI during the early 1960s. (Marine Publishing Co. Collection)

Fleet No. & Name Vessel Name	Type of Vessel	Year Built	Type of Engine	Cargo Cap. or Gross*	Overall Length	Breadth	Depth or Draft*
C-20 — CHRISTOPHER LADD, PUT-IN-BAY, OH							
Ladler	DB	1950	B	100	100' 00"	26' 00"	5' 06"*
Mervine II	TB	1942	D	22*	46' 08"	14' 00"	5' 01"*
C-21 — CLEVELAND FIRE DEPT., CLEVELAND, OH							
Anthony J. Celebrezze	FB	1961	D		66' 00"	17' 00"	5' 00"
C-22 — CLIFF TYNER, BARBEAU, MI							
Neebish Islander	CF	1950	D	49*	55' 00"	20' 07"	6' 00"
(Lillifred '50 - '56)							
(Last operated in 1995 — Currently laid up at Neebish Island, MI.)							
C-23 — CLINTON RIVER CRUISE CO., CLINTON TOWNSHIP, MI							
Clinton	ES	1949	D	12*	44' 00"	11' 01"	4' 00"*
Gibralter	ES	1984	D	47*	64' 11"	22' 00"	3' 00"*
C-24 — CLIPPER CRUISE LINES, INC., ST. LOUIS, MO							
Clipper Adventurer	PA	1975	D	4,364*	328' 01"	53' 03"	23' 00"
(Alla Tarasova '75 - '97)							
Nantucket Clipper	PA	1984	D	96*	207' 00"	37' 00"	11' 06"
Yorktown Clipper	PA	1988	D	97*	257' 00"	43' 00"	12' 05"
C-25 — CLUB CANAMAC CRUISES, TORONTO, ON							
Aurora Borealis	ES	1983	D	277*	101' 00"	24' 00"	6' 00"*
Jaguar II	ES	1968	D	142*	95' 03"	20' 00"	9' 00"
(Jaguar '68 - '86)							
Seaflight I	HY	1994	D	135*	113' 02"	33' 10"	5' 11"
(Katran-1 '94 - '98)							
Seaflight II	HY	1996	D	135*	113' 02"	33' 10"	5' 11"
(Katran-4 '96 - '98)							
Stella Borealis	ES	1989	D	356*	118 '00"	26' 00"	7' 00"
C-26 — COASTWISE TRADING CO., INC., CHICAGO, IL							
Great Lakes {2}	TK	1982	B	75,000	414' 00"	60' 00"	30' 00"
(Amoco Great Lakes '82 - '85)							
Michigan {10}	TB	1982	D	293*	107' 08"	34' 00"	16' 00"
(Amoco Michigan '82 - '85)							
[Great Lakes/Michigan overall dimensions together]					454' 00"	60' 00"	30' 00"
C-27 — COLUMBIA YACHT CLUB, CHICAGO, IL							
Abegweit {1}	CF	1947	D	6,694*	372' 06"	61' 00"	24' 09"
(Abegweit {1} '47 - '81, Abby '81 - '97)							
(Former CN Marine, Inc. vessel which last operated in 1981.)							
(Currently in use as a floating club house in Chicago, IL.)							
C-28 — CONSTANTINOS MAKAYDAKIS, ATHENS, GREECE							
The Straits of Mackinac	CF	1928	R	736*	202' 11"	48' 00"	16' 07"
(Last operated in 1968 — 5 year survey expired September, 1971.)							
(Currently laid up in Sturgeon Bay, WI.)							
C-29 — CONTESSA CRUISE LINES, L.L.C., LAFAYETTE, LA							
Arthur K. Atkinson	PA	1917	D	3,241*	384' 00"	56' 00"	20' 06"
(Ann Arbor No. 6 '17 - '59)							
(Last operated in 1984 — 5 year survey expired August, 1985.)							
(Currently laid up in Ludington, MI.)							
Viking {2}	PA	1925	D	2,713*	360' 00"	56' 03"	21' 06"
(Ann Arbor No. 7 '25 - '64)							
(Last operated 11 April, 1982 — 5 year survey expires May, 2001.) (Currently laid up in Erie, PA.)							
C-30 — CONTINENTAL MARINE, INC., LEMONT, IL							
Brandon E.	TB	1945	D	19*	42' 01"	12' 10"	5' 02"*
C-31 — CORP. OF PROFESSIONAL GREAT LAKES PILOTS, ST. CATHARINES, ON							
J. W. Cooper	PB		D				
Juleen I	PB		D				
Mrs. C.	PB		D				
C-32 — CROISIERES AML, INC., QUEBEC, PQ							
Cavalier des Mers	ES	1974	D	128*	105' 00"	21' 00"	4' 08"
Cavalier Grand Fleuve	ES	1987	D	499*	145' 00"	30' 00"	5' 06"
Cavalier Maxim	ES	1962	D	752*	191' 02"	42' 00"	11' 07"
(Osborne Castle '62 - '78, Le Gobelet D' Argent '78 - '88, Gobelet D' Argent '88 - '89, Le Maxim '89 - '92)							

Fleet No. & Name Vessel Name	Type of Vessel	Year Built	Type of Engine	Cargo Cap. or Gross*	Overal Length	Breadth	Depth or Draft*
Cavalier Royal	ES	1971	D	283*	125' 00"	24' 00"	5' 00"
Louis-Joliet	ES	1938	D	2,436*	170' 01"	70' 00"	17' 00"
M/V Montreal	ES	1975	D	281*	106' 00"	24' 00"	
(Island Queen {1} '75 - '79, Miss Kingston II '79 - '84)							
Miss Olympia	ES	1972	D	29*	62' 08"	14' 00"	4' 08"
Nouvelle-Orleans	ES	1989	D	234*	90' 00"	25' 00"	5' 03"
Tandem	ES	1991	D	102*	66' 00"	22' 00"	2' 02"
Transit	ES	1992	D	102*	66' 00"	22' 00"	2' 08"
Ville Marie II	ES	1947	R	887*	176' 00"	66' 00"	13' 06"
(Laviolette '47 - '76, Bluewater Belle '76 - '79, Cadedonia '79 - '82)							

C-33 — CROISIERES DES ISLES DE SOREL, INC., STE. ANNE DE SOREL, PQ

Le Survenant III	ES	1974	D	105*	65' 00"	13' 00"	5' 00"

C-34 — CROISIERES M/S JACQUES CARTIER, TROIS RIVIERES, PQ

Jacques Cartier	ES	1924	D	441*	135' 00"	35' 00"	10' 00"
Le Draveur	ES	1992	D	79*			

C-35 — CROISIERES MARJOLAINE, INC., CHICOUTIMI, PQ

Marjolaine II	ES	1904	D		92' 00"	27' 00"	9' 00"

C-36 — CROISIERES RICHELIEU, INC., SAINT-JEAN-SUR-RICHELIEU, PQ

Fort Saint-Jean II	ES	1967	D	109*	62' 09"	19' 10"	
Miss Montreal	ES	1973	D	64*	43' 06"	16' 00"	10' 04"

D-1 — DALE T. DEAN — WALPOLE - ALGONAC FERRY LINE, PORT LAMBTON, ON

City of Algonac	CF	1990	D	92*	80' 04"	26' 01"	6' 09"
Lowell D.	CF	1946	D	38*	48' 07"	17' 06"	5' 02"
Walpole Islander	CF	1986	D	71*	74' 00"	33' 00"	7' 00"

D-2 — DALMIG MARINE, INC., QUEBEC, PQ

Dalmig	CF	1957	D	538*	175' 10"	40' 01"	11' 10"
(Pierre de Saurel '57 - '87)							

D-3 — DAN MINOR & SONS, INC., PORT COLBORNE, ON

Andrea Marie I	TB	1963	D	87*	75' 02"	24' 07"	7' 03"
Susan Michelle	TB	1995	D	89*	79' 10"	20' 11"	6' 02"
Welland	TB	1954	D	94*	86' 00"	20' 00"	8' 00"

D-4 — DAVID MALLOCH, SCUDDER, ON

Cemba	TK	1960	D	151	50' 00"	15' 06"	7' 06"

D-5 — DAWES MARINE TUG & BARGE, INC., NORTH TONAWANDA, NY

Apache	TB	1954	D	119*	71' 00"	19' 06"	9' 06"
(Lewis Castle '54 - '97)							
Fourth Coast	TB	1957	D	17*	40' 00"	12' 06"	4' 00"
Sand Pebble	TB	1969	D	30*	48' 00"	15' 00"	8' 00"
Tommy Ray	TB	1954	D	19*	45' 00"	12' 05"	6' 00"

D-6 — DEAN CONSTRUCTION CO.LTD., BELLE RIVER, ON

Americo Dean	TB	1956	D	15*	45' 00"	15' 00"	5' 00"
Annie M. Dean	TB	1981	D	58*	50' 00"	19' 00"	5' 00"
Neptune III	TB	1939	D	23*	53' 10"	15' 06"	5' 00"
Wayne Dean	TB	1946	D	10*	45' 00"	13' 00"	5' 00"

D-7 — DETOUR MARINE, INC., DETOUR, MI

Resolute	TB	1935	D	17*	36' 10"	12' 05"	4' 00"*

D-8 — DETROIT CITY FIRE DEPT., DETROIT, MI

Curtis Randolph	FB	1979	D	85*	77' 10"	21' 06"	9' 03"

D-9 — DIAMOND JACK'S RIVER TOURS, GROSSE ILE, MI

Diamond Belle	ES	1958	D	93*	93' 06"	25' 10"	10' 01"
(Mackinac Islander '58 - '90, Sir Richard '90 - '91)							
Diamond Jack	ES	1955	D	82*	72' 00"	25' 00"	8' 00"
(Emerald Isle {1} '55 - '91)							
Diamond Queen	ES	1956	D	94*	92' 00"	25' 00"	10' 00"
(Mohawk '56 - '96)							

D-10 — DIRK SPLILLMAKER, EAST LANSING, MI

Verendrye	RV	1958	D	297*	167' 06"	34' 00"	16' 07"
(CCGS Verendrye '58 - '86, 500 '86 - '92)							
(Currently laid up in Toronto, ON.)							

Fleet No. & Name Vessel Name	Type of Vessel	Year Built	Type of Engine	Cargo Cap. or Gross*	Overal Length	Breadth	Depth or Draft*
D-11 — DISSEN & JUHN CORP., MACEDON, NY							
Constructor	TB	1950	D	14*	39' 00"	11' 00"	5' 00"
James W. Rickey	TB	1935	D	24*	46' 00"	14' 00"	7' 00"
Portside Belle	TB	1953	D	13*	35' 00"	10' 06"	6' 00"
D-12 — DOW CHEMICAL CO., LUDINGTON, MI							
DC 710	TK	1969	B	25,500	260' 00"	50' 00"	9' 00"
E-63	TK	1980	B	60,000	407' 00"	60' 00"	20' 00"
D-13 — DUC d' ORLEANS CRUISE BOAT, CORUNNA, ON							
Duc d' Orleans	ES	1943	D	112*	112' 00"	17' 10"	6' 03"
(HMCS Duc d' Orleans [ML-105] '43 - '48)							
D-14 — DUROCHER DOCK & DREDGE, INC., CHEBOYGAN, MI							
ACBL 1613	DB	1966	B	1,200	195' 02"	35' 02"	10' 04"
ACBL 1614	DB	1966	B	1,200	195' 02"	35' 02"	10' 04"
Betty D.	TB	1953	D	14*	40' 00"	13' 00"	6' 00"
Champion {3}	TB	1974	D	125*	75' 00"	24' 00"	9' 06"
General	TB	1954	D	119*	71' 00"	19' 06"	9' 06"
(U.S. Army ST-1999 '54 - '61, USCOE Au Sable '61 - '84, Challenger {3} '84 - '87)							
Joe Van	TB	1955	D	32*	57' 09"	16' 06"	9' 00"
Meagan Beth	TB	1982	D	94*	60' 00"	22' 00"	9' 00"
MOBRO 2000	DB	1980	B	2,400	180' 00"	52' 00"	11' 04"
MOBRO 2001	DB	1980	B	2,400	180' 00"	52' 00"	11' 04"
MOBRO 2005	DB	1980	B	2,400	180' 00"	52' 00"	11' 04"
Nancy Anne	TB	1969	D	73*	60' 00"	20' 00"	6' 00"
Ray Durocher	TB	1943	D	20*	45' 06"	12' 05"	7' 06"
Samson II	CS	1959	B	700	90' 00"	50' 00"	7' 02"
E-1 — EASTERN CANADA TOWING LTD., HALIFAX, NS							
Point Carroll	TB	1973	D	366*	127' 00"	30' 05"	14' 05"
Point Chebucto	TT	1992	D	412*	110' 00"	33' 00"	17' 00"
Pointe Aux Basques	TB	1972	D	396*	105' 00"	33' 06"	19' 06"
Pointe Comeau	TT	1976	D	391*	104' 00"	40' 00"	19' 00"
Pointe Sept-Iles	TB	1980	D	424*	105' 00"	34' 06"	19' 06"
Point Halifax	TT	1986	D	417*	110' 00"	36' 00"	19' 00"
Point Vibert	TB	1961	D	236*	96' 03"	28' 00"	14' 06"
(Foundation Vibert '61 - '73)							
Point Vigour	TB	1962	D	207*	98' 05"	26' 10"	13' 05"
(Foundation Vigour '62 - '74)							
Point Vim	TB	1962	D	207*	98' 05"	26' 10"	13' 05"
(Foundation Vim '62 - '74)							
E-2 — EASTERN UPPER PENINSULA TRANSIT AUTHORITY, SAULT STE. MARIE, MI							
Drummond Islander	CF	1947	D	99*	84' 00"	30' 00"	8' 03"
Drummond Islander III	CF	1989	D	96*	108' 00"	37' 00"	12' 03"
Neebish Islander II	CF	1946	D	90*	89' 00"	29' 06"	6' 09"
(Sugar Islander '46 - '95)							
Sugar Islander II	CF	1995	D	223*	114' 00"	40' 00"	10' 00"
Thunder Bay	TB	1953	D	15*	45' 00"	13' 00"	7' 00"
E-3 — EDELWEISS CRUISE DINING, MILWAUKEE, WI							
Edelweiss I	ES	1988	D	87*	64' 08"	18' 00"	6' 00"
Edelweiss II	ES	1989	D	89*	73' 08"	20' 00"	7' 00"
E-4 — EDWARD E. GILLEN CO., MILWAUKEE, WI							
Andrew J.	TB	1950	D	25*	47' 00"	15' 07"	8' 00"
Edith J.	TB	1962	D	19*	45' 03"	13' 00"	8' 00"
Edward E. Gillen III	TB	1988	D	95*	75' 00"	26' 00"	9' 06"
Harbor Builder	DB	1930	B	662*	150' 00"	42' 05"	12' 05"
A variety of cargo barges are also available.							
E-5 — EDWIN M. ERICKSON, BAYFIELD, WI							
Outer Island	PK	1942	D	300	112' 00"	32' 00"	8' 06"
(Pluswood '42 - '46)							
E-6 — EGAN MARINE CORP., LEMONT, IL							
Alice E.	TB	1950	D	183*	100' 00"	26' 00"	9' 00"
(L. L. Wright '50 - '55, Martin '55 - '74, Mary Ann '74 - '77, Judi C. '77 - '94)							
Becky E.	TB	1943	D	146*	81' 01"	24' 00"	9' 10"
(DPC 51 '43 - '44, WSA 6 '44 - '46, Chas E. Trout '46 - '78, Naomi Marie '78 - '80, South Haven '80 - '90)							

Fleet No. & Name Vessel Name	Type of Vessel	Year Built	Type of Engine	Cargo Cap. or Gross*	Overal Length	Breadth	Depth or Draft*
Crow	TB	1963	D	152*	84' 06"	25' 00"	11' 06"
Daniel E.	TB	1967	D	70*	70' 00"	18' 06"	6' 08"
(Foster M. Ford '67 - '84)							
Denise E.	TB	1912	D	138*	80' 07"	21' 06"	10' 03"
(Caspian '12 - '48, Trojan '48 - '81, Cherokee {1} '81 - '93)							
Derek E.	TB	1907	D	85*	72' 06"	20' 01"	10' 06"
(John Kelderhouse '07 - '25, Sachem '25 - '90)							
Ethel E.	TB	1913	D	96*	81' 00"	20' 00"	12' 06"
(Michigan {4} '13 - '78, Ste. Marie II '78 - '81, Dakota '81 - '92)							
Lisa E.	TB	1963	D	75*	65' 06"	20' 00"	8' 06"
(Dixie Scout '63 - '90)							
Robin E.	TB	1889	D	123*	84' 09"	19' 00"	9' 00"
(Asa W. Hughes 1889 - '13, Triton {1} '13 - '81, Navajo {2} '81 - '92)							
Susan E.	TB	1921	D	96*	81' 00"	20' 00"	12' 06"
(Oregon {1} '21 - '78, Ste. Marie I '78 - '81, Sioux {2} '81 - '91)							

E-7 — EMPIRE CRUISE LINES, U. S. A., ST. THOMAS, ON

Marine Star	PA	1945	T	12,773*	520' 00"	71' 06"	43' 06"
(USNS Marine Star '45 - '55, Aquarama '55 - '94)							

(Last operated in 1962 — 5 year survey expired May, 1965.) (Currently laid up in Lackawanna, NY.)

E-8 — EMPIRE SANDY, INC., TORONTO, ON

Empire Sandy	3S	1943	W	438*	140' 00"	32' 08"	14' 00"
(Empire Sandy '43 - '48, Ashford '48 - '52, Chris M. '52 - '79)							
Wayward Princess	ES	1976	D	325*	92' 00"	26' 00"	10' 00"
(Cayuga II '76 - '82)							

E-9 — EMPRESS OF CANADA ENTERPRISES LTD., TORONTO, ON

Empress of Canada	ES	1980	D	399*	116' 00"	28' 00"	6' 06"*
(Island Queen V {2} '80 - '89)							

E-10 — EMPRESS RIVER CASINO, JOLIET, IL

Empress	GA	1992	D	1,136*	214' 00"	66' 00"	6' 07"*
Empress II	GA	1993	D	1,248*	230' 00"	67' 00"	6' 08"*
Empress III	GA	1994	D	1,126*	288' 00"	76' 00"	10' 07"*

E-11 — ERIE ISLANDS PETROLEUM, INC., PUT-IN-BAY, OH

Cantankerous	TK	1955	D	323	53' 00"	14' 00"	5' 00"*

E-12 — ERIE SAND & GRAVEL CO., ERIE, PA

J. S. St. John	SC	1945	D	680	174' 00"	32' 02"	15' 00"
(USS YO-178 '45 - '51, Lake Edward '51 - '67)							

ERIE NAVIGATION CO. - MANAGED BY ERIE SAND & GRAVEL CO.

Day Peckinpaugh	CC	1921	D	1,490	254' 00"	36' 00"	14' 00"
(Interwaterways Line Incorporated 101 '21 - '32, I.L.I. 101 '32 - '36, Richard J. Barnes '36 - '58)							

(Last operated 9 September, 1994 — 5 year survey expired August, 1995.)
(Currently laid up in Erie, PA.)

John R. Emery	SC	1905	D	490	140' 00"	33' 00"	14' 00"
(Trenton {1} '05 - '25)							

ERIE SAND STEAMSHIP CO. - MANAGED BY ERIE SAND & GRAVEL CO.

Richard Reiss	SU	1943	D	14,900	620' 06"	60' 03"	35' 00"
(Adirondack '43 - '43, Richard J. Reiss {2} '43 - '86)							

F-1 — FAMILLE DUFOUR, BEAUPRE, PQ

Famille DuFour	ES	1992	D	451*	132' 00"	29' 00"	11' 00"
Famille DuFour II	PC	1995	D	465*	127' 06"	34' 09"	10' 06"
Marie-Clarisse	2S	1930	W	126*	130' 00"	21' 04"	11' 05"*

F-2 — FAUST CORP., DETROIT, MI

Linnhurst	TB	1930	D	11*	37' 06"	10' 06"	4' 08"

F-3 — FEDNAV LTD., MONTREAL, PQ

CANARCTIC SHIPPING CO. LTD. - A DIVISION OF FEDNAV LTD.

Arctic	BC	1978	D	26,440	692' 04"	75' 05"	49' 05"
Arctic Kalvik	SB	1983	D	4,391	288' 09"	57' 05"	32' 10"
(Kalvik '83 - '97)							

FEDERAL TERMINALS LTD. - A DIVISION OF FEDNAV LTD.

Brochu	TT	1973	D	390*	100' 00"	36' 00"	14' 06"
Vachon	TT	1973	D	390*	100' 00"	36' 00"	14' 06"

Listings continued on Page 72

Colors of the Great Lakes & Seaway Smokestacks

Algoma Central Marine Corp.
Div. of Algoma Central Corp.
St. Catharines, ON

Basic Marine
Escanaba, MI

Canadian Coast Guard
Ottawa, ON

Croisieres AML Inc.
Quebec, PQ

Erie Sand & Gravel Co.
Erie Sand Steamship Co.
Erie, PA

Algoma Tankers Ltd.
Div. of Algoma Central Corp.
Dartmouth, NS

Beaver Island Transit Co.
Charlevoix, MI

Canadian Dredge & Dock Inc.
Don Mills, ON

Croisieres Nordik, Inc.
Div. of Transport Desgagnes, Inc.
Quebec, PQ

Essroc Canada, Inc.
Downsville, ON

American Canadian
Caribbean Line, Inc.
Warren, RI

Bethlehem Steel Corp.
Chesterton, IN

Central Marine Logistics, Inc.
Highland, IN

Dean Construction Co.
Belle River, ON

Fednav Ltd.
Montreal, PQ

American Steamship Co.
Williamsville, NY

Bigane Vessel Fueling Co.
Chicago, IL

Chicago Fire Department
Chicago, IL

City of Detroit Fire Department
Detroit, MI

Fraser Shipyards, Inc.
Superior, WI

American Tug & Transit Co.
Bay City, MI

Black Creek Shipping Co.
Port Dover, ON

Cleveland Fire Department
Cleveland, OH

Diamond Jack River Tours
Detroit, MI

Gaelic Tug Boat Co.
Grosse Ile, MI

Andrie, Inc.
Muskegon, MI

Buffalo Fire Department
Buffalo, NY

Cleveland Tankers (1991), Inc.
Cleveland, OH

Duluth - Superior Excursions
Duluth, MN

Gananoque Boat Line
Gananoque, ON

Arnold Transit Co.
Mackinac Island, MI

Busch Marine
Carrollton, MI

Clipper Cruise Lines
Subsidiary of Intrav
St. Louis, MO

Durocher Dock & Dredge, Inc.
Cheboygan, MI

Edward E. Gillen Co.
Milwaukee, WI

Atlantic Towing Ltd.
Div. of Irvingdale Shipping Ltd.
St. John, NB

Canada Steamship Lines, Inc.
Montreal, PQ

Coastwise Trading Co.
East Chicago, IN

Eastern Canada Towing Ltd.
Halifax, NS

Goodtime Transit Boats, Inc.
Cleveland, OH

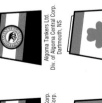

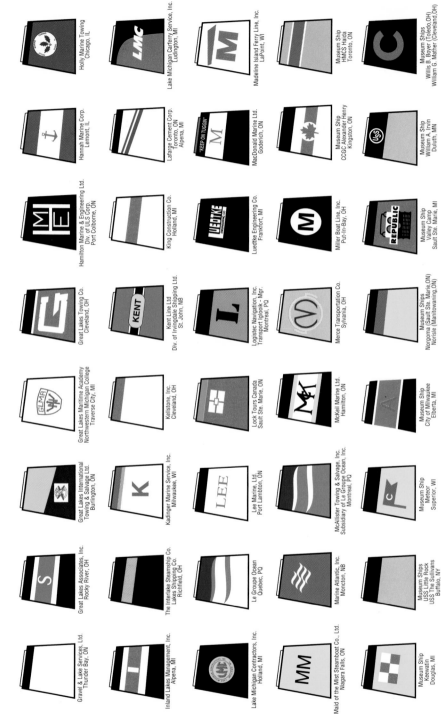

Holly Marine Towing
Chicago, IL

Hannah Marine Corp.
Lemont, IL

Hamilton Marine & Engineering Ltd.
Div. of ULS Corp.
Port Colborne, ON

Great Lakes Towing Co.
Cleveland, OH

Great Lakes Maritime Academy
Northwestern Michigan College
Traverse City, MI

Great Lakes International
Towing & Salvage Ltd.
Burlington, ON

Great Lakes Associates, Inc.
Rocky River, OH

Gravel & Lake Services, Ltd.
Thunder Bay, ON

Lake Michigan Carferry Service, Inc.
Ludington, MI

Lafarge Cement Corp.
Toronto, ON
Alpena, MI

King Construction Co.
Holland, MI

Kent Line Ltd.
Div. of Irvingdale Shipping Ltd.
St. John, NB

Kellstone, Inc.
Cleveland, OH

Kadinger Marine Service, Inc.
Milwaukee, WI

The Interlake Steamship Co.
Lakes Shipping Co.
Richfield, OH

Inland Lakes Management, Inc.
Alpena, MI

Madeline Island Ferry Line, Inc.
LaPoint, WI

MacDonald Marine Ltd.
Goderich, ON

Luedtke Engineering Co.
Frankfort, MI

Logistec Navigation, Inc.
Transport Igloolik - Mgr.
Montreal, PQ

Lock Tours Canada
Sault Ste. Marie, ON

Lee Marine, Ltd.
Port Lambton, ON

Le Groupe Ocean
Quebec, PQ

Lake Michigan Contractors, Inc.
Holland, MI

Museum Ship
HMCS Haida
Toronto, ON

Museum Ship
CCGC Alexander Henry
Kingston, ON

Miller Boat Line, Inc.
Put-In-Bay, OH

Merce Transportation Co.
Sylvania, OH

McKeil Marine Ltd.
Hamilton, ON

McAllister Towing & Salvage, Inc.
Subsidiary of Le Groupe Ocean, Inc.
Montreal, PQ

Marine Atlantic, Inc.
Moncton, NB

Maid of the Mist Steamboat Co., Ltd.
Niagara Falls, ON

Museum Ship
Willis B. Boyer (Toledo, OH)
William G. Mather (Cleveland, OH)

Museum Ship
William A. Irvin
Duluth, MN

Museum Ship
Valley Camp
Sault Ste. Marie, MI

Museum Ships
Norgoma (Sault Ste. Marie, ON)
Norisle (Manitowaning, ON)

Museum Ship
City of Milwaukee
Elberta, MI

Museum Ship
Meteor
Superior, WI

Museum Ships
USS Little Rock
USS The Sullivans
Buffalo, NY

Museum Ship
Keewatin
Douglas, MI

Muskoka Lakes Navigation & Hotel Co. Gravenhurst, ON

Nadro Marine Services Port Dover, ON

Neuman Boat Line, Inc. Sandusky, OH

Ojibway Norton Co. Cleveland, OH

Ontario Ministry of Transportation & Communication Kingston, ON

Ontario Northland Transportation Commission Owen Sound, ON

Osborne Materials Co. Mentor, OH

Navigation Sonamar Algoma Central Corp.-Mgr. Sault Ste. Marie, ON

N.M. Paterson & Sons Ltd. Thunder Bay, ON

Pelee Island Transportation Services Pelee Island, ON

Provmar Fuels, Inc. Div. of ULS Corporation Toronto, ON

Purvis Marine Ltd. Sault Ste. Marie, ON

Purvis Marine Ltd. Sault Ste. Marie, ON

Rigel Shipping Canada, Inc. Rigel Shipping Co., Inc Shediac, NB

P. & H Shipping Div. of Parrish & Heimbecker Ltd. Mississauga, ON

P.M. Marine Ludington, MI

Selvick Marine Towing Corp. Sturgeon Bay, WI

Shell Canadian Tankers Ltd. Montreal, PQ

Shepler's Mackinac Island Ferry Services Mackinaw City, MI

Soo Locks Boat Tours Sault Ste. Marie, MI

Southdown, Inc. Cleveland, OH

Roen Salvage Co. Sturgeon Bay, WI

Sea Fox Thousand Islands Tours Kingston, ON

St. Lawrence Seaway Development Corp. Massena, NY

Shell Canadian Tankers Ltd. Montreal, PQ

Société des Traversiers du Québec Québec, PQ

Star Line Fleet St. Ignace, MI

Transport Igloolik, Inc. Montreal, PQ

St. Lawrence Cruise Lines, Inc. Kingston, ON

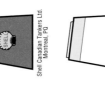

St. Lawrence Seaway Management Corp. Cornwall, ON

St. Mary's Cement Co. Toronto, ON

Toronto Metropolitan Park Dept. Toronto, ON

Transport Desgagnes, Inc. Quebec, PQ

Upper Lakes Towing Company, Inc. Escanaba, MI

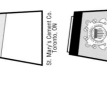

Trois Rivieres Remorqueurs Ltee. Trois Rivieres, PQ

Upper Lakes Group Jackes Shipping, Inc. ULS Marbulk, Inc. Ottawa, ON

United States Army Corps of Engineers Great Lakes and Ohio River Division Chicago, IL

United States Coast Guard 9th Coast Guard District Cleveland, OH

United States Environmental Protection Agency Bay City, MI

University of Michigan Center for Great Lakes & Aquatic Sciences Ann Arbor, MI

USS Great Lakes Fleet, Inc. Duluth, MN

Colors of Major International Seaway Fleets

AG Shipmanagement Ltd.
London, England

Akmar Shipping & Trading S.A.
Istanbul, Turkey

Alba Shipping Ltd. A/S
Aalborg, Denmark

Anglo-Georgian Shipping Co. Ltd.
London, England

Artemis Shipping, Inc.
Monrovia, Liberia

Atlantska Plovidba
Dubrovnik, Croatia

Aurora Shipping, Inc.
Manila, Philippines

Azov Sea Shipping Co.
Mariupol, Ukraine

B&N Sea Partner AB
Skärhamn, Sweden

Bay Ocean Management, Inc.
Englewood Cliffs, NJ

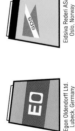
Bergen Bulk Carriers A/S
Bergen, Norway

Bison Shipmanagement
& Chartering Co. Pte. Ltd.
Singapore

Black Star Line
Hamburg, Germany

C. A. Crosbie Shipping Ltd.
Montreal, PQ

Canadian Forest
Navigation Co. Ltd.
Montreal, PQ

Cape Shipping S.A.
Piraeus, Greece

Cebi Metal Shipping
& Trading Ltd.
Istanbul, Turkey

Cere Hellenic Shipping Enterprises
Piraeus, Greece

Christensen Canadian African Lines
Montreal, PQ

Continental Commercial
Enterprises, Inc.
Monrovia, Liberia

Cosco (H.K.) Shipping Co. Ltd.
Hong Kong

Densan Shipping Co. Ltd.
Istanbul, Turkey

Det Nordenfjeldske D/S AS
Trondheim, Norway

Diana Shipping Agencies S.A.
Piraeus, Greece

Egon Oldendorff Ltd.
Lübeck, Germany

Eidsiva Rederi ASA
Oslo, Norway

ER Denizcilik Sanayi Nakliyat ve
Ticaret A.S.
Istanbul, Turkey

Fatalios Shipping S.A.
Piraeus, Greece

Fednav International Ltd.
Montreal, PQ

Gourdomichalis Maritime S.A.
Piraeus, Greece

Hapag Lloyd
Hamburg, Germany

Jebsens Ship
Management Ltd.
Bergen, Norway

J. Lauritzen A/S
Copenhagen, Denmark

Johan Hagenaes & Co.
Fednav Ltd. – Mgr.
Montreal, PQ

Knutsen Shipping
Haugesund, Norway

Laurin Maritime, Inc.
Houston, TX

Lithuanian Shipping Co.
Klaipeda, Lithuania

Lynx Shipping Co.
Athens, Greece

M.T.M. Ship Management
Pte. Ltd.
Singapore

Mammoet Shipping Ltd.
Amsterdam, Netherlands

Policlip (Luxembourg) S.A.
Luxembourg, Luxembourg

Pacific International Lines (Pte.) Ltd.
Singapore

Pacific Basin Agencies Ltd.
Hong Kong

Orion Schiffahrts-Gesellschaft
Hamburg, Germany

Olympic Shipping and Management S.A.
Monte Carlo, Monaco

Oceanbulk Maritime S.A.
Athens, Greece

Navigation Bulgare Ltd.
Varna, Bulgaria

Murmansk Shipping Co.
Murmansk, Russia

Societe Anonyme Monegasque d' Administration Maritime et Aerienne
Monte Carlo, Monaco

Sidemar Servizi Accessori S.p.A.
Genoa, Italy

Seastar Navigation Co. Ltd.
Athens, Greece

Scanscot Shipping Services GmbH
Hamburg, Germany

Rigel Shipping Canada, Inc.
Rigel Shipping Co., Inc.
Shediac, NB

Reinauer Transportation Co.
Staten Island, NY

R.O. Brodogradiliste
Rijeka, Yugoslavia

Polish Steamship Co.
Szczecin, Poland

Transmar Shipping Enterprises S.A.
Athens, Greece

Thenamaris Ships Management, Inc.
Athens, Greece

Teo Shipping Corp.
Piraeus, Greece

Stolt Nielsen Tankers
Greenwich, CT

Split Ship Management, Ltd.
Split, Croatia

Shipping Corp. of India Ltd.
Bombay, India

Sherinar Management Co. Ltd.
Athens, Greece

Sohtorik Denizcilik ve Ticaret A.S.
Istanbul, Turkey

Wagenborg Shipping B.V.
Delfzijl, Netherlands

V. Ships (Cyprus) Ltd.
Limassol, Cyprus

Viken Shipping Co. A/S
Bergen, Norway

Vale de Rio Doce Navigation Ltd.
Rio de Janeiro, Brazil

Univan Ship Management Ltd.
Hong Kong

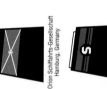

Space does not permit listing every potential international visitor to the Great Lakes and Seaway. Therefore we have included only the stack markings of the fleets that make regular transits of the St. Lawrence Seaway and Great Lakes system.

House Flags of Great Lakes & Seaway Fleets

Algoma Central
Marine Corp.

American Steamship
Co.

Atlantic Towing Ltd.
Kent Line Ltd.

Bethlehem Steel
Corp.

Black Creek
Shipping Co.

Canada Steamship
Lines, Inc.

Cleveland Tankers,
(1991) Inc.

Erie Navigation Co.
Erie Sand & Gravel

Gaelic Tug Boat Co.

Great Lakes
Associates Inc.

Great Lakes Towing
Co.

Inland Lakes
Management, Inc.

Interlake Steamship
Co.
Lakes Shipping Co.

LaFarge Cement
Corp.

McKeil Marine Ltd.

Oglebay Norton Co.

Ontario Northland
Transportation
Commission

P. & H. Shipping

N.M. Paterson
& Sons Ltd.

Purvis Marine Ltd.

Seaway Bulk Carriers

Seaway Self
Unloaders

Southdown Inc.

Transport
Desgagnes, Inc.

Upper Lakes Group,
Inc.

USS Great Lakes
Fleet, Inc.

Most merchant vessels fly the flag
of the nation in which they are
registered on the aft-most mast. In
foreign waters, the flag of the host
country is usually flown at the
vessel's foremast.

Flags of Nations in the Marine Trade

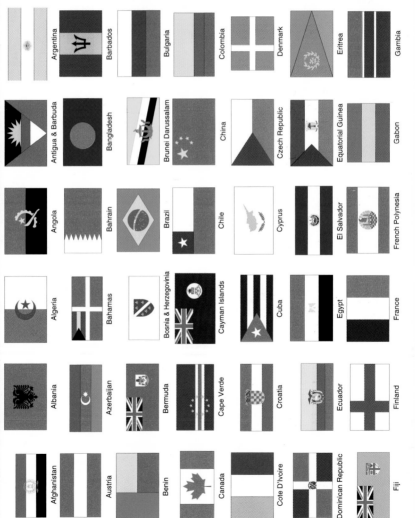

Australia	Armenia	Argentina	Antigua & Barbuda	Angola	Algeria
Belize	Belgium	Barbados	Bangladesh	Bahrain	Bahamas
Cameroon	Cambodia	Bulgaria	Brunei Darussalam	Brazil	Bosnia & Herzegovina
Costa Rica	Congo	Colombia	China	Chile	Cayman Islands
Dominica	Djibouti	Denmark	Czech Republic	Cyprus	Cuba
Ethiopia	Estonia	Eritrea	Equatorial Guinea	El Salvador	Egypt
Georgia	Germany	Gambia	Gabon	French Polynesia	France

Albania	Azerbaijan	Bermuda	Cape Verde	Croatia	Ecuador	Finland
Afghanistan	Austria	Benin	Canada	Cote D'Ivoire	Dominican Republic	Fiji

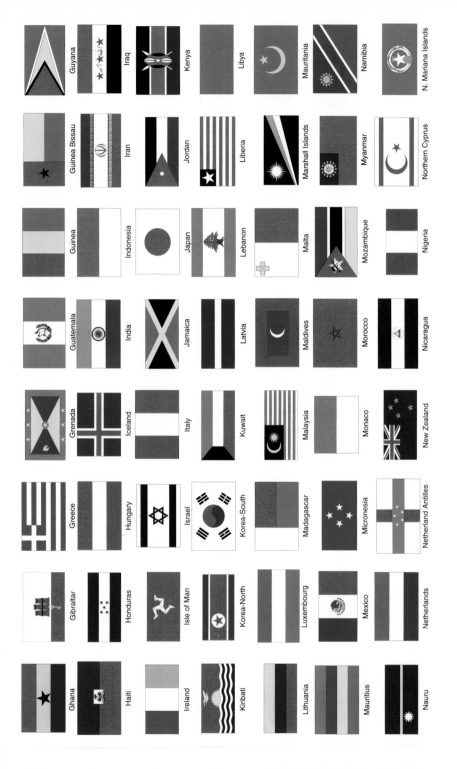

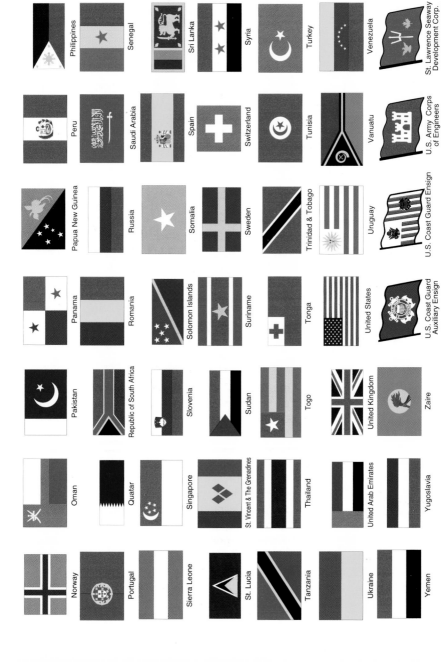

Poland
Seychelles
St. Christopher Nevis
Taiwan
Tuvalu
Vietnam
St. Lawrence Seaway Management Corp.

Philippines
Senegal
Sri Lanka
Syria
Turkey
Venezuela
St. Lawrence Seaway Development Corp.

Peru
Saudi Arabia
Spain
Switzerland
Tunisia
Vanuatu
U.S. Army Corps of Engineers

Papua New Guinea
Russia
Somalia
Sweden
Trinidad & Tobago
Uruguay
U.S. Coast Guard Ensign

Panama
Romania
Solomon Islands
Suriname
Tonga
United States
U.S. Coast Guard Auxiliary Ensign

Pakistan
Republic of South Africa
Slovenia
Sudan
Togo
United Kingdom
Zaire

Oman
Quatar
Singapore
St. Vincent & The Grenadines
Thailand
United Arab Emirates
Yugoslavia

Norway
Portugal
Sierra Leone
St. Lucia
Tanzania
Ukraine
Yemen

ALL HANDS ON DECK

... at the Great Lakes Maritime Academy

Forget the want ads - your perfect job may be waiting aboard a Great Lakes vessel. There are shortages of qualified personnel - especially in the engine departments - to sail the lakes, reports the **Great Lakes Maritime Academy** at Northwestern Michigan College in Traverse City, MI.

The Maritime Academy, which has been training Great Lakes seamen since 1969 and is one of only six such state facilities authorized by the federal government to train future officers for the U.S. Merchant Marine, offers two career paths. Cadets who choose the "deck" program train to become pilots and mates; those who choose the "engine" program train to become powerplant engineers, operating the diesel or steam engines that propel the mighty lakers.

Courses include seamanship, navigation and piloting, as well as steam and diesel engineering, and include 270 days afloat training aboard Great Lakes freighters. Only 50 students are admitted to the program each year, and there are no age or marital restrictions. Graduates serve with every company operating on the Great Lakes and as pilots for ocean-going ships sailing the lakes. Many have reached the pinnacle of their profession, and are masters or chief engineers aboard Great Lakes freighters. Interested in a life on the lakes? Call (800) 748-0566, ext.1200, for more information.

BOOKS FOR BOATS

Locks Library Serves Seamen

The **American Merchant Marine Library Association** provides an important service for Great Lakes sailors by lending books and magazines to crewmembers on board U.S.-flag vessels passing through the Soo Locks at Sault Ste. Marie, MI.

From a historic sandstone building on the locks grounds, the AMMLA - the "Public Library of the High Seas" - distributes hundreds of books each year to the men and women sailing the lakes. Adventures and westerns rate high on the reading lists but news magazines and, yes, even Playboy, are popular too.

In addition to the service at the Soo Locks, AMMLA libraries operate at five U.S. saltwater ports. Since the library relies on donations, surplus books and current magazines are always welcome.

Alpena returns to her namesake port after delivering a cargo of cement to Duluth. (Roger LeLievre)

ALPENA

Vessel Spotlight

Alpena is a classic steamer sailing for Inland Lakes Management and carrying LaFarge cement out of her namesake city.

Alpena's career began as the ore carrier **Leon Fraser** of the United States Steel fleet, entering service in 1942 after construction at the now-defunct Great Lakes Engineering Works in Detroit. She was the first of five "super" class lakers constructed to meet the demands of World War II. Fraser sailed for U.S. Steel until the end of the 1981 season, then sat idle in Lorain, OH, until October 1989, when she was towed to Fraser Shipyards in Superior, WI, for conversion to a cement carrier.

Shortened by 120 feet and renamed Alpena, she re-entered service in June 1991. Alpena had the largest capacity for cement on the lakes until LaFarge's barge **Integrity** began sailing in 1996. Alpena's original steam turbine moves her between LaFarge's many storage silos around the lakes from Bath, Ontario, to the east, Duluth to the west, and Chicago to the south.

- Rod Burdick

Fleet No. & Name Vessel Name	Type of Vessel	Year Built	Type of Engine	Cargo Cap. or Gross*	Overal Length	Breadth	Depth or Draft*
FEDNAV INTERNATIONAL LTD. - A DIVISION OF FEDNAV LTD.							
Federal Baffin	BC	1995	D	43,732	623' 04"	100' 00"	54' 06"
Federal Franklin	BC	1995	D	43,706	623' 04"	100' 00"	54' 06"
Federal Maas {2}	BC	1997	D	34,372	656' 02"	77' 01"	48' 11"
Federal Rhine {2}	BC	1997	D	34,372	656' 02"	77' 01"	48' 11"
Federal Saguenay {2}	BC	1996	D	34,372	656' 02"	77' 01"	48' 11"
Federal Schelde {2}	BC	1997	D	34,372	656' 02"	77' 01"	48' 11"
Federal St. Laurent {2}	BC	1996	D	34,372	656' 02"	77' 01"	48' 11"
Federal Sumida	BC	1998	D		738' 02"	106' 00"	
ALL TRUST SHIPPING CO. - CHARTERED BY FEDNAV INTERNATIONAL LTD.							
Federal Calliope	BC	1978	D	30,353	622' 07"	76' 05"	47' 05"
(Federal Saguenay {1} '78 - '95)							
Federal Dora	BC	1978	D	30,350	622' 07"	76' 05"	47' 05"
(Federal St. Laurent {1} '78 - '95)							
ATLANTSKA PLOVIDBA D.D. - CHARTERED BY FEDNAV INTERNATIONAL LTD.							
Orsula	BC	1996	D	34,198	656' 02"	77' 01"	48' 11"
(Federal Calumet {2} '96 - '97)							
Petka	BC	1986	D	34,685	728' 09"	75' 11"	48' 05"
BAY OCEAN MANAGEMENT, INC. - CHARTERED BY FEDNAV INTERNATIONAL LTD.							
Lake Carling	BC	1992	D	26,264	591' 01"	75' 09"	45' 07"
(Ziemia Cieszynska '92 - '93)							
Lake Champlain	BC	1992	D	26,264	591' 01"	75' 09"	45' 07"
(Ziemia Lodzka '92 - '92)							
Lake Charles	BC	1990	D	26,209	591' 01"	75' 09"	45' 07"
(Ziemia Gornoslaska '90 - '91)							
Lake Erie	BC	1980	D	35,630	729' 11"	76' 02"	47' 01"
(Federal Ottawa '80 - '95)							
Lake Michigan	BC	1981	D	38,294	729' 11"	76' 03"	47' 01"
(Federal Maas {1} '81 - '95)							
Lake Ontario	BC	1980	D	35,630	729' 11"	76' 03"	47' 01"
(Federal Danube '80 - '95)							
Lake Superior	BC	1981	D	35,630	729' 11"	76' 03"	47' 01"
(Federal Thames '81 - '95)							
EIDSIVA REDERI ASA - CHARTERED BY FEDNAV INTERNATIONAL LTD.							
Federal Oslo	BC	1985	D	29,462	601' 00"	76' 00"	48' 11"
(Paolo Pittaluga '85 - '91)							
Federal Vibeke	BC	1981	D	30,900	617' 04"	76' 00"	47' 07"
(Nosira Lin '81 - '89, Dan Bauta '89 - '89, Kristianiafjord '89 - '93)							
JUGOSLAVENSKA OCEANSKA PLOVIDBA - CHARTERED BY FEDNAV INT. LTD.							
Grant Carrier	BC	1984	D	30,850	617' 04"	75' 11"	47' 07"
KYLCO MARITIME LTD. - CHARTERED BY FEDNAV INTERNATIONAL LTD.							
Millenium Condor	BC	1981	D	27,036	627' 07"	75' 03"	44' 03"
(Eggarlock '81 - '82, Holck-Larsen '82 - '98)							
Millenium Eagle	BC	1983	D	28,788	606' 11"	75' 11"	48' 01"
(Mangal Desai '83 - '98)							
Millenium Falcon	BC	1981	D	27,048	627' 07"	75' 03"	44' 03"
(Oak Star '81 - '82, Soren Toubro '82 - '98)							
Millenium Hawk	BC	1984	D	28,791	606' 11"	75' 11"	48' 01"
(LT Argosy '84 - '98)							
Millenium Osprey	BC	1984	D	28,786	606' 11"	75' 11"	48' 01"
(LT Odyssey '84 - '98)							
PACIFIC BASIN AGENCIES LTD. - CHARTERED BY FEDNAV INTERNATIONAL LTD.							
Federal Bergen	BC	1984	D	29,159	593' 00"	76' 00"	47' 00"
(High Peak '84 - '90, Federal Bergen '90 - '92, Thunder Bay '92 - '93)							
SPAR SHIPPING A.S. - CHARTERED BY FEDNAV INTERNATIONAL LTD.							
Spar Garnet	BC	1984	D	30,686	589' 11"	75' 10"	50' 11"
(Mary Anne '84 - '93, Federal Vigra '93 - '97)							
Spar Jade	BC	1984	D	30,674	589' 11"	75' 10"	50' 11"
(Fiona Mary '84 - '93, Federal Aalesund '93 - '97)							
Spar Opal	BC	1984	D	28,214	585' 00"	75' 10"	48' 05"
(Lake Shidaka '84 - '91, Consensus Atlantic '91 - '92, Federal Matane '92 - '97)							
UNIVAN SHIP MANAGEMENT LTD. - CHARTERED BY FEDNAV INTERNATIONAL LTD.							
Federal Fraser	BC	1983	D	35,315	730' 00"	75' 09"	48' 00"
(Selkirk Settler '83 - '91, Federal St. Louis '91 - '91)							
Federal MacKenzie	BC	1983	D	35,315	730' 00"	75' 09"	48' 00"
(Canada Marquis '83 - '91, Federal Richelieu '91 - '91)							

Fleet No. & Name Vessel Name	Type of Vessel	Year Built	Type of Engine	Cargo Cap. or Gross*	Overall Length	Breadth	Depth or Draft*
Lady Hamilton	BC	1983	D	34,500	730' 00"	75' 09"	48' 00"
(Saskatchewan Pioneer '83 - '95)							

VANGUARD ENTERPRISE CO. LTD. - CHARTERED BY FEDNAV INTERNATIONAL LTD.

Federal Agno	BC	1985	D	29,643	599' 09"	75' 11"	48' 07"
(Federal Asahi '85 - '89)							

VIKEN SHIPPING CO. A/S - CHARTERED BY FEDNAV INTERNATIONAL LTD.

Daviken	BC	1987	D	34,752	729' 00"	75' 11"	48' 05"
(Malinska '87 - '97)							
Federal Fuji	BC	1986	D	29,536	599' 09"	75' 11"	48' 07"
Federal Polaris	BC	1985	D	29,536	599' 09"	75' 11"	48' 07"
Goviken	BC	1987	D	34,752	729' 00"	75' 11"	48' 05"
(Omisalj '87 - '97)							
Inviken	BC	1984	D	30,052	621' 05"	75' 01"	47' 11"
(Bar '84 - '97)							
Utviken	BC	1985	D	30,052	621' 05"	75' 01"	47' 11"
(Bijelo Polje '85 - '92, C. Blanco '92 - '95)							

CHARTERED BY FEDNAV INTERNATIONAL LTD.

Mecta Sea	BC	1984	D	28,166	584' 08"	75' 11"	48' 05"
(Socrates '84 - '92, Union '92 - '97)							
Tecam Sea	BC	1984	D	28,166	584' 08"	75' 11"	48' 05"
(Alam University '84 - '98)							

F-4 — FERRISS MARINE CONTRACTING CORP., DETROIT, MI

Magnetic	TB	1925	D	30*	55' 00"	14' 00"	6' 06"
Norma B.	TB	1940	D	14*	43' 00"	15' 00"	4' 00"

F-5 — FRASER SHIPYARDS, INC., SUPERIOR, WI

Brenda L.	TB	1941	D	11*	36' 00"	10' 00"	3' 08"
(Harbour I '41 - '58, Su-Joy III '58 -'78)							
Maxine Thompson	TB	1959	D	30*	47' 04"	13' 00"	6' 06"
(Susan A. Fraser '59 - '78)							
Murray R.	TB	1946	D	17*	42' 10"	12' 00"	4' 07"
Phil Milroy	TB	1957	D	41*	47' 11"	16' 08"	8' 04"
(Barney B. Barstow '57 - '78)							
Reuben Johnson	TB	1912	D	71*	78' 00"	17' 00"	11' 00"
(Buffalo {1} '12 - '28, USCOE Churchill '28 - '46, USCOE Buffalo {1} '46 - '74, Todd Fraser '74 - '78)							
Todd L.	TB	1965	D	22*	42' 10"	12' 00"	5' 06"
(Robert W. Fraser '65 - '78)							
Wally Kendora	TB	1956	D	24*	43' 00"	12' 00"	5' 06"
(Byron S. Nelson '56 - '65)							
Wells Larson	TB	1953	D	22*	42' 10"	12' 00"	5' 06"
(E. C. Knudsen '53 - '74)							

F-6 — FROST ENGINEERING CO., FRANKFORT, MI

Captain George	TB	1929	D	61*	63' 00"	17' 00"	7' 08"
(USCOE Captain George '29 - '68, Captain George '68 - '73, Kurt R. Luetdke '73 - '91)							

G-1 — G. J. TAYLOR, OAKVILLE, ON

Nelvana {1}	ES	1963	D	61*	55' 10"	16' 00"	5' 00"

G-2 — GAELIC TUG BOAT CO., GROSSE ILE, MI

Carolyn Hoey	TB	1951	D	146*	90' 00"	25' 00"	11' 00"
(Atlas '51 - '84 Susan Hoey {1} '84 - '85, Atlas '85 - '87)							
G.T.B. No. 1	BC	1956	B	2,500	248' 00"	43' 00"	12' 00"
L.S.C. 236	TK	1946	B	10,000	195' 00"	35' 00"	10' 06"
Marysville	TK	1973	B	16,000	200' 00"	50' 00"	12' 06"
Patricia Hoey {2}	TB	1949	D	146*	88' 06"	25' 00"	11' 00"
(Propeller '49 - '82, Bantry Bay '82 - '91)							
Roger Stahl	TB	1944	D	148*	110' 00"	26' 05"	15' 05"
(USCG Kennebec [WYT-61] '44 - '44, USCG Kaw [WYT-61] '44 - '80, Kaw '80 - '97)							
Shannon	TB	1944	D	145*	101' 00"	28' 00"	13' 00"
(USS Connewango [YTB-338] '44 - '77)							

G-3 — GALACTICA 001 ENTERPRISES LTD., TORONTO, ON

Enterprise 2000	ES	1998	D				
Galactica 001	ES	1957	D	67*	50' 00"	16' 00"	6' 03"

G-4 — GALLAGHER MARINE CONSTRUCTION CO., INC., ESCANABA, MI

Bee Jay	TB	1939	D	19*	45' 00"	13' 00"	7' 00"

Fleet No. & Name Vessel Name	Type of Vessel	Year Built	Type of Engine	Cargo Cap. or Gross*	Overall Length	Breadth	Depth or Draft*

G-5 — GANANOQUE BOAT LINE LTD., GANANOQUE, ON

Thousand Islander	ES	1972	D	200*	104' 00"	22' 00"	5' 00"
Thousand Islander II	ES	1973	D	200*	100' 00"	22' 00"	5' 00"
Thousand Islander III	ES	1975	D	376*	118' 00"	28' 00"	6' 00"
Thousand Islander IV	ES	1976	D	347*	118' 00"	28' 00"	6' 00"
Thousand Islander V	ES	1979	D	246*	88' 00"	24' 00"	5' 00"

G-6 — GARY ZULAUF, OSHAWA, ON

Rhea	MS	1943	D	245*	136' 00"	24' 06"	10' 00"

(USS YMS-299 '43 - '47, USS Rhea [AMS-52/MSCO-52] '47 - '60)
   (The Rhea earned 3 Battle Stars during World War II as the USS YMS-299.)

G-7 — GENESEE MARINE, INC.

Spirit of Rochester	ES	1975	D	80*	124' 03"	28' 06"	7' 03"

(American Eagle '75 - '83, Island Clipper {1} '83 - '94)

G-8 — GEORGIAN BAY CRUISE CO., PARRY SOUND, ON

Chippewa {8}	PA	1954	D		65' 00"	16' 00"	6' 06"

G-9 — GILLESPIE OIL & TRANSIT, INC., ST. JAMES, MI

American Girl	PK	1922	D	40	64' 00"	14' 00"	8' 03"
Oil Queen	TK	1949	B	620	65' 00"	16' 00"	6' 00"

G-10 — GODERICH ELEVATORS LTD., GODERICH, ON

Willowglen	BC	1943	R	16,300	620' 06"	60' 00"	35' 00"

(Mesabi '43 - '43, Lehigh {3} '43 - '81, Joseph X. Robert '81 - '82)
   (Last operated 21 December, 1992 — 5 year survey expired October, 1997.)
   (Currently in use as a stationary grain storage vessel in Goderich, ON.)

G-11 — GOODTIME ISLAND CRUISES, INC., SANDUSKY, OH

Goodtime I	ES	1960	D	81*	111' 00"	29' 08"	9' 05"

G-12 — GOODTIME TRANSIT BOATS, INC., CLEVELAND, OH

Goodtime III	ES	1990	D	95*	161' 00"	40' 00"	11' 00"

G-13 — GRAND VALLEY STATE UNIVERSITY, ALLENDALE, MI

D. J. Angus	RV	1986	D	14*	45' 00"	14' 00"	4' 00"*
W. G. Jackson	RV	1996	D	80*	64' 10"	20' 00"	5' 00"*

G-14 — GRAVEL & LAKE SERVICES LTD., THUNDER BAY, ON

Donald Mac	TB	1914	D	69*	71' 00"	17' 00"	10' 00"
F. A. Johnson	TB	1953	B	439*	150' 00"	32' 00"	10' 00"

(Capt. Charles T. Parker '52 - '54, Rapid Cities '54 - '69, S. P. Renolds '69 - '70)

George N. Carleton	TB	1943	D	97*	82' 00"	21' 00"	11' 00"

(Bansaga '43 - '64)

Peninsula	TB	1944	D	261*	111' 00"	27' 00"	13' 00"

(HMCS Norton [W-31] '44 - '45, W.A.C. 1 '45 - '46)

Robert John	TB	1945	D	98*	82' 00"	20' 01"	11' 00"

(Bansturdy '45 - '66)

Wolf River	BC	1956	D	5,880	349' 02"	43' 07"	25' 04"

(Tecumseh {2} '56 - '67, New York News {3} '67 - '86, Stella Desgagnes '86 - '93, Beam Beginner '94 - '95)

G-15 — GREAT LAKES ASSOCIATES, INC., CLEVELAND, OH

Kinsman Enterprise {2}	BC	1927	T	16,000	631' 00"	65' 00"	33' 00"

(Harry Coulby {2} '27 - '89)
   (Last operated 13 December 1995 — 5 year survey expired May, 1998.) (Laid up in Buffalo, NY.)

Kinsman Independent {3}	BC	1952	T	18,800	642' 03"	67' 00"	35' 00"

(Charles L. Hutchinson {3} '52 - '62, Ernest R. Breech '62 - '88)

G-16 — GREAT LAKES INTERNATIONAL TOWING & SALVAGE, INC., BURLINGTON, ON

Ecosse	TB	1979	D	145*	91' 00"	26' 00"	8' 06"

(R. & L. No. 1 '79 - '96)

G-17 — GREAT LAKES MARITIME ACADEMY, TRAVERSE CITY, MI — (616)-922-1200

Anchor Bay	TV	1953	D	23*	45' 00"	13' 00"	7' 00"*
GLMA Barge	TV	1960	B	25	80' 00"	20' 00"	7' 00"
Northwestern {2}	TV	1969	D	12*	55' 00"	15' 00"	6' 06"

(USCOE North Central '69 - '98)

G-18 — GREAT LAKES SCHOONER CO., TORONTO, ON

Challenge	3S	1980	W	76*	96' 00"	16' 06"	8' 00"
True North of Toronto	2S	1947	W	95*	115' 00"	20' 00"	10' 06"

(Eenhorn '47 - '86, Unicorn of St. Helier '86 - '96)

Canada Steamship Lines' Ferbec, eastbound in the St. Lawrence River 7 July 1998. (Angela S. Clayton)

Fleet No. & Name Vessel Name	Type of Vessel	Year Built	Type of Engine	Cargo Cap. or Gross*	Overal Length	Breadth	Depth or Draft*
G-19 — GREAT LAKES SHIPWRECK HISTORICAL SOCIETY, SAULT STE. MARIE, MI							
Antiquarian	RV		D		40' 00"	12' 00"	4' 00"
David Boyd	RV	1982	D	23*	47' 00"	17' 00"	3' 00"*
G-20 — GREAT LAKES TOWING CO., CLEVELAND, OH							
Alabama {2}	TB	1916	D	98*	81' 00"	21' 03"	12' 05"
Alaska	TB	1912	D	71*	74' 00"	19' 06"	12' 00"
(Gary {1} '12 - '34, Green Bay '34 - '81, Oneida '81 - '87, Iroquois {2} '87 - '90)							
Arizona	TB	1931	D	98*	81' 00"	21' 03"	12' 05"
Arkansas {2}	TB	1909	D	98*	81' 00"	21' 03"	12' 05"
(Yale '09 - '48)							
California	TB	1926	D	98*	81' 00"	21' 03"	12' 05"
Colorado	TB	1928	D	98*	81' 00"	21' 03"	12' 05"
Delaware {4}	TB	1924	D	98*	81' 00"	21' 03"	12' 05"
Florida	TB	1926	D	98*	81' 00"	21' 03"	12' 05"
(Florida '26 - '83, Pinellas '83 - '84)							
Idaho	TB	1931	D	98*	81' 00"	20' 00"	12' 06"
Illinois {2}	TB	1914	D	98*	81' 00"	20' 00"	12' 06"
Indiana	TB	1911	D	98*	81' 00"	20' 00"	12' 06"
Iowa	TB	1915	D	98*	81' 00"	20' 00"	12' 06"
Kansas	TB	1927	D	98*	81' 00"	20' 00"	12' 06"
Kentucky {2}	TB	1929	D	98*	81' 00"	20' 00"	12' 06"
Louisiana	TB	1917	D	97*	81' 00"	20' 00"	12' 06"
Maine {1}	TB	1921	D	98*	81' 00"	20' 00"	12' 06"
(Maine {1} '21 - '82, Saipan '82 - '83, Hillsboro '83 - '84)							
Maryland {2}	TB	1925	D	98*	81' 00"	21' 03"	12' 05"
(Maryland {2} '25 - '82, Tarawa '82 - '83, Pasco '83 - '84)							
Massachusetts	TB	1928	D	98*	84' 04"	20' 00"	12' 06"
Michigan {9}	TB	1915	D	99*	81' 00"	20' 00"	12' 06"
(Missouri {1} '15 - '83, Polk '83 - '84)							
Minnesota {1}	TB	1911	D	98*	81' 00"	20' 00"	12' 06"
Mississippi	TB	1916	D	97*	81' 00"	20' 00"	12' 06"
Missouri {2}	TB	1927	D	149*	95' 00"	24' 00"	13' 06"
(Rogers City {1} '27 - '56, Dolomite {1} '56 - '81, Chippewa {7} '81 - '90)							
Montana	TB	1929	D	98*	84' 04"	20' 00"	12' 06"
Nebraska	TB	1929	D	98*	84' 04"	20' 00"	12' 06"
New Hampshire {2}	TB	1951	D	149*	88' 07"	24' 10"	10' 09"
(Messenger '51 - '84, Patricia Hoey {1} '84 - '90)							
New Jersey	TB	1924	D	98*	81' 00"	20' 00"	12' 06"
(New Jersey '24 - '52, Petco-21 '52 - '53)							
New Mexico {1}	TB	1910	D	97*	81' 00"	20' 00"	12' 06"
(W. L. Mercereau '10 - '38)							
New York	TB	1913	D	98*	81' 00"	20' 00"	12' 06"
North Carolina {2}	TB	1952	D	145*	95' 06"	24' 00"	13' 06"
(Limestone '52 - '83, Wicklow '83 - '90)							
North Dakota	TB	1910	D	97*	81' 00"	20' 00"	12' 06"
(John M. Truby '10 - '38)							
Ohio {3}	TB	1903	D	194*	118' 00"	24' 00"	13' 06"
(M.F.D. No. 15 '03 - '52, Laurence C. Turner '52 - '73)							
Oklahoma	TB	1913	D	97*	81' 00"	20' 00"	12' 06"
(T. C. Lutz {2} '13 - '34)							
Oregon {2}	TB	1952	D	149*	88' 07"	24' 10"	10' 09"
(Jennifer George '52 - '82, Galway Bay '82 - '90)							
Pennsylvania {3}	TB	1911	D	98*	81' 00"	20' 00"	12' 06"
Rhode Island	TB	1930	D	98*	84' 04"	20' 00"	12' 06"
South Carolina	TB	1925	D	102*	86' 00"	21' 00"	11' 00"
(Welcome {2} '25 - '53, Joseph H. Callan '53 - '72 South Carolina '72 - '82, Tulagi '82 - '83)							
Superior {3}	TB	1912	D	147*	97' 00"	22' 00"	12' 05"
Tennessee	TB	1917	D	98*	81' 00"	20' 00"	12' 06"
Texas	TB	1916	D	97*	81' 00"	20' 00"	12' 06"
Vermont	TB	1914	D	98*	81' 00"	20' 00"	12' 06"
Virginia {2}	TB	1914	D	97*	81' 00"	20' 00"	12' 06"
Washington {1}	TB	1925	D	97*	81' 00"	20' 00"	12' 06"
Wisconsin {4}	TB	1897	D	106*	90' 03"	21' 00"	12' 03"
(America {3} 1897 - '82, Midway '82 - '83)							
Wyoming	TB	1929	D	98*	84' 04"	20' 00"	12' 06"

Fleet No. & Name Vessel Name	Type of Vessel	Year Built	Type of Engine	Cargo Cap. or Gross*	Overal Length	Breadth	Depth or Draft*
G-21 — GREELY GOODTIME CHARTERS, INC., TORONTO, ON							
Yankee Lady	ES	1965	D	56*	42' 10"	16' 06"	9' 02"
(Peggy Vee V '65 - '88)							
Yankee Lady II	ES	1980	D	68*	75' 00"	16' 00"	9' 08"
(Blue Chip II '80 - '89)							
H-1 — HALRON OIL CO., INC., GREEN BAY, WI							
Mr. Micky	TK	1940	B	10,500	195' 00"	35' 00"	10' 00"
H-2 — HAMILTON HARBOUR COMMISSIONERS, HAMILTON, ON							
Judge McCombs	TB	1948	D	10*	36' 00"	10' 03"	4' 00"
H-3 — HANK VAN ASPERT, WINDSOR, ON							
Queen City {2}	PA	1911	D	248*	116' 00"	23' 00"	12' 07"
(Polana '11 - '30, Jalobert '30 - '54, Macassa {2} '54 - '65)							
(Last operated in 1982 — Currently laid up in LaSalle, ON.)							
H-4 — HANNAH MARINE CORP., LEMONT, IL							
Daryl C. Hannah {2}	TB	1956	D	268*	102' 00"	28' 00"	8' 00"
(Cindy Jo '56 - '66, Katherine L. '66 - '93)							
Donald C. Hannah	TB	1962	D	191*	91' 00"	29' 00"	11' 06"
Hannah D. Hannah	TB	1955	D	134*	86' 00"	24' 00"	10' 00"
(Harbor Ace '55 - '61, Gopher State '61 - '71, Betty Gale '71 - '93)							
Hannah 1801	TK	1967	B	18,550	240' 00"	50' 00"	12' 00"
Hannah 1802	TK	1967	B	18,550	240' 00"	50' 00"	12' 00"
Hannah 2801	TK	1980	B	28,665	275' 00"	54' 00"	17' 06"
Hannah 2901	TK	1962	B	17,400	264' 00"	52' 06"	12' 06"
Hannah 2902	TK	1962	B	17,360	264' 00"	52' 06"	12' 06"
Hannah 2903	TK	1962	B	17,350	264' 00"	52' 06"	12' 06"
Hannah 3601	TK	1972	B	35,360	290' 00"	60' 00"	18' 03"
Hannah 5101	TK	1978	B	49,660	360' 00"	60' 00"	22' 06"
James A. Hannah	TB	1945	D	593*	149' 00"	33' 00"	16' 00"
(U.S. Army LT-280 '45 - '65, Muskegon {1} '65 - '71)							
Kristin Lee Hannah	TB	1945	D	602*	149' 00"	33' 00"	16' 00"
(U.S. Army LT-815 '45 - '64, Henry Foss '64 - '84, Kristin Lee '84 - '93)							
Margaret M.	TB	1956	D	167*	89' 06"	24' 00"	10' 00"
(Shuttler '56 - '60, Margaret M. Hannah '60 - '84)							
Mark Hannah	TB	1969	D	191*	127' 05"	32' 01"	14' 03"
(Lead Horse '69 - '73, Gulf Challenger '73 - '80, Challenger {2} '80 - '93)							
Mary E. Hannah	TB	1945	D	612*	149' 00"	33' 00"	16' 00"
(U.S. Army LT-821 '45 - '47, Brooklyn '47 - '66, Lee Reuben '66 - '75)							
Mary Page Hannah {2}	TB	1972	D	99*	59' 08"	24' 01"	10' 03"
(Kings Squire '72 - '78, Juanita D. '78 - '79 Katherine L. '79 - '93)							
No. 25	TK	1949	B	19,500	254' 00"	54' 00"	11' 00"
No. 26	TK	1949	B	19,500	254' 00"	54' 00"	11' 00"
No. 28	TK	1957	B	20,725	240' 00"	50' 00"	12' 06"
No. 29 {2}	TK	1952	B	22,000	254' 00"	54' 00"	11' 06"
Peggy D. Hannah	TB	1920	D	145*	108' 00"	25' 00"	14' 00"
(William A. Whitney '20 - '92)							
H-5 — HARBOR LIGHT CRUISE LINES, INC., TOLEDO, OH							
Sandpiper	ES	1984	D	19*	65' 00"	16' 00"	4' 00"
H-6 — HARRY GAMBLE SHIPYARDS, PORT DOVER, ON							
H. A. Smith	TB	1944	D	24*	55' 00"	16' 00"	5' 06"
J. A. Cornett	TB	1937	D	60*	65' 00"	17' 00"	9' 00"
H-7 — HOLLY MARINE TOWING, CHICAGO, IL							
Blackie B.	TB	1952	D	146*	85' 00"	25' 00"	11' 00"
(Bonita {2} '52 - '85, Susan Hoey {2} '85 - '95)							
Chris Ann	TB	1981	D	45*	51' 09"	17' 00"	6' 01"
(Captain Robbie '81 - '90, Philip M. Pearse '90 - '97)							
Holly Ann	TB	1926	D	220*	108' 00"	26' 00"	15' 00"
(Wm. A. Lydon '26 - '92)							
Katie Ann	TB	1924	D	99*	85' 00"	21' 06"	10' 09"
(Martha C. '24 - '52, Langdon C. Hardwicke '52 - '82, Wabash {2} '82 - '93)							
Laura Lynn	TB	1950	D	146*	82' 00"	25' 00"	10' 07"
(Navajo {1} '50 - '53, Seaval '53 - '64, Mary T. Tracy '64 - '69, Yankee '69 - '70, Minn '70 - '74, William S. Bell '74 - '83, Newcastle '83 - '93)							

Cuyahoga, inbound at Erie, PA, 21 April 1996. (Jim Thoreson)

Fleet No. & Name Vessel Name	Type of Vessel	Year Built	Type of Engine	Cargo Cap. or Gross*	Overall Length	Breadth	Depth or Draft*
L-1 — LAKE MICHIGAN CARFERRY SERVICE, INC., LUDINGTON, MI							
Badger [43] {2}	CF	1953	S	4,244*	410' 06"	59' 06"	24' 00"
Spartan [42] {2}	CF	1952	S	4,244*	410' 06"	59' 06"	24' 00"
(Last operated 20 January, 1979 — 5 year survey expired January, 1981.)							
(Currently laid up in Ludington, MI.)							
Wynken, Blynken and Nod	CF	1957	D	73*	61' 01"	28' 10"	8' 06"
(Rebel '57 - '94)							
PERE MARQUETTE SHIPPING CO. - A DIV. OF LAKE MICHIGAN CARFERRY SERVICE, INC.							
Undaunted	TB	1944	D	860*	143' 00"	33' 01"	17' 00"
(USS Undaunted [ATR-126, ATA-199] '44 - '63, USMA Kings Pointer '63 - '93, Krystal K. '93 - '97)							
Pere Marquette 41	BC	1941	B	4,545	400' 00"	58' 00"	23' 06"
(City of Midland 41 '41 - '97)							
[Pere Marquette 41/Undaunted overall dimensions together]					494' 00"	58' 00"	23' 06"
L-2 — LAKE MICHIGAN CONTRACTORS, INC., HOLLAND, MI							
Art Lapish	TB	1954	D	15*	44' 03"	12' 08"	5' 04"
Captain Barnaby	TB	1956	D	146*	94' 00"	27' 00"	11' 09"
(William C. Gaynor '56 - '87)							
Cherokee	DB	1943	B	1,500	155' 00"	50' 00"	13' 00"
Curly B.	TB	1956	D	131*	84' 00"	26' 00"	9' 02"
(Waverly '56 - '74, Bother Collins '74 - '80)							
G. W. Falcon	TB	1936	D	22*	49' 07"	13' 08"	6' 02"
Illinois {3}	DS	1971	B	521*	140' 00"	50' 00"	9' 00"
Iroquois {3}	DS	1950	B	495*	120' 00"	30' 00"	7' 00"
James Harris	TB	1943	D	18*	41' 09"	12' 05"	5' 07"
John Henry	TB	1954	D	66*	70' 00"	20' 06"	9' 07"
(U.S. Army ST-2013 '54 - '80)							
Ojibway {2}	DS	1954	B	517*	120' 00"	50' 00"	10' 00"
PBI	DS	1957	B	216*	96' 05"	35' 00"	6' 00"
Shirley Joy	TB	1978	D	98*	72' 00"	26' 00"	7' 06"
(Douglas B. Mackie '78 - '97)							
Sioux {1}	DS	1954	B	518*	120' 00"	50' 00"	10' 00"
A variety of derrick barges are also available.							
L-3 — LAKE MICHIGAN HARDWOOD CO., LELAND, MI							
Glen Shore	PK	1957	D	105	68' 00"	21' 00"	6' 00"
L-4 — LAKE SUPERIOR EXCURSIONS, BEAVER BAY, MN							
Grampa Woo III	ES	1978	D		115' 00"	22' 00"	5' 00"*
(Southern Comfort '78 - '97)							
L-5 — LAKE TOWING, INC., AVON, OH							
Jiggs	TB	1911	D	45*	61' 00"	16' 00"	8' 00"
Johnson	TB	1976	D	287*	140' 06"	40' 00"	15' 06"
Johnson II	TB	1975	D	311*	194' 00"	40' 00"	17' 00"
2361	BC	1967	B	3,600	236' 00"	50' 00"	15' 10"
3403	SU	1963	B	9,500	340' 00"	62' 06"	25' 04"
L-6 — LAKES PILOTS ASSOCIATION, PORT HURON, MI							
Huron Belle	PB	1979	D	21*	50' 00"	16' 00"	7' 09"
Huron Maid	PB	1976	D		46' 00"	16' 00"	
L-7 — LAURIN MARITIME (AMERICA), INC., HOUSTON, TX							
Mountain Blossom	TK	1986	D	70,020	527' 07"	74' 11"	39' 04"
Nordic Blossom	TK	1981	D	152,216	505' 03"	74' 07"	45' 04"
(Nordic Sun '81 - '89, Nordic '89 - '94)							
Sunny Blossom	TK	1986	D	92,326	527' 07"	74' 11"	39' 05"
L-8 — LE BATEAU-MOUCHE, MONTREAL, PQ							
Le Bateau-Mouche	ES	1992	D	190*	108' 00"	22' 00"	3' 00"
L-9 — LE BRUN CONSTRUCTORS LTD., THUNDER BAY, ON							
Henry T.	DB	1932	B	1,000	120' 00"	44' 00"	11' 00"
L-10 — LE GROUPE OCEAN, INC., QUEBEC, PQ							
Betsiamites	SU	1969	B	11,600	402' 00"	75' 00"	24' 00"
Captain Ioannis S.	TB	1973	D	722*	136' 08"	35' 08"	22' 00"
(Sistella '73 - '78, Sandy Cape '78 - '80)							
Elmglen {2}	BC	1952	B	21,425	678' 00"	68' 03"	36' 03"
(John O. McKellar {2} '52 - '84)							
(Currently laid up in Quebec, PQ.)							

Fleet No. & Name Vessel Name	Type of Vessel	Year Built	Type of Engine	Cargo Cap. or Gross*	Overal Length	Breadth	Depth or Draft*
Lac St-Francois	BC	1979	B	1,200	195' 00"	35' 00"	12' 00"
McAllister No. 3	DB	1956	B	1,000	165' 00"	38' 00"	9' 00"
Nanook	GC	1946	B	736	225' 00"	38' 00"	12' 06"
Ocean Abys	DB	1948	B	1,000	140' 00"	40' 00"	9' 00"
Ocean Bravo	TB	1970	D	320*	110' 00"	28' 06"	17' 00"
(Takis V. '70 - '80, Donald P. '80 - '80, Nimue '80 - '83, Donald P. '83 - '98)							
Ocean Charlie	TB	1973	D	448*	123' 02"	31' 06"	18' 09"
(Leonard W. '73 - '98)							
Ocean Echo II	TB	1969	D	438*	104' 08"	35' 05"	18' 09"
(Atlantic '69 - '75, Laval '75 - '96)							
Ocean Foxtrot	TB	1971	D	700*	184' 05"	38' 05"	16' 07"
(Polor Shore '71 - '77, Canmar Supplier VII '77 - '95)							
Ocean Intrepide	TT	1998	D	178*	74' 08"	30' 01"	14' 09"
Ocean Jupiter	TT	1998	D	178*	74' 08"	30' 01"	14' 09"

McALLISTER TOWING & SALVAGE, INC. - A SUBSIDIARY OF LE GROUPE OCEAN, INC.

Basse-Cote	DB	1932	B	400	201' 00"	40' 00"	12' 00"
Cathy McAllister	TB	1954	D	225*	101' 10"	26' 00"	13' 08"
Gercon #1	DS	1940	B	500	110' 00"	30' 00"	9' 00"
McAllister No. 50	CS	1931	B		100' 00"	45' 00"	10' 00"
Navcomar #1	DB	1955	B	500	135' 00"	35' 00"	9' 00"
Ocean Alpha	TB	1960	D	202*	91' 06"	27' 03"	12' 06"
(Jerry G. '60 - '98)							
Ocean Golf	TB	1959	D	152*	103' 00"	25' 10"	11' 09"
(Scranton '59 - '59, Helen M. McAllister '59 - '97)							
Ocean Hercule	TB	1976	D	448*	120' 00"	32' 00"	19' 00"
(Stril Pilot '76 - '81, Spirit Sky '81 - '86, Ierland '86 - '89, Ierlandia '89 - '95, Charles Antoine '95 - '97)							
OKA No. 12	CS	1956	B	1,000	165' 00"	38' 00"	9' 00"
P. S. Barge No. 1	BC	1923	B	3,000	258' 06"	43' 01"	20' 00"
(Edwin T. Douglas '23 - '60)							
Queng #1	DB	1924	B	500	100' 00"	38' 00"	9' 00"
Salvage Monarch	TB	1959	D	219*	97' 09"	28' 00"	14' 06"

SOREL TUGBOATS, INC. - A SUBSIDIARY OF McALLISTER TOWING & SALVAGE, INC.

Omni-Atlas	CS	1913	B	479*	133' 00"	42' 00"	10' 00"
Omni-Richelieu	TB	1969	D	144*	83' 00"	24' 06"	13' 06"
(Port Alfred II '69 - '82)							
Omni Sorel	TB	1962	D	71*	72' 00"	19' 00"	12' 00"
(Angus M. '62 - '92)							
Omni St-Laurent	TB	1957	D	161*	99' 02"	24' 09"	12' 06"
(Diligent '57 - '89)							

L-11 — LEE MARINE LTD., PORT LAMBTON, ON

Hammond Bay	ES	1992	D	43*	54' 00"	16' 00"	3' 00"
(Scrimp & Scrounge '92 - '95)							
Nancy A. Lee	TB	1939	D	9*	40' 00"	12' 00"	3' 00"

L-12 — LOCK TOURS CANADA BOAT CRUISES, SAULT STE. MARIE, ON.

Chief Shingwauk	ES	1965	D	109*	70' 00"	24' 00"	4' 06"

L-13 — LUEDTKE ENGINEERING CO., FRANKFORT, MI

Alan K. Luedtke	TB	1944	D	149*	86' 04"	23' 00"	10' 03"
(U.S. Army ST-527 '44 - '55, USCOE Two Rivers '55 - '90)							
Chris E. Luedtke	TB	1936	D	18*	45' 00"	12' 03"	6' 00"
Erich R. Luedtke	TB	1939	D	18*	45' 00"	12' 03"	6' 00"
Gretchen B.	TB	1943	D	18*	45' 00"	12' 03"	6' 00"
Karl E. Luedtke	TB	1928	D	32*	59' 03"	14' 09"	8' 00"
Kurt Luedtke	TB	1956	D	96*	72' 00"	22' 06"	7' 06"
(Jere C. '56 - '90)							
Paul L. Luedtke	TB	1935	D	18*	42' 06"	11' 09"	6' 09"

M-1 — M. C. M. MARINE, INC., SAULT STE. MARIE, MI

Drummond Islander II	CF	1961	D	97*	65' 00"	36' 00"	9' 00"
Mackinaw City	TB	1943	D	23*	38' 00"	11' 05"	4' 07"
Wolverine	TB	1952	D		42' 05"	12' 05"	5' 00"

M-2 — MacDONALD MARINE LTD., GODERICH, ON

Debbie Lyn	TB	1950	D	10*	45' 00"	14' 00"	10' 00"
Donald Bert	TB	1953	D	11*	45' 00"	14' 00"	10' 00"
Dover	TB	1931	D	70*	84' 00"	17' 00"	6' 00"
Ian Mac	TB	1955	D	12*	45' 00"	14' 00"	10' 00"

Fleet No. & Name Vessel Name	Type of Vessel	Year Built	Type of Engine	Cargo Cap. or Gross*	Overal Length	Breadth	Depth or Draft*
M-3 — MADELINE ISLAND FERRY LINE, INC., LaPOINTE, WI							
Island Queen {2}	CF	1966	D	90*	75' 00"	34' 09"	10' 00"
Madeline	CF	1984	D	97*	90' 00"	35' 00"	8' 00"
Nichevo II	CF	1962	D	89*	65' 00"	32' 00"	8' 09"
M-4 — MAID OF THE MIST STEAMBOAT CO. LTD., NIAGARA FALLS, ON							
Maid of the Mist	ES	1987	D	54*	65' 00"	16' 00"	7' 00"
Maid of the Mist III	ES	1972	D	54*	65' 00"	16' 00"	7' 00"
Maid of the Mist IV	ES	1976	D	74*	72' 00"	16' 00"	7' 00"
Maid of the Mist V	ES	1983	D	74*	72' 00"	16' 00"	7' 00"
Maid of the Mist VI	ES	1990	D	155*	78' 09"	29' 06"	7' 00"
Maid of the Mist VII	ES	1997	D	160*	80' 00"	30' 00"	7' 00"
M-5 — MALCOLM MARINE, ST. CLAIR, MI							
Manitou {2}	TB	1943	D	491*	110' 00"	26' 05"	11' 06"
(USCG Manitou [WYT-60] '43 - '84)							
M-6 — MANITOU ISLAND TRANSIT, LELAND, MI							
Manitou Isle	PK	1946	D	10	52' 00"	14' 00"	8' 00"
(Namaycush '46 - '59)							
Mishe-Mokwa	CF	1966	D	49*	65' 00"	17' 06"	8' 00"
(LaSalle '66 - '80)							
M-7 — MANSON CONSTRUCTION CO., INC., NORTH TONAWANDA, NY							
Burro	TB	1965	D	19*	36' 00"	13' 03"	5' 01"
J. G. II	TB	1944	D	16*	42' 03"	13' 00"	5' 06"
Marcey	TB	1966	D	22*	42' 00"	12' 06"	6' 10"
M-8 — MARINE ATLANTIC, INC., MONCTON, NB							
Atlantic Freighter	RR	1978	D	8,661	495' 05"	71' 01"	48' 01"
(Tor Felicia '78 - '78, Merzario Grecia '78 - '83, Stena Grecia '83 - '86)							
Caribou	CF	1986	D	27,213*	587' 04"	84' 01"	27' 06"
Joseph & Clara Smallwood	CF	1989	D	27,614*	587' 03"	84' 01"	22' 02"
M-9 — MARINE CONTRACTING CORP., PORT CLINTON, OH							
Ambridge 528	DB	1937	B	409	114' 10"	26' 10"	7' 10"*
Ambridge 529	DB	1937	B	409	114' 10"	26' 10"	7' 10"*
Clyde	DB	1922	B	727	150' 00"	40' 00"	9' 06"*
GL 170	DB	1955	B	455	120' 00"	36' 00"	6' 00"*
Pioneerland	TB	1943	D	45*	59' 06"	17' 00"	7' 06"*
Prairieland	TB	1955	D	29*	50' 00"	15' 07"	6' 05"*
Timberland	TB	1946	D	19*	44' 00"	13' 05"	6' 11"*
M-10 — MARINE MANAGEMENT, INC., BRUSSELS, WI							
Nathan S.	TB	1954	D	76*	66' 00"	19' 00"	9' 00"
(Sanita '54 - '77, Soo Chief '77 - '81, Susan M. Selvick '81 - '91)							
Nicole S.	TB	1949	D	146*	88' 07"	24' 10"	10' 09"
(Evening Star '49 - '86, Protector '86 - '94)							
M-11 — MARINE TECH OF DULUTH, INC., DULUTH, MN							
B. Yetter	DR	1986	B	338*	120' 00"	48' 00"	7' 00"
Jason	TB	1945	D	21*	48' 00"	12' 01"	7' 00"
(Ashland {2} '44 - '72, Charles F. Liscomb '72 - '94)							
Nancy Ann	TB	1910	D	51*	64' 03"	16' 09"	8' 06"
(Chattanooga '10 - '79, Howard T. Hagen '79 - '94)							
M-12 — MARINE TOWING, INC., PORT CLINTON, OH							
Retriever	TB	1960	D	13*	38' 00"	12' 01"	5' 04"*
M-13 — MARIPOSA CRUISE LINE, TORONTO, ON							
Captain Matthew Flinders	ES	1982	D	696*	144' 00"	40' 00"	8' 06"
Mariposa Belle	ES	1970	D	195*	93' 00"	23' 00"	8' 00"
(Niagara Belle '70 - '73)							
Northern Spirit I	ES	1983	D	489*	136' 00"	31' 00"	9' 00"
(New Spirit '83 - '89, Pride of Toronto '89 - '92)							
Oriole	ES	1987	D	200*	75' 00"	23' 00"	9' 00"
Rosemary	ES	1960	D	52*	68' 00"	15' 06"	6' 08"
Showboat Royal Grace	ES	1988	D	135*	58' 00"	18' 00"	4' 00"
Torontonian	ES	1962	D	68*	68' 00"	18' 06"	6' 08"
(Shiawassie '62 - '82)							

Fleet No. & Name Vessel Name	Type of Vessel	Year Built	Type of Engine	Cargo Cap. or Gross*	Overall Length	Breadth	Depth or Draft*
M-14 — MARITIME INVESTING LLC., GLADSTONE, MI							
Manitowoc	TF	1926	B	27 rail cars	371' 03"	67' 03"	22' 06"
Roanoke {2}	TF	1930	B	30 rail cars	381' 06"	58' 03"	22' 06"
(City of Flint 32 '30 - '70)							
Windsor {2}	TF	1930	B	28 rail cars	370' 05"	65' 00"	21' 06"
(Above three last operated 1 May, 1994 — Above three currently laid up in Toledo, OH.)							
Pere Marquette 10	TF	1945	B	27 rail cars	400' 00"	53' 00"	22' 00"
(Last operated 7 October, 1994 — Currently laid up in Port Huron, MI.)							
M-15 — MARTIN GAS & OIL, BEAVER ISLAND, MI							
West Shore {2}	CF	1947	D	94*	64' 10"	30' 00"	9' 03"
M-16 — McASPHALT INDUSTRIES LTD., SCARBOROUGH, ON							
McAsphalt 401	TK	1966	B	48,000	300' 00"	60' 00"	23' 00"
(Pittson 200 '66 - '73, Pointe Levy '73 - '87)							
M-17 — McKEIL MARINE LTD., HAMILTON, ON							
Anvantage	TB	1969	D	367*	116' 10"	32' 09"	16' 03"
(Sea Lion '69 - ?)							
Albert B.	DB		B	475	120' 00"	32' 00"	8' 00"
Argue Martin	TB	1895	D	71*	69' 00"	19' 06"	9' 00"
(Ethel 1895 - '38, R. C. Co. Tug No.1 '38 - '58, R. C. L. Tug No. 1 '58 - '62)							
Atomic	TB	1945	D	96*	82' 00"	20' 00"	10' 00"
Beaver D.	TB	1955	D	15*	36' 02"	14' 09"	4' 04"
Billie M.	TB	1897	D	35*	58' 00"	16' 00"	7' 00"
Black Carrier	DB	1908	B	1,200	200' 06"	43' 01"	10' 00"
Cargo Carrier #1	DB		B	500	90' 00"	30' 00"	10' 00"
Cargo Carrier #2	DB		B	1,000	90' 00"	60' 00"	10' 00"
Cargo Master	CS		B	600	136' 00"	50' 00"	9' 00"
Carolyn Jo	TB	1941	D	60*	65' 06"	17' 00"	7' 00"
([Unnamed] '41 - '56, Sea Hound '56 - '80)							
Colinette	TB	1943	D	64*	65' 00"	16' 00"	7' 00"
(Ottawa {1} '43 - '57, Lac Ottawa '57 - '66)							
CSL Trillium	BC	1966	B	18,064	489' 10"	75' 00"	37' 05"
(Caribbean '66 - '92, Pacnav Princess '92 - '94, CSL Trillium I '94 - '95)							
Doug McKeil {2}	TB	1943	D	196*	130' 00"	30' 00"	15' 01"
(U.S. Army LT-643 '44 - '77, Taurus '77 - '90, Gaelic Challenge '90 - '95, Frankie D. '95 - '97, Dawson B. '97 - '98)							
Duchess V	TB	1955	D	18*	55' 00"	16' 00"	6' 08"
Dufresne M-58	TB	1944	D	40*	58' 08"	14' 08"	6' 02"
Erie West	DB	1951	B	1,800	290' 00"	50' 00"	12' 00"
Escort Protector	TB	1972	D	719*	171' 00"	38' 00"	16' 00"
(Nordic VI '72 - '73, Fednav 6 '73 - '81, Seafed Avalon '81 - '83, Arctic Mallik '83 - '90)							
Escorte	TT	1964	D	120*	85' 00"	23' 08"	11' 00"
(USS Menasha [YTB/YTM-773, YTM-761] '64 - '92, Menasha {1} '92 - '95)							
Evans McKeil	TB	1936	D	284*	110' 07"	25' 06"	11' 06"
(Alhajuela '36 - '70, Barbara Ann {2} '70 - '89)							
Flo-Mac	TB	1960	D	15*	40' 00"	13' 00"	6' 00"
Florence McKeil	TB	1962	D	207*	98' 05"	26' 00"	9' 07"
(T. 4 '62 - ?, Feuille D' Erable ? - ?, Foundation Viceroy ? - ?)							
Glenbrook	TB	1944	D	91*	81' 00"	20' 00"	9' 07"
Glenevis	TB	1944	D	91*	81' 00"	20' 00"	9' 07"
Greta V	TB	1951	D	14*	44' 00"	12' 00"	5' 00"
Handy Andy	DB		B	700	100' 00"	44' 00"	11' 00"
Handy Boy	DB		B	350			
Jarrett McKeil	TB	1956	D	197*	91' 08"	27' 04"	13' 06"
(Robert B. No. 1 '56 - '97)							
Jean Raymond	DB	1941	B	6,800	409' 00"	57' 00"	18' 00"
Jerry Newberry	TB	1956	D	244*	98' 00"	28' 02"	14' 04"
(Foundation Victor '56 - '73, Point Victor '73 - '77, Kay Cole '77 - '95)							
John Spence	TB	1972	D	719*	171' 00"	38' 00"	15' 01"
(Mary B. VI '72 - '81, Mary B. '81 - '82, Mary B. VI '82 - '83, Artic Tuktu '83 - '94)							
Kate B.	TB	1950	D	12*	46' 00"	12' 10"	3' 00"
Konigsberg	TB		D	91*	41' 07"	13' 02"	7' 07"
Lac Como	TB	1944	D	63*	65' 00"	16' 10"	7' 10"
(Tanac 74 '44 - '64)							
Lac Erie	TB	1944	D	65*	65' 00"	16' 10"	7' 07"

Myron C. Taylor locks through the Black Rock Lock at Buffalo, NY.
(Brian C. Wroblewski)

Fleet No. & Name Vessel Name	Type of Vessel	Year Built	Type of Engine	Cargo Cap. or Gross*	Overal Length	Breadth	Depth or Draft*
Lac Manitoba	TB	1944	D	65*	65' 00"	16' 10"	7' 07"
(Tanac 75 '44 - '52, Manitoba '52 - '57)							
Lac Vancouver	TB	1943	D	65*	65' 00"	16' 10"	7' 07"
(Vancouver '43 - '74)							
Le Vent	DB	1969	B	13,920	379' 09"	63' 03"	33' 08"
Macassa Bay	ES		D	210*	74' 05"	25' 00"	10' 04"
McAllister 252	DB	1969	B	2,636*	250' 00"	76' 01"	16' 01"
Miss Shawn Simpson	ES		D	30*	55' 02"	13' 02"	5' 00"
Ocean Hauler	BK	1943	B	8,500/88,735	382' 07"	69' 07"	25' 07"
Offshore Supplier	TB	1979	D	127*	92' 00"	25' 00"	11' 06"
(Elmore M. Misener '79 - '94)							
Pacific Standard	TB	1967	D	451*	127' 08"	31' 00"	15' 06"
(Irishman '67 - '76, Kwakwani '76 - '78, Lorna B. '78 - '81)							
Paul E. No. 1	TB	1945	D	97*	80' 00"	20' 00"	9' 07"
(W.A.C. 4 '45 - '46, E. A. Rockett '46 - '76)							
Peter Kamingoak	DB	1975	B	12,000	351' 03"	91' 00"	20' 08"
St. Clair {2}	TF	1927	B	27 rail cars	400' 00"	54' 00"	22' 00"
(Pere Marquette 12 '27 - '70)							
Stormont	TB	1953	D	108*	80' 00"	20' 00"	9' 07"
Salty Dog No. 1	TK	1945	B	88,735	313' 00"	68' 03"	26' 07"
Sault au Couchon	BC	1969	B	10,000	422' 11"	74' 10"	25' 07"
Sillery	EV	1963	D	9,415	175' 00"	36' 00"	14' 00"
(Imperial Verdun '63 - '79)							
S.M.T.B. No. 7	EV	1969	B	7,502	150' 00"	33' 00"	14' 00"
Techno Venture	TB	1939	D	470*	138' 03"	30' 07"	15' 01"
(Dragonet '39 - '61, Foundation Venture '61 - '73, M.I.L. Venture '73 - '79)							
Toledo	TK	1962	B	6,388	135' 00"	34' 00"	9' 00"
Toni D.	TB	1959	D	15*	50' 00"	16' 00"	5' 00"
Vortice	TB	1976	D	767*	152' 00"	39' 04"	20' 03"
(Musketeer Fury '76 - '78, Tender Panther '78 - '79, Margarita '79 - '83)							
Wyn Cooper	TB		D		48' 00"	13' 00"	4' 00"
Wyatt McKeil	TB	1950	D	237*	102' 06"	26' 00"	13' 06"
(Otis Wack '50 - '97)							
REMORQUEURS ET BARGES MONTREAL LTEE - A SUBSIDIARY OF McKEIL MARINE LTD.							
Cavalier	TB	1944	D	18*	40' 00"	10' 05"	4' 08"
D. C. Everest	CS	1953	D	3,017	259' 00"	43' 06"	21' 00"
(D. C. Everest '53 - '81, Condarrell '82 - '89)							
Wilmac	TB	1959	D	16*	40' 00"	13' 00"	3' 07"

M-18 — McMULLEN & PITZ CONSTRUCTION CO., MANITOWOC, WI

Dauntless	TB	1937	D	25*	52' 06"	15' 06"	5' 03"

M-19 — MENASHA TUGBOAT CO., SARNIA, ON

Menasha {2}	TB	1949	D	147*	78' 00"	24' 00"	9' 08"
(W. C. Harms '49 - '54, Hamilton '54 - '86, Ruby Casho '86 - '88, W. C. Harms '88 - '97)							

M-20 — MERCURY CRUISE LINES, PALATINE, IL

Chicago's First Lady	ES	1991	D	62*	96' 00"	22' 00"	9' 00"
Skyline Princess	ES	1956	D	56*	59' 04"	16' 00"	4' 08"
Skyline Queen	ES	1959	D	45*	61' 05"	16' 10"	6' 00"

M-21 — MILLER BOAT LINE, INC., PUT-IN-BAY, OH

Islander {3}	CF	1983	D	92*	90' 03"	38' 00"	8' 03"
Put-In-Bay {3}	CF	1997	D	95*	96' 00"	38' 06"	9' 06"
South Bass	CF	1989	D	95*	96' 00"	38' 06"	9' 06"
Wm. Market	CF	1993	D	95*	96' 00"	38' 06"	8' 09"

M-22 — MILWAUKEE BULK TERMINALS, INC., MILWAUKEE, WI

MBT 10	DB	1994	B	1,960	200' 00"	35' 00"	11' 07"*
MBT 20	DB	1994	B	1,960	200' 00"	35' 00'	11' 07"*
MBT 33	DB	1976	B	3,793	240' 00"	52' 06"	14' 06"*

M-23 — MORTON SALT CO., CHICAGO, IL

Morton Salt 74	DB	1974	B	2,101	195' 00"	35' 00"	12' 00"

M-24 — MUSKOKA LAKES NAVIGATION & HOTEL CO., GRAVENHURST, ON

Segwun	PA	1887	R	168*	128' 00"	24' 00"	7' 06"
(Nipissing {2} 1887 - '25)							
Wanda III	ES	1915	R	60*	94' 00"	12' 00"	5' 00"

Fleet No. & Name Vessel Name	Type of Vessel	Year Built	Type of Engine	Cargo Cap. or Gross*	Overall Length	Breadth	Depth or Draft*
N-1 — N. M. PATERSON & SONS LTD., THUNDER BAY, ON							
Cartierdoc {2}	BC	1959	D	29,100	730' 00"	75' 09"	40' 02"
(Ems Ore '59 - '76, Montcliffe Hall '76 - '88)							
Comeaudoc	BC	1960	D	26,750	730' 00"	75' 06"	37' 09"
(Murray Bay {2} '60 - '63)							
(Last operated 4 December, 1996 — 5 year survey expires July, 2001.)							
(Currently laid up in Montreal, PQ.)							
Mantadoc {2}	BC	1967	D	17,650	607' 09"	62' 00"	36' 00"
Paterson {2}	BC	1985	D	32,600	736' 06"	75' 10"	42' 00"
Quedoc {3}	BC	1965	D	28,050	730' 00"	75' 00"	39' 02"
(Beavercliffe Hall '65 - '88)							
(Last operated 20 December, 1991 — 5 year survey expired June, 1993.)							
(Currently laid up in Thunder Bay, ON.)							
Vandoc {2}	BC	1964	D	16,000	605' 00"	62' 00"	33' 10"
(Sir Denys Lowson '64 - '79)							
(Last operated 21 December, 1991 — Currently laid up in Thunder Bay, ON.)							
Windoc {2}	BC	1959	D	29,100	730' 00"	75' 09"	40' 02"
(Rhine Ore '59 - '76, Steelcliffe Hall '76 - '88)							
N-2 — NADRO MARINE SERVICES LTD., PORT DOVER, ON							
Bert Verge	TB	1959	D	22*	43' 07"	14' 00"	4' 06"
C. West Pete	TB	1956	D	28*	63' 00"	17' 03"	5' 06"
Lois T.	TB	1943	D	32*	63' 00"	16' 06"	7' 06"
(Kolbe '43 - '86)							
Miseford	TB	1915	D	116*	85' 00"	20' 00"	10' 06"
Nadro Clipper	TB	1939	D	64*	70' 00"	23' 00"	6' 06"
(Stanley Clipper '39 - '94)							
Progress	TB	1948	D	123*	86' 00"	21' 00"	10' 00"
(P. J. Murer '48 - '81, Michael D. Misner '81 - '93, Thomas A. Payette '93 - '96)							
Terry S.	TB	1958	D	16*	52' 00"	17' 00"	6' 00"
Vac	TB	1942	D	37*	65' 00"	21' 00"	6' 06"
N-3 — NELSON CONSTRUCTION CO., LaPOINTE, WI							
Eclipse	TB	1937	D	23*	47' 00"	13' 00"	6' 00"
N-4 — NEUMAN CRUISE & FERRY LINE, SANDUSKY, OH							
Commuter	CF	1960	D	81*	64' 06"	33' 00"	9' 00"
Emerald Empress	ES	1994	D	94*	151' 00"	33' 00"	10' 06"
Endeavor	CF	1987	D	98*	101' 00"	34' 06"	10' 00"
Kelley Islander	CF	1969	D	95*	100' 00"	34' 03"	8' 00"
N-5 — NICHOLSON TERMINAL & DOCK CO., RIVER ROUGE, MI							
Charles E. Jackson	TB	1956	D	12*	35' 00"	10' 06"	5' 01"
Detroit {1}	TF	1904	B	22 rail cars	308' 00"	76' 09"	19' 06"
N-6 — NORTHUMBERLAND / BAY FERRIES LTD., CHARLOTTETOWN, PEI							
Confederation {2}	CF	1993	D	8,060*	374' 08"	61' 07"	17' 09"
Holiday Island	CF	1971	D	3,037*	325' 00"	67' 06"	16' 06"
Incat 046	CF	1997	D	5,060*	300' 00"	85' 03"	12' 01"
Princess of Acadia	CF	1971	D	10,051*	480' 01"	66' 00"	12' 06"
O-1 — OAK GROVE MARINE AND TRANSPORTATION, INC., CLAYTON, NY							
Maple Grove	PK	1954	D	55	75' 00"	21' 00"	5' 06"*
Oak Grove	PK	1953	D	18	53' 02"	14' 00"	4' 00"*
O-2 — ODYSSEY CRUISES, CHICAGO, IL							
Odyssey II	ES	1993	D	101*	200' 00"	41' 00"	9' 00"*
O-3 — OGLEBAY NORTON CO., CLEVELAND, OH							
Armco	SU	1953	T	25,500	767' 00"	70' 00"	36' 00"
Buckeye {3}	SU	1952	T	22,300	698' 00"	70' 00"	37' 00"
(Sparrows Point '52 - '91)							
Columbia Star	SU	1981	D	78,850	1,000' 00"	105' 00"	56' 00"
Courtney Burton	SU	1953	T	22,300	690' 00"	70' 00"	37' 00"
(Ernest T. Weir {2} '53 - '78)							
David Z. Norton {3}	SU	1973	D	19,650	630' 00"	68' 00"	36' 11"
(William R. Roesch '73 - '95)							
Earl W. Oglebay	SU	1973	D	19,650	630' 00"	68' 00"	36' 11"
(Paul Thayer '73 - '95)							
Fred R. White Jr.	SU	1979	D	23,800	636' 00"	68' 00"	40' 00"

Fleet No. & Name / Vessel Name	Type of Vessel	Year Built	Type of Engine	Cargo Cap. or Gross*	Overall Length	Breadth	Depth or Draft*
Joseph H. Frantz	SU	1925	D	13,600	618' 00"	62' 00"	32' 00"
Middletown	SU	1942	T	26,300	730' 00"	75' 00"	39' 03"
(Marquette '42 - '42, USS Neshanic [AO-71] '43 - '47, Gulfoil '47 - '61, Pioneer Challenger '61 - '62)							
Oglebay Norton	SU	1978	D	78,850	1,000' 00"	105' 00"	56' 00"
(Burns Harbor {1} '78 - '78, Lewis Wilson Foy '78 - '91)							
Reserve	SU	1953	T	25,500	767' 00"	70' 00"	36' 00"
Wolverine {4}	SU	1974	D	19,650	630' 00"	68' 00"	36' 11"

O-4 — ONTARIO MINISTRY OF TRANS. & COMMUNICATION, KINGSTON, ON

Amherst Islander {2}	CF	1955	D	184*	106' 00"	38' 00"	10' 00"
(Currently laid up in Kingston, ON.)							
Frontenac II	CF	1962	D	666*	181' 00"	45' 00"	10' 00"
(Charlevoix {2} '62 - '92)							
Glenora	CF	1952	D	209*	127' 00"	33' 00"	9' 00"
(The St. Joseph Islander '52 - '74)							
The Quinte Loyalist	CF	1954	D	209*	127' 00"	32' 00"	8' 00"
Wolfe Islander III	CF	1975	D	985*	205' 00"	68' 00"	6' 00"

O-5 — ONTARIO WATERWAYS CRUISES, INC., ORILLIA, ON

Kawartha Voyager	PA	1983	D	264*	108' 00"	22' 00"	5' 00"

O-6 —ORILLIA BOAT CRUISES LTD., ORILLIA, ON

Lady Belle II	ES	1967	D	89*	65' 00"	19' 00"	5' 00"
(Lady Midland '67 - '82)							
Island Princess	ES	1989	D	194*	65' 00"	27' 00"	5' 00"

O-7 — OSBORNE MATERIALS CO., MENTOR, OH

Emmet J. Carey	SC	1948	D	900	114' 00"	23' 00"	11' 00"
(Beatrice Ottinger '48 - '63, James B. Lyons '63 - '88)							
F. M. Osborne {2}	SC	1910	D	500	150' 00"	29' 00"	11' 03"
(Grand Island {1} '10 - '58, Lesco '58 - '75)							

O-8 — OWEN SOUND TRANSPORTATION CO. LTD., OWEN SOUND, ON

Chi-Cheemaun	CF	1974	D	6,991*	365' 05"	61' 00"	21' 00"

ONTARIO NORTHLAND MARINE SERVICES - OWEN SOUND TRANSPORTATION CO. LTD., MGR.

Nindawayma	CF	1976	D	6,197*	333' 06"	55' 00"	36' 06"
(Monte Cruceta '76 - '76, Monte Castillo '76 - '78, Manx Viking '78 - '87, Manx '87 - '88, Skudenes '88 - '89, Ontario No.1 {2} '89 - '89)							
(Last operated in 1992 — 5 year survey expired January 1996.)							
(Currently laid up in Owen Sound, ON.)							

PELEE ISLAND TRANSPORTATION SERVICES
A DIVISION OF OWEN SOUND TRANSPORTATION CO. LTD.

Jiimaan	CF	1992	D	2,830*	176' 09"	42' 03"	13' 06"
Pelee Islander	CF	1960	D	334*	145' 00"	32' 00"	10' 00"

P-1 — P.& H. SHIPPING - A DIV. OF PARRISH & HEIMBECKER LTD., MISSISSAUGA, ON

Mapleglen {2}	BC	1960	T	26,100	715' 03"	75' 00"	37' 09"
(Carol Lake '60 - '87, Algocape {1} '87 - '94)							
Oakglen {2}	BC	1954	T	22,950	714' 06"	70' 03"	37' 03"
(T. R. McLagan '54 - '90)							

P-2 — PEMBINA EXPLORATION LTD., PORT COLBORNE, ON

Louis J. Coulet	DV	1957	D	2,099*	259' 00"	43' 11"	22' 06"
(Coniscliffe Hall {2} '57 - '74, Coniscliffe '74 - '75, Telesis '75 - '98)							
(Currently laid up in Port Dover, ON.)							

P-3 — PICTURED ROCKS CRUISES, INC., MUNISING, MI

Grand Island {2}	ES	1989	D	51*	68' 00"	16' 01"	5' 01"
Miners Castle	ES	1974	D	72*	68' 00"	17' 00"	5' 00"
Miss Superior	ES	1984	D	76*	68' 00"	17' 00"	5' 00"
Pictured Rocks	ES	1972	D	47*	60' 00"	14' 00"	4' 04"

P-4 — PIERRE GAGNE CONTRACTING LTD., THUNDER BAY, ON

Saguenay {2}	SU	1964	D	30,500	730' 00"	75' 02"	44' 08"
(Last operated 30 November, 1992 — Currently laid up in Thunder Bay, ON.)							

P-5 — PITTS INTERNATIONAL, INC., DON MILLS, ON

Flo Cooper	TB	1962	D	97*	80' 00"	21' 00"	10' 09"

P-6 — PLAUNT TRANSPORTATION CO., INC., CHEBOYGAN, MI

Kristen D.	CF	1988	D	83*	64' 11"	36' 00"	6' 05"

Fleet No. & Name Vessel Name	Type of Vessel	Year Built	Type of Engine	Cargo Cap. or Gross*	Overal Length	Breadth	Depth or Draft*
P-7 — P. M. C. L. 30,000 ISLAND BOAT CRUISES, MIDLAND, ON							
Miss Midland	ES	1974	D	123*	68' 07"	19' 04"	6' 04"
Serendipity Princess	ES	1982	D	93*	69' 00"	23' 00"	4' 03"*
(Trent Voyageur '82 - '87, Serendipity Lady '87 - '95)							
P-8 — PORT CITY PRINCESS, INC., MUSKEGON, MI							
Port City Princess	ES	1966	D	79*	64' 09"	30' 00"	5' 06"
(Island Queen {1} '66 - '87)							
P-9 — PORT DALHOUSIE PIERS, INC., ST. CATHARINES, ON							
Normac	PA	1902	D	462*	124' 06"	25' 00"	18' 00"
(James R. Elliot '02 - '31)							
(Former Owen Sound Trans. Commision vessel which last operated in 1968.)							
(Currently in use as a floating restaurant in Port Dalhousie, ON.)							
P-10 — PORTOFINO RESTAURANT, INC., WYANDOTTE, MI							
Friendship	ES	1968	D	78*	69' 06"	23' 05"	7' 04"
(Peche Island V '68 - '71, Papoose V '71 - '82)							
P-11 — PURVIS MARINE LTD., SAULT STE. MARIE, ON							
Adanac	TB	1913	D	108*	80' 03"	19' 02"	10' 06"
(Edward C. Whalen '13 - '66, John McLean '66 - '95)							
Anglian Lady	TB	1953	D	398*	136' 06"	30' 00"	14' 01"
(Hamtun '53 - '72, Nathalie Letzer '72 - '88)							
Avenger IV	TB	1962	D	293*	120' 00"	30' 05"	17' 05"
(Avenger '62 - '85)							
Charles W. Johnson	DB	1916	B	1,685	245' 00"	43' 00"	14' 00"
(Iocolite '16 - '47, Imperial Kingston '47 - '61)							
Chief Wawatam	DB	1911	B	4,500	347' 00"	62' 03"	15' 00"
G.L.B. No. 1	DB	1953	B	3,215	305' 00"	50' 00"	12' 00"
G.L.B. No. 2	DB	1953	B	3,215	305' 02"	50' 00"	12' 00"
Goki	TB	1940	D	24*	57' 00"	12' 08"	7' 00"
Malden	DB	1946	B	1,075	150' 00"	41' 09"	10' 03"
Martin E. Johnson	TB	1959	D	26*	46' 00"	16' 00"	5' 09"
McKeller	CS	1935	B	200	90' 00"	33' 00"	8' 00"
Osprey	TB	1944	D	36*	45' 00"	13' 06"	7' 00"
P.M.L. Alton	DB	1951	B	150	93' 00"	30' 00"	8' 00"
P.M.L. Salvager	DB	1945	B	5,200	341' 00"	54' 00"	27' 00"
([Unnamed '45 - '55, Balsambranch '55 - '73, M.I.L. Balsam '73 - '77, Techno Balsam '77 - '77, DDS Salvager '77 - '88)							
P.M.L. 357	DB	1944	B	600	138' 00"	38' 00"	11' 00"
P.M.L. 2501	TK	1980	B	25,000	302' 00"	52' 00"	17' 00"
Rocket	TB	1901	D	39*	70' 00"	15' 00"	8' 00"
Sheila P.	TB	1940	D	15*	40' 00"	14' 00"	
Tecumseh II	DB	1976	B	2,500	180' 00"	54' 00"	12' 00"
Wilfred M. Cohen	TB	1948	D	284*	104' 00"	28' 00"	14' 06"
(A. T. Lowmaster '48 - '75)							
W. I. Scott Purvis	TB	1938	D	206*	96' 06"	26' 04"	10' 04"
(Orient Bay '38 - '75, Guy M. No. 1 '75 - '90)							
W. J. Ivan Purvis	TB	1938	D	191*	100' 06"	25' 06"	9' 00"
(Magpie '38 - '66, Dana T. Bowen '66 - '75)							
Yankcanuck {2}	CS	1963	D	4,760	324' 03"	49' 00"	26' 00"
P-12 — PUT-IN-BAY BOAT LINE CO., PUT-IN-BAY, OH							
Jet Express	PC	1989	D	93*	92' 08"	28' 06"	8' 04"
Jet Express II	PC	1992	D	85*	92' 06"	28' 06"	8' 04"
R-1 — RIGEL SHIPPING CANADA, INC., SHEDIAC, NB							
Diamond Star	TK	1992	D	68,019	405' 11"	58' 01"	34' 09"
(Elbestern '92 - '93)							
Emerald Star	TK	1992	D	68,019	405' 11"	58' 01"	34' 09"
(Emsstern '92 - '92)							
RIGEL SHIPPING NORWAY - OWNER							
Jade Star	TK	1993	D	68,019	405' 11"	58' 01"	34' 09"
(Jadestern '93 - '94)							
R-2 — ROCKPORT BOAT LINE (1994) LTD., ROCKPORT, ON							
Ida M.	ES	1970	D	29*	55' 00"	14' 00"	3' 00"
Ida M. II	ES	1973	D	116*	63' 02"	22' 02"	5' 00"

Tug Mary E. Hannah with a barge in the Welland Canal. (Al Hart)

Fleet No. & Name Vessel Name	Type of Vessel	Year Built	Type of Engine	Cargo Cap. or Gross*	Overal Length	Breadth	Depth or Draft*
R-3 — ROEN SALVAGE CO., STURGEON BAY, WI							
Chas Asher	TB	1967	D	10*	50' 00"	18' 00"	8' 00"
John R. Asher	TB	1943	D	93*	70' 00"	20' 00"	8' 06"
(U.S. Army ST-71 '43 - '46, Russell 8 '46 - '64, Reid McAllister '64 - '67, Donegal '67 - '85)							
Spuds	TB	1944	D	19*	42' 00"	12' 06"	6' 00"
Stephen M. Asher	TB	1954	D	60*	65' 00"	19' 01"	5' 04"
(Captain Bennie '54 - '82, Dumar Scout '82 - '87)							
A variety of barges are also available.							
R-4 — RUGARE'S SIGHTSEEING CRUISES & FERRY SERVICE, ERIE, PA							
Little Toot	ES	1950	D	17*	55' 00"	13' 06"	3' 10"*
R-5 — RUSSELL ISLAND TRANSIT CO., ALGONAC, MI							
Islander {2}	CF	1982	D		41' 00"	15' 00"	3' 06"
R-6 — RYBA MARINE CONSTRUCTION CO., CHEBOYGAN, MI							
Alcona	TB	1957	D	18*	40' 00"	12' 06"	5' 06"
Amber Mae	TB	1922	D	67*	65' 00"	14' 01"	10' 00"
Derrick No. 4	CS	1956	B		122' 06"	41' 02"	8' 08"
Harbor Master	CS	1979	B	100*	70' 00"	27' 00"	4' 00"
Kathy Lynn	TB	1944	D	140*	85' 00"	24' 00"	9' 06"
(U.S. Army ST-693 '44 - '79, Sea Islander '79 - '91)							
Jarco 1402	CS	1981	B	473*	140' 00"	39' 00"	9' 00"
RC1	DS	1935	B		102' 00"	32' 00"	7' 00"
RC2	DS	1935	B		102' 00"	32' 00"	7' 00"
Relief	CS	1924	B	1,000	160' 00"	40' 00"	9' 00"
Rochelle Kaye	TB	1963	D	52*	51' 06"	19' 04"	7' 00"
(Jaye Anne '63 - ?, Katanni ? - '97)							
Tonawanda	CS	1935	B	600	120' 00"	45' 00"	8' 00"
S-1 — SCIO SHIPPING, INC., NEW YORK, NY							
Island Gem	BC	1984	D	28,005	584' 08"	76' 02"	48' 05"
Island Skipper	BC	1984	D	28,031	584' 08"	76' 02"	48' 05"
Island Sky	BC	1976	D	19,467	512' 07"	74' 02"	42' 04"
S-2 — SEA FOX THOUSAND ISLANDS TOURS, KINGSTON, ON							
Sea Fox II	ES	1988	D	55*	39' 08"	20' 00"	2' 00"*
Limestone Clipper	ES	1968	D	110*	85' 00"	30' 06"	7' 03"
(Peche Island II '68 - '71, Papoose III '71 - '96)							
S-3 — SEARS OIL CO., ROME, NY							
Midstate I	TB	1942	D	106*	86' 00"	24' 00"	12' 00"
Midstate II	TB	1945	D	137*	89' 00"	24' 00"	12' 06"

S-4 — SEAWAY BULK CARRIERS, WINNIPEG, MB
PARTNERSHIP BETWEEN ALGOMA CENTRAL CORP. AND UPPER LAKES GROUP, INC.*

ALGOMA CENTRAL CORP.	UPPER LAKES GROUP, INC.	
Algocape {2}	Canadian Leader	Canadian Voyager
Algocen {2}	Canadian Mariner	Gordon C. Leitch {2}
Algogulf {2}	Canadian Miner	Montrealais
Algoisle	Canadian Prospector	Quebecois
Algonorth	Canadian Provider	Seaway Queen
Algontario	Canadian Ranger	
Algoriver	Canadian Trader	
Algosound	Canadian Venture	

S-5 — SEAWAY SELF UNLOADERS, ST. CATHARINES, ON
PARTNERSHIP BETWEEN ALGOMA CENTRAL CORP. AND UPPER LAKES GROUP, INC.*

ALGOMA CENTRAL CORP.		UPPER LAKES GROUP, INC.
Agawa Canyon	Algoville	Canadian Century
Algobay	Algoway {2}	Canadian Enterprise
Algolake	Algowest	Canadian Navigator
Algomarine	Algowood	Canadian Olympic
Algoport	Capt. Henry Jackman	Canadian Progress
Algorail {2}	John B. Aird	Canadian Transfer
Algosoo {2}		Canadian Transport {2}
Algosteel {2}		James Norris

* SEE RESPECTIVE FLEETS FOR VESSEL DETAILS

Fleet No. & Name Vessel Name	Type of Vessel	Year Built	Type of Engine	Cargo Cap. or Gross*	Overall Length	Breadth	Depth or Draft*
S-6 — SELVICK MARINE TOWING CORP.,STURGEON BAY, WI							
Baldy B.	TB	1932	D	36*	62' 00"	16' 01"	7' 00"
Bonnie G. Selvick	TB	1928	D	95*	86' 00"	21' 00"	12' 00"
(E. James Fucik '28 - '77)							
Carla Anne Selvick	TB	1908	D	191*	96' 00"	23' 00"	11' 02"
(S.O. Co. No. 19 '08 - '16, S.T. Co. No. 19 '16 - '18, Socony 19 '18 - '47, Esso Tug No. 4 '47 - '53,							
McAllister 44 '53 - '55, Roderick McAllister '55 - '84)							
Escort	TB	1955	D	26*	50' 00"	15' 00"	7' 03"
John M. Selvick	TB	1898	D	256*	118' 00"	24' 00"	12' 07"
(Illinois {1} 1898 - '41, John Roen III '41 - '74)							
Mary Page Hannah {1}	TB	1950	D	461*	143' 00"	33' 01"	14' 06"
(U.S. Army ATA-230 '49 - '72, G. W. Codrington '72 - '73, William P. Feeley {2} '73 - '73,							
William W. Stender '73 - '78)							
Moby Dick	DB	1952	B	835	121' 00"	33' 02"	10' 06"
Sharon M. Selvick	TB	1945	D	28*	45' 06"	13' 00"	7' 01"
Timmy L.	TB	1939	D	148*	110' 00"	25' 00"	13' 00"
(USCG Naugatuck [WYT/WYTM-92] '39 - '80, Timmy B. '80 - '84)							
William C. Selvick	TB	1944	D	142*	85' 00"	22' 11"	10' 04"
(U.S. Army ST-500 '44 - '49, Sherman H. Serre '49 - '77)							
S-7 — SHAKER CRUISE LINES, TORONTO, ON							
Lake Runner	CF	1984	D	316*	124' 07"	26' 06"	12' 10"
(Marine Courier '84 - '97)							
Sprint Runner	HY	1990	D		90' 07"	20' 04"	6' 07"*
(Sunrise II '90 - '96, Sunrise VI '96 - '98)							
Wave Runner	HY	1990	D		90' 07"	20' 04"	6' 07"*
(Sunrise I '90 - '96, Sunrise V '96 - '98)							
S-8 — SHAMROCK CHARTERING CO., GROSSE POINT, MI							
Helene	ES	1927	D	109*	106' 00"	17' 00"	6' 06"*
S-9 — SHELL CANADIAN TANKERS LTD., MONTREAL, PQ							
Horizon Montreal	RT	1958	D	32,900	315' 00"	45' 07"	24' 07"
(Tyee Shell '58 - '69, Arctic Trader '69 - '83, Rivershell {4} '83 - '95)							
S-10 — SHEPLER'S MACKINAC ISLAND FERRY SERVICE, MACKINAW CITY, MI							
Capt. Shepler	PF	1986	D	71*	78' 00"	21' 00"	7' 10"
Felicity	PF	1972	D	84*	65' 00"	18' 01"	8' 03"
Sacre Bleu	PK	1959	D	92*	94' 10"	31' 00"	9' 09"
(Put-In-Bay {2} '59 - '94)							
The Hope	PF	1975	D	87*	77' 00"	20' 00"	8' 03"
The Welcome	PF	1969	D	66*	60' 06"	16' 08"	8' 02"
Wyandot	PF	1979	D	99*	77' 00"	20' 00"	8' 00"
S-11 — SHIPWRECK TOURS, INC., MUNISING, MI							
Miss Munising	ES	1967	D	50*	60' 00"	14' 00"	4' 04"
S-12 — SHORELINE MARINE CO., CHICAGO, IL							
Marlyn	ES	1961	D	85*	65' 00"	25' 00"	7' 00"*
Shoreline II	ES	1987	D	89*	75' 00"	26' 00"	7' 01"
S-13 — SIVERTSON'S GRAND PORTAGE - ISLE ROYALE TRANS. LINES, INC., SUPERIOR, WI							
A. E. Clifford	TB	1946	D	33*	45' 00"	15' 00"	7' 00"
Hiawatha {1}	TB	1938	D	63*	58' 00"	15' 00"	8' 00"
(Apostle Islands '38 - '60)							
Linda Beth	TB	1948	D	13*	39' 05"	11' 05"	4' 02"
Provider	ES	1959	D		46' 00"	13' 05"	5' 05"
Voyageur II	ES	1970	D		63' 00"	18' 00"	5' 00"
Wenonah	ES	1960	D	91*	70' 07"	19' 04"	9' 07"
(Jamacia '60 - '64)							
S-14 — SOCIETE DES TRAVERSIERS DU QUEBEC, QUEBEC, PQ							
Alphonse des Jarnins	CF	1971	D	1,741*	214' 00"	71' 06"	20' 00"
Armand Imbeau	CF	1980	D	1,285*	203' 07"	72' 00"	18' 04"
Camille Marcoux	CF	1974	D	6,122*	310' 09"	62' 09"	39' 00"
Catherine-Legardeur	CF	1985	D	1,348*	205' 09"	71' 10"	18' 10"
Felix-Antoine-Savard	CF	1997	D	2,489*	272' 00"	70' 00"	
Grue Des Iles	CF	1981	D	447*	155' 10"	41' 01"	12' 06"
Jos Deschenes	CF	1980	D	1,287*	203' 07"	72' 00"	18' 04"

Fleet No. & Name Vessel Name	Type of Vessel	Year Built	Type of Engine	Cargo Cap. or Gross*	Overal Length	Breadth	Depth or Draft*
Joseph Savard	CF	1985	D	1,445*	206' 00"	71' 10"	18' 10"
Lomer Gouin	CF	1971	D	1,741*	214' 00"	71' 06"	20' 00"
Lucien L.	CF	1967	D	867*	220' 10"	61' 06"	15' 05"
Radisson {1}	CF	1954	D	1,043*	164' 03"	72' 00"	10' 06"
Trois Rivieres	CF	1961	D	882*	200' 00"	70' 06"	10' 00"

S-15 — SOCIETE DU PORT DE MONTREAL, MONTREAL, PQ

Maisonneuve	TB	1972	D	103*	63' 10"	20' 07"	9' 03"

S-16 — SOO LOCKS BOAT TOURS, SAULT STE. MARIE, MI
    AMERICAN AND CANADIAN LOCK TOURS, INC. - OWNER

Bide-A-Wee {3}	ES	1955	D	99*	64' 07"	23' 00"	7' 11"
Hiawatha {2}	ES	1959	D	99*	64' 07"	23' 00"	7' 11"
Holiday	ES	1957	D	99*	64' 07"	23' 00"	7' 11"

    FAMOUS SOO LOCK CRUISES, INC. - OWNER

LeVoyageur	ES	1959	D	70*	65' 00"	25' 00"	7' 00"
Nokomis	ES	1959	D	70*	65' 00"	25' 00"	7' 00"

S-17 — SOUTHDOWN, INC., CLEVELAND, OH

C.T.C. No.1	CC	1943	R	16,300	620' 06"	60' 00"	35' 00"

  (McIntyre '43 - '43, Frank Purnell {1} '43 - '64, Steelton {3} '64 - '78, Hull No. 3 '78 - '79, Pioneer {3} '79 - '82)
  (Last operated 12 November, 1981.)
  (Currently in use as a stationary cement storage/transfer vessel in S. Chicago, IL.)

Medusa Challenger	CC	1906	S	10,250	552' 01"	56' 00"	31' 00"

  (William P. Snyder '06 - '26, Elton Hoyt II {1} '26 - '52, Alex D. Chisholm '52 - '66)

Medusa Conquest	CC	1937	B	8,500	437' 06"	55' 00"	28' 00"

  (Red Crown '37 - '62, Amoco Indiana '62 - '87)
  HANNAH MARINE CORP. - CHARTERED BY SOUTHDOWN, INC.

Susan W. Hannah	TB	1977	D	174*	121' 06"	34' 06"	18' 02"

  (Lady Elda '77 - '78, Kings Challenger '78 - '78, ITM No. 1 '78 - '81, Kings Challenger '81 - '86)

S-18 — SPECIALTY RESTAURANTS CORP., ANAHEIM, CA

Lansdowne	TF	1884	B	1,571*	319' 00"	41' 03"	13' 00"

  (Last operated in 1974 — Currently laid up in Buffalo, NY.)

S-19 — ST. LAWRENCE CRUISE LINES, INC., KINGSTON, ON

Canadian Empress	PA	1981	D	463*	108' 00"	30' 00"	8' 00"

S-20 — ST. LAWRENCE SEAWAY MANAGEMENT CORP., CORNWALL, ON

La Prairie	TB	1975	D	110*	70' 06"	25' 09"	11' 08"
VM/S Hercules	GL	1962	D	2,107	200' 00"	75' 00"	18' 08"
VM/S Iroquois	TB		D				
VM/S Massinouve	TB		D				

S-21 — ST. LAWRENCE SEAWAY DEVELOPMENT CORP., MASSENA, NY

Eighth Sea	TB	1958	D	17*	40' 00"	12' 06"	4' 00"
Performance	TB	1997	D		50' 00"	16' 07"	7' 06"
Robinson Bay	TB	1958	D	213*	103' 00"	26' 10"	14' 06"

S-22 — ST. MARY'S CEMENT CO., TORONTO, ON

Sea Eagle II	TB	1979	D	560*	132' 00"	35' 00"	19' 00"

  (Sea Eagle '79 - '81, Canmar Sea Eagle '81 - '91)

St. Mary's Cement II	CC	1978	B	19,513	496' 06"	76' 00"	35' 00"

  (Velasco '78 - '81, Canmar Shuttle '81 - '90)

St. Mary's Cement III	CC	1980	B	4,800	335' 00"	76' 08"	17' 09"

  (Bigorange XVI '80 - '84, Says '84 - '85, Al-Sayb-7 '85 - '86, Clarkson Carrier '86 - '94)
  GREAT LAKES INT. TOWING & SALVAGE, INC. CHARTERED BY ST. MARY'S CEMENT CO.

Petite Forte	TB	1969	D	368*	127' 00"	32' 00"	14' 06"

  (E. Bronson Ingram '69 - '72, Jarmac 42 '720 - '73, Scotsman '73 - '81, Al Battal '81 - '86)

S-23 — ST. MARY'S HOLDINGS, INC., DETROIT, MI

Lewis G. Harriman	CC	1923	R	5,500	350' 00"	55' 00"	28' 00"

  (John W. Boardman '23 - '65)
  (Last operated 20 April 1980 — 5 year survey expired September 1997.)
  (Currently in use as a non-powered cement storage vessel in Green Bay, WI.)

St. Mary's Cement	CC	1986	B	9,400	360' 00"	60' 00"	23' 03"

  MERCE TRANSPORTATION CO. - CHARTERED BY ST. MARY'S HOLDING'S, INC.

Triton {2}	TB	1941	D	197*	135' 00"	30' 00"	17' 06"

  (USS Tuscarora [AT-77, YT-341, YTB-341, ATA-245] '41 - '79, Challenger {1} '79 - '86)

Fleet No. & Name / Vessel Name	Type of Vessel	Year Built	Type of Engine	Cargo Cap. or Gross*	Overal Length	Breadth	Depth or Draft*
S-24 — STAR LINE MACKINAC ISLAND FERRY, ST. IGNACE, MI							
Cadillac {5}	PF	1990	D	73*	64' 07"	20' 00"	7' 07"
Joliet {3}	PF	1993	D	83*	64' 08"	22' 00"	8' 03"
La Salle {4}	PF	1983	D	55*	65' 00"	20' 00"	7' 05"
Marquette {5}	PF	1979	D	55*	62' 03"	22' 00"	7' 01"
Nicolet {2}	PF	1985	D	51*	65' 00"	20' 00"	7' 05"
Radisson {2}	PF	1988	D	97*	80' 00"	23' 06"	7' 00"
S-25 — STEAMER COLUMBIA FOUNDATION, DETROIT, MI							
Columbia {2}	PA	1902	R	968*	216' 00"	60' 00"	13' 06"
(Last operated 2 September, 1991 — 5 year survey expired January, 1998.) (Currently laid up in Ecorse, MI.)							
S-26 — STEAMER STE. CLAIRE FOUNDATION, DETROIT, MI							
Ste. Claire	PA	1910	R	870*	197' 00"	65' 00"	14' 00"
(Last operated 2 September, 1991 — 5 year survey expired May, 1993.) (Currently laid up in Ecorse, MI.)							
S-27 — STEVEN WALLACE, PENETANGUISHENE, ON							
Georgian Storm	TB	1931	D	167*	91' 00"	24' 02"	12' 00"
(Capitaine Simard '31 - '57, Renee Simard '57 - '86)							
S-28 — STOLT PARCEL TANKERS, INC., HOUSTON, TX							
Stolt Alliance	TK	1985	D	65,540	404' 06"	65' 08"	36' 09"
(Shoun Hope '85 - '89)							
Stolt Aspiration	TK	1987	D	72,213	422' 11"	66' 04"	36' 01"
(Golden Angel '87 - '87)							
Stolt Kent	TK	1998	D	110,965	487' 00"		
Stolt Taurus	TK	1985	D	65,303	404' 06"	67' 04"	36' 09"
(Shoun Taurus '85 - '89)							
T-1 — TALL SHIP ADVENTURE, CHARLEVOIX, MI							
Appledore	2S	1989	W		85' 00"	19' 00"	9' 00"*
T-2 — TECHNO-NAVIGATION LTEE., SILLERY, PQ							
Petrel V	SV	1947	D	955*	195' 00"	30' 01"	16' 00"
(Akurey '47 - '67, Akeroy '67 - '68, Petrel '68 - '76) (Currently laid up in Quebec, PQ.)							
Techno St-Laurent	TB	1944	D	261*	111' 00"	27' 00"	13' 00"
(HMCS Riverton [W-47/ATA-528] '44 - '79)							
T-3 — TEE DEE ENTERPRISES, INC., CHICAGO, IL							
Anita Dee	ES	1972	D	97*	90' 00"	21' 00"	8' 10"
Anita Dee II	ES	1990	D	81*	140' 00"	33' 00"	8' 06"
T-4 — THE ISLE ROYALE LINE, COPPER HARBOR, MI							
Isle Royale Queen III	PK	1959	D	15	85' 00"	18' 04"	9' 05"
T-5 — THOMAS W. MARSHALL, TORONTO, ON							
Still Watch	SV	1960	D	390*	134' 02"	28' 00"	13' 09"
(CCGS Ville Marie '60 - '85, Heavenbound '85 - '95) (Currently laid up in Toronto, ON.)							
T-6 — THORNTON CONSTRUCTION CO., INC.HANCOCK, MI							
Shannon 66-5	TB	1950	D	21*	49' 00"	16' 00"	5' 00"*
T-7 — THUNDER BAY MARINE SERVICE LTD., THUNDER BAY, ON							
Agoming	CS	1926	B	155*	100' 00"	34' 00"	9' 00"
Coastal Cruiser	TB	1939	D	29*	65' 00"	18' 00"	12' 00"
Glenada	TB	1944	D	107*	80' 06"	25' 00"	10' 01"
Robert W.	TB	1949	D	48*	60' 00"	16' 00"	8' 06"
Rosalee D.	TB	1943	D	22*	55' 00"	16' 00"	10' 00"
T-8 — THUNDER BAY TUG SERVICES LTD., THUNDER BAY, ON							
Valour	TB	1958	D	246*	97' 08"	28' 02"	13' 10"
(Foundation Valour '58 - '83, Point Valour '83 - '92)							
T-9 — TORONTO DRYDOCK CORP., TORONTO, ON							
Menier Consol	FD	1962	B	2,575*	304' 07"	49' 06"	25' 06"
(Last operated 13 September, 1984.)							
T-10 — TORONTO FIRE DEPARTMENT, TORONTO, ON							
Wm. Lyon Mackenzie	FB	1964	D	102*	81' 01"	20' 00"	10' 00"

Gordon C. Leitch meets Canadian Miner in the pool between the Snell and Eisenhower locks on the St. Lawrence Seaway. (Terry Beahen)

Algosoo inbound for Toledo on the Maumee River. *(Jim Hoffman)*

ALGOSOO

Vessel Spotlight

Algosoo is a standard (730' x 75') Seaway-size Canadian self-unloader, part of the Algoma Central Marine/Seaway Self-Unloaders partnership. Built in 1974 at the former Collingwood Shipyards on Georgian Bay, Algosoo was the last "traditional" style laker built on the lakes - pilothouse foward, propulsion aft. Her maiden voyage was in December 1974. Algosoo is the second vessel on the lakes to carry the name - the first was scrapped in 1967. Her name's familiar fleet prefix - "Algo" couples with "Soo," honoring the city of Sault Ste. Marie, ON, home of the Algoma Steel mill.

Algosoo suffered a serious fire during winter lay-up, 1986, in which her aft-end cabins were gutted and self-unloading equipment damaged. She was repaired by October 1986, and returned to service.

Algosoo hauls a variety of cargoes from iron ore to salt. Look for her around the lakes from the Seaway to Lake Michigan. A common trip sees the Algosoo carrying taconite from a Gulf of St. Lawrence port to the steel mills of Lorain, OH, or Burns Harbor, IN.

- Rod Burdick

Fleet No. & Name Vessel Name	Type of Vessel	Year Built	Type of Engine	Cargo Cap. or Gross*	Overall Length	Breadth	Depth or Draft*
T-11 — TORONTO HARBOUR COMMISSIONERS, TORONTO, ON							
Fred Scandrett	TB	1963	D	52*	62' 00"	17' 00"	8' 00"
(C. E. "Ted" Smith '63 - '70)							
J. G. Langton	TB	1934	D	15*	45' 00"	12' 00"	5' 00"
Maple City	CF	1951	D	135*	70' 06"	36' 04"	5' 11"
Ned Hanlan II	TB		D				
William Rest	TB	1961	D	62*	65' 00"	18' 06"	10' 06"
Windmill Point	CF	1954	D	118*	65' 00"	36' 00"	10' 00"
T-12 — TORONTO METROPOLITAN PARK DEPARTMENT, TORONTO, ON							
Ongiara	PF	1963	D	180*	78' 00"	36' 00"	9' 09"
Sam McBride	PF	1939	D	412*	129' 00"	34' 11"	6' 00"
Thomas Rennie	PF	1950	D	419*	129' 00"	32' 11"	6' 00"
Trillium	PF	1910	R	611*	150' 00"	30' 00"	8' 04"
William Inglis	PF	1935	D	238*	99' 00"	24' 10"	6' 00"
(Shamrock {2} '35 - '35)							
T-13 — TORONTO PADDLEWHEEL CRUISES LTD., TORONTO, ON							
Jubilee Queen	ES	1986	D	269*	122' 00"		
(Pioneer Princess III '86 - '89)							
Pioneer Princess	ES	1984	D	74*	56' 00"		
Pioneer Queen	ES	1968	D	110*	85' 00"	30' 06"	7' 03"
(Peche Island III '68 - '71, Papoose IV '71 - '96)							
T-14 — TRANSPORT DESGAGNES, INC., QUEBEC, PQ							
CROISIERES NORDIK, INC. - A DIVISION OF TRANSPORT DESGAGNES, INC.							
Nordik Passeur	RR	1962	D	627	285' 04"	62' 00"	20' 01"
(Confederation {1} '62 - '93, Hull 28 '93 - '94)							
(5 year survey expired 11 April, 1994 — Currently laid up in Quebec, PQ.)							
DESGAGNES SHIPPING INTERNATIONAL, INC.							
A DIVISION OF TRANSPORT DESGAGNES, INC.							
Anna Desgagnes	RR	1986	D	17,850	565' 00"	75' 00"	45' 00"
(Truskavets '86 - '96)							
DESGAGNES TANKERS, INC. - A DIVISION OF TRANSPORT DESGAGNES, INC.							
Petrolia Desgagnes	TK	1975	D	97,725	441' 05"	56' 06"	32' 10"
(Jorvan '75 - '79, Lido '79 - '84, Ek-Sky '84 - '98)							
Thalassa Desgagnes	TK	1976	D	104,667	441' 05"	56' 06"	32' 10"
(Joasla '76 - '79, Orinoco '79 - '82, Rio Orinoco '82 - '93)							
GROUP DESGAGNES, INC. - A DIVISION OF TRANSPORT DESGAGNES, INC.							
Amelia Desgagnes	GC	1976	D	7,000	355' 00"	49' 00"	30' 06"
(Soodoc {2} '76 - '90)							
Catherine Desgagnes	GC	1962	D	8,350	410' 03"	56' 04"	31' 00"
(Gosforth '62 - '72, Thorold {4} '72 - '85)							
Cecelia Desgagnes	GC	1971	D	7,875	374' 10"	54' 10"	34' 06"
(Carl Gorthon '71 - '81, Federal Pioneer '81 - '85)							
Jacques Desgagnes	GC	1960	D	1,250	208' 10"	36' 00"	14' 00"
(Loutre Consol '60 - '77)							
Mathilda Desgagnes	GC	1959	D	6,920	360' 00"	51' 00"	30' 02"
(Eskimo '59 - '80)							
Melissa Desgagnes	GC	1975	D	7,000	355' 00"	49' 00"	30' 06"
(Ontadoc {2} '75 - '90)							
Nordik Express	CF	1974	D	1,697	219' 11"	44' 00"	16' 01"
(Theriot Offshore IV '74 - '77, Scotoil 4 '77 - '79, Tartan Sea '79 - '87)							
T-15 — TRANSPORT IGLOOIK, INC., MONTREAL, PQ							
Aivik	HL	1980	D	4,860	359' 08"	63' 08"	38' 09"
(Mont Ventoux '80 - '90, Aivik '90 - '91, Unilifter '91 - '92)							
LOGISTEC NAVIGATION, INC. - MANAGED BY TRANSPORT IGLOOIK, INC.							
Lucien-Paquin	GC	1969	D	12,802	459' 05"	70' 06"	42' 01"
(Boreland '69 - '79, Sunemerillon '79 - '82, Mesange '82 - '85)							
T-16 — TRAVERSE TALL SHIP CO., TRAVERSE CITY, MI							
Malabar	2S	1975	W	100*	105' 00"	22' 00"	8' 00"
Manitou {1}	PA	1983	W	78*	114' 00"	21' 00"	9' 00"
T-17 — TROIS RIVIERES REMORQUEURS LTEE., TROIS RIVIERES, PQ							
Andre H.	TB	1963	D	317*	126' 00"	28' 06"	15' 06"
(Foundation Valiant '63 - '73, Point Valiant '73 - '95)							
Duga	TB	1977	D	403*	111' 00"	33' 00"	16' 01"

Fleet No. & Name Vessel Name	Type of Vessel	Year Built	Type of Engine	Cargo Cap. or Gross*	Overall Length	Breadth	Depth or Draft*
R. F. Grant	TB	1969	D	78*	71' 00"	17' 00"	8' 00"
Robert H.	TB	1944	D	261*	111' 00"	27' 00"	13' 00"

T-18 — TRUMP INDIANA, INC., GARY, IN

Trump Casino	GA	1996	D	1,434*	238' 02"	76' 00"	17' 06"

T-19 — 30,000 ISLANDS CRUISE LINES, INC., PARRY SOUND, ON

Island Queen V {3}	ES	1990	D	526*	130' 00"	35' 00"	6' 06"

U-1 — UNCLE SAM BOAT TOURS, ALEXANDRIA, NY

Alexandria Belle	ES	1988	D	72*	104' 00"	32' 00"	7' 08"*
Island Duchess	ES	1988	D	60*	110' 00"	27' 08"	8' 08"*
Island Wanderer	ES	1971	D	57*	62' 05"	22' 00"	7' 02"
Uncle Sam Jr.	ES	1958	D	30*	50' 00"	10' 00"	4' 00"*
Uncle Sam II	ES	1958	D	75*	63' 00"	17' 06"	5' 04"
Uncle Sam VII	ES	1976	D	55*	60' 04"	22' 00"	7' 01"

U-2 — UNISPEED GROUP, INC., MONTREAL, PQ

Phoenician Trader	GC	1969	D	12,898	496' 09"	66' 09"	39' 02"

U-3 — U. S. ARMY CORPS OF ENGINEERS - GREAT LAKES & OHIO RIVER DIV., CHICAGO, IL
U. S. ARMY CORPS OF ENGINEERS - BUFFALO DISTRICT

Buffalo	TB	1953	D	23*	45' 00"	13' 00"	7' 00"*
Cheraw	TB	1970	D	356*	109' 00"	30' 06"	16' 03"
Chetek	TB	1973	D	356*	109' 00"	30' 06"	16' 03"
McCauley	CS	1948	B		112' 00"	52' 00"	3' 00"*
Simonsen	CS	1954	B		142' 00"	58' 00"	5' 00"*
Tonawanda	CS	1935	B		120' 00"	45' 00"	3' 00"*
Washington	TB	1952	D	390*	107' 00"	26' 06"	14' 10"

U. S. ARMY CORPS OF ENGINEERS - CHICAGO DISTRICT

Kenosha	TB	1954	D	82*	70' 00"	20' 00"	9' 08"
Manitowoc	CS	1976	B		132' 00"	44' 00"	8' 00"*
Racine	TB	1931	D	61*	66' 03"	18' 05"	7' 08"

U. S. ARMY CORPS OF ENGINEERS - DETROIT DISTRICT

D. L. Billmaier	TB	1968	D	345*	109' 00"	30' 06"	16' 03"
Duluth	TB	1954	D	82*	70' 00"	20' 00"	9' 08"
Fairchild	TB	1953	D	23*	45' 00"	13' 00"	7' 00"*
Forney	TB	1944	D	163*	86' 00"	23' 00"	10' 04"
Hammond Bay	TB	1953	D	23*	45' 00"	13' 00"	7' 00"*
Harvey	CS	1961	B		122' 00"	40' 00"	4' 10"*
H. J. Schwartz	CS	1995	B		150' 00"	48' 00"	7' 04"*
Huron	CS	1954	B		100' 00"	34' 00"	4' 06"*
James M. Bray	SV	1924	D	194*	128' 00"	31' 00"	8' 00"
(Deck Cargo Barge 20 '24 - '85)							
Michigan	CS	1971	B		120' 00"	33' 00"	3' 06"*
Nicolet	CS	1971	B		120' 00"	42' 00"	5' 00"*
Owen M. Frederick	TB	1942	D	56*	65' 00"	17' 00"	7' 06"
Paj	SV	1955	D	151*	120' 06"	34' 02"	6' 05"
(Deck Cargo Barge No. 30 '55 - '86)							
Paul Bunyan	GL	1945	B		150' 00"	65' 00"	12' 00"*
Shelter Bay	TB	1953	D	23*	45' 00"	13' 00"	7' 00"*
Tawas Bay	TB	1953	D	23*	45' 00"	13' 00"	7' 00"*
Whitefish Bay	TB	1953	D	23*	45' 00"	13' 00"	7' 00"*

U-4 — U. S. COAST GUARD - 9TH COAST GUARD DISTRICT, CLEVELAND, OH

Acacia **WLB-406**	BT	1944	D	1,025*	180' 00"	37' 00"	17' 00"
(Launched as Thistle [WAGL-406])							
Biscayne Bay **WTGB-104**	IB	1979	D	662*	140' 00"	37' 06"	12' 00"*
Bramble **WLB-392**	BT	1944	D	1,025*	180' 00"	37' 00"	17' 00"
Bristol Bay **WTGB-102**	IB	1979	D	662*	140' 00"	37' 06"	12' 00"*
Buckthorn **WLI-642**	BT	1963	D	200*	100' 00"	24' 00"	4' 08"*
CGB 12000	BT	1991	B	700*	120' 00"	50' 00"	6' 00"*
CGB 12001	BT	1991	B	700*	120' 00"	50' 00"	6' 00"*
Katmai Bay **WTGB-101**	IB	1978	D	662*	140' 00"	37' 06"	12' 00"*
Mackinaw **WAGB-83**	IB	1944	D	5,252*	290' 00"	74' 00"	29' 00"
(Launched as Manitowoc [WAG-83])							
Mobile Bay **WTGB-103**	IB	1979	D	662*	140' 00"	37' 06"	12' 00"*
Neah Bay **WTGB-105**	IB	1980	D	662*	140' 00"	37' 06"	12' 00"*
Sundew **WLB-404**	BT	1944	D	1,025*	180' 00"	37' 00"	17' 00"

Fleet No. & Name Vessel Name	Type of Vessel	Year Built	Type of Engine	Cargo Cap. or Gross*	Overal Length	Breadth	Depth or Draft*

U-5 — U. S. DEPT. OF THE INTERIOR - U. S. FISH & WILDLIFE SERV., ANN ARBOR, MI

Cisco	RV	1951	D		60' 06"	16' 08"	7' 08"
Grayling	RV	1977	D		75' 00"	22' 00"	9' 10"
Kaho	RV	1961	D		64' 10"	17' 10"	9' 00"
Musky II	RV	1960	D	25*	45' 00"	14' 04"	5' 00"
Siscowet	RV	1946	D	54*	57' 00"	14' 06"	7' 00"

U-6 — U. S. ENVIRONMENTAL PROTECTION AGENCY, WASHINGTON D. C.

Lake Guardian	RV	1989	D	282*	180' 00"	40' 00"	11' 00"
(Marsea Fourteen '81 - '90)							

U-7 — U. S. NATIONAL PARK SERVICE - ISLE ROYALE NATIONAL PARK, HOUGHTON, MI

Beaver	GC	1952	B	550	110' 00"	32' 00"	6' 05"
Charlie Mott	PF	1953	D	28*	56' 00"	14' 00"	4' 07"
Greenstone	TK	1977	B	30	81' 00"	24' 00"	6' 01"
J. E. Colombe	TB	1953	D	25*	45' 00"	12' 05"	5' 03"
Ranger III	PK	1958	D	140	165' 00"	34' 00"	15' 03"

U-8 — U. S. NAVAL SEA CADET CORPS, WHITE LAKE, MI

Grey Fox	TV	1985	D	213*	120' 00"	25' 00"	12' 00"*
(USS TWR-825 '85 - '97)							
Pride of Michigan	TV	1979	D	70*	80' 06"	7' 08"	5' 03"*
(USS YP-673 '79 - '89)							

U-9 — UNIVERSITE DU QUEBEC, RIMOUSKI, PQ

Alcide C. Horth	RV	1965	D	135*	89' 02"	22' 09"	11' 00"
(Villmont No. 2 '65 - '83, Raymond Moore '83 - '90)							

U-10 — UNIVERSITY OF MICHIGAN, ANN ARBOR, MI

Laurentian	RV	1977	D	129*	80' 00"	21' 06"	11' 00"

U-11 — UNIVERSITY OF MINNESOTA - DULUTH, DULUTH, MN

Blue Heron	RV	1985	D	175*	119' 06"	28' 00"	15' 06"

U-12 — UNIVERSITY OF WISCONSIN - SUPERIOR, SUPERIOR, WI

L. L. Smith Jr.	RV	1950	D	38*	57' 06"	16' 06"	6' 06"

U-13 — UPPER CANADA STEAMBOATS, INC., BROCKVILLE, ON

Miss Brockville	ES		D		48' 00"	10' 00"	4' 00"
Miss Brockville IV	ES		D		45' 00"	10' 00"	5' 00"
Miss Brockville V	ES		D		62' 00"	13' 00"	5' 00"
Miss Brockville VI	ES		D		38' 00"	8' 00"	3' 00"
Miss Brockville VII	ES		D		66' 00"	15' 00"	5' 00"
Miss Brockville VIII	ES		D		48' 00"	12' 00"	5' 00"

U-14 — UPPER LAKES BARGE LINE, INC., BARK RIVER, MI

McKee Sons	SU	1945	B	19,900	579' 02"	71' 06"	38' 06"
(USNS Marine Angel '45 - '52)							
Olive M. Moore	TB	1928	D	297*	125' 00"	27' 01"	13' 09"
(John F. Cushing '28 - '66, James E. Skelly '66 - '66)							

U-15 — UPPER LAKES GROUP, INC., TORONTO, ON
HAMILTON MARINE & ENGINEERING LTD. - A DIV. OF UPPER LAKES GROUP, INC.

James E. McGrath	TB	1963	D	90*	77' 00"	20' 00"	10' 09"

JACKES SHIPPING, INC. - A DIVISION OF UPPER LAKES GROUP, INC.

Canadian Trader	BC	1969	D	28,300	730' 00"	75' 00"	39' 08"
(Ottercliffe Hall '69 - '83, Royalton {2} '83 - '85, Ottercliffe Hall '85 - '88, Peter Misener '88 - '94)							
Canadian Venture	BC	1965	D	28,050	730' 00"	75' 00"	39' 02"
(Lawrencecliffe Hall {2} '65 - '88, David K. Gardiner '88 - '94)							
Gordon C. Leitch {2}	BC	1968	D	29,700	730' 00"	75' 00"	42' 00"
(Ralph Misener '68 - '94)							

MARBULK SHIPPING, INC. - A DIVISION OF UPPER LAKES GROUP, INC.

Ambassador	SU	1983	D	37,800	730' 00"	75' 10"	50' 00"
(Canadian Ambassador '83 - '85)							
Nelvana	SU	1983	D	74,973	797' 05"	105' 11"	66' 04"
Pioneer	SU	1981	D	37,900	730' 00"	75' 10"	50' 00"
(Canadian Pioneer '81 - '86)							

PROVMAR FUELS, INC. - A DIVISION OF UPPER LAKES GROUP, INC.

Hamilton Energy	RT	1965	D	8,622	201' 05"	34' 01"	14' 09"
(Partington '65 - '79, Shell Scientist '79 - '81, Metro Sun '81 - '85)							

Fleet No. & Name Vessel Name	Type of Vessel	Year Built	Type of Engine	Cargo Cap. or Gross*	Overal Length	Breadth	Depth or Draft*
Provmar Terminal	TK	1959	B	60,000	403' 05"	55' 06"	28' 05"
(Varangnes '59 - '70, Tommy Wiborg '70 - '74, Ungava Transport '74 - '85)							
(Last operated in 1984.) (Currently in use as a stationary fuel storage barge in Hamilton, ON.)							
Provmar Terminal II	TK	1948	B	73,740	408' 08"	53' 00"	26' 00"
(Imperial Sarnia {2} '48 - '89)							
(Last operated 13 December, 1986.) (In use as a stationary fuel storage barge in Hamilton, ON.)							
ULS CORPORATION - A DIVISION OF UPPER LAKES GROUP, INC.							
Canadian Century	SU	1967	D	31,600	730' 00"	75' 00"	45' 00"
Canadian Enterprise	SU	1979	D	35,100	730' 00"	75' 08"	46' 06"
Canadian Leader	BC	1967	T	28,300	730' 00"	75' 00"	39' 08"
(Feux - Follets '67 - '72)							
Canadian Mariner	BC	1963	T	27,700	730' 00"	75' 00"	39' 03"
(Newbrunswicker '63 - '68, Grande Hermine '68 - '72)							
Canadian Miner	BC	1966	D	28,050	730' 00"	75' 00"	39' 01"
(Maplecliffe Hall '66 - '88, Lemoyne {2} '88 - '94)							
Canadian Navigator	SU	1967	D	31,600	729' 10"	75' 10"	40' 06"
(Demeterton '67 - '75, St. Lawrence Navigator '75 - '80)							
Canadian Olympic	SU	1976	D	35,100	730' 00"	75' 00"	46' 06"
Canadian Progress	SU	1968	D	32,700	730' 00"	75' 00"	46' 06"
Canadian Prospector	BC	1964	D	30,500	730' 00"	75' 10"	40' 06"
(Carlton '64 - '75, Federal Wear '75 - '75, St. Lawrence Prospector '75 - '79)							
Canadian Provider	BC	1963	T	27,450	730' 00"	75' 00"	39' 02"
(Murray Bay {3} '63 - '94)							
Canadian Ranger	GU	1943	D	25,900	730' 00"	75' 00"	39' 03"
([Fore Section] Grande Ronde '43 - '48, Kate N. L. '48 - '61, Hilda Marjanne '61 - '84)							
([Stern Section] Chimo '67 - '83)							
Canadian Transfer	SU	1943	D	16,029	650' 06"	60' 00"	35' 00"
([Fore Section] J. H. Hillman Jr. '43 - '74, Crispin Oglebay {2} '74 - '95, Hamilton '95 - '96,							
* Hamilton Transfer '96 - '98)*							
([Stern Section] Cabot '65 - '83, Canadian Explorer '83 - '98)							
Canadian Transport {2}	SU	1979	D	35,100	730' 00"	75' 08"	46' 06"
Canadian Voyager	BC	1963	T	27,050	730' 00"	75' 00"	39' 02"
(Black Bay '63 - '94)							
James Norris	SU	1952	U	18,600	663' 06"	67' 00"	35' 00"
Montrealais	BC	1962	T	27,800	730' 00"	75' 00"	39' 00"
(Montrealer '62 - '62)							
Quebecois	BC	1963	T	27,800	730' 00"	75' 00"	39' 00"
Seaway Queen	BC	1959	T	24,300	713' 03"	72' 00"	37' 00"
BARBER SHIP MANAGEMENT - MANAGED BY UPPER LAKES GROUP, INC.							
Thornhill	SU	1981	D	37,939	635' 11"	90' 08"	48' 07"
(Frotabrasil '81 - '87, Athos '87 - '89, Chennai Perumai '89 - '93)							
U-16 — UPPER LAKES TOWING, INC., ESCANABA, MI							
Joseph H. Thompson	SU	1944	B	21,200	706' 06"	71' 06"	38' 06"
(USNS Marine Robin '44 - '52)							
Joseph H. Thompson Jr.	TB	1990	D	841*	146' 06"	38' 00"	35' 00"
William H. Donner	CS	1914	R	9,400	524' 00"	54' 00"	30' 00"
(Last operated in 1969 — Currently laid up in Menominee, MI.)							
U-17 — USS GREAT LAKES FLEET, INC., DULUTH, MN							
Arthur M. Anderson	SU	1952	T	25,300	767' 00"	70' 00"	36' 00"
Calcite II	SU	1929	D	12,650	604' 09"	60' 00"	32' 00"
(William G. Clyde '29 - '61)							
Cason J. Callaway	SU	1952	T	25,300	767' 00"	70' 00"	36' 00"
Edgar B. Speer	SU	1980	D	73,700	1,004' 00"	105' 00"	56' 00"
Edwin H. Gott	SU	1979	D	74,100	1,004' 00"	105' 00"	56' 00"
George A. Sloan	SU	1943	D	15,800	620' 06"	60' 00"	35' 00"
(Hill Annex '43 - '43)							
John G. Munson {2}	SU	1952	T	25,550	768' 03"	72' 00"	36' 00"
Myron C. Taylor	SU	1929	D	12,450	603' 09"	60' 00"	32' 00"
Ojibway {1}	SB	1945	D	65*	53' 00"	28' 00"	7' 00"
Philip R. Clarke	SU	1952	T	25,300	767' 00"	70' 00"	36' 00"
Roger Blough	SU	1972	D	43,900	858' 00"	105' 00"	41' 06"
GLF GREAT LAKES CORP. - A DIVISION OF USS GREAT LAKES FLEET, INC.							
Presque Isle {2}	TB	1973	D	1,578*	153' 03"	54' 00"	31' 03"
Presque Isle {2}	SU	1973	B	57,500	974' 06"	104' 07"	46' 06"
[Presque Isle {2} overall dimensions together]					1,000' 00"	104' 07"	46' 06"

Columbia Star enters the piers at Duluth.
(Kenneth Newhams, Duluth Shipping News)

Fleet No. & Name Vessel Name	Type of Vessel	Year Built	Type of Engine	Cargo Cap. or Gross*	Overal Length	Breadth	Depth or Draft*
V-1 — VERREAULT NAVIGATION, INC., LES MACHINS, PQ							
I.V. No. 9	GC	1936	D	320	110' 00"	23' 10"	8' 05"
(A.C.D. '36 - '69)							
I.V. No.10	GC	1936	D	320	110' 00"	23' 10"	8' 05"
(G.T.D. '36 - '69)							
I.V. No. 14	GC	1937	D	229	113' 00"	22' 05"	8' 06"
(Kermic '37 - '74)							
Keta V	TB	1961	D	236*	98' 00"	26' 00"	12' 06"
(Kelligrews '61 - '89, Verreault '89 - '89, Verreault No. 25 '89 - '89)							
Port Mechins	DR	1949	R	1,321	200' 00"	40' 02"	18' 00"
(Haffar '49 - '61, Lockeport '61 - '92)							
V-2 — VINCENT KLAMERUS EXCAVATING, DRUMMOND ISLAND, MI							
Lime Island	TB	1957	D	21*	42' 10"	12' 00"	5' 06"*
V-3 — VISTA FLEET, DULUTH, MN							
Vista King	ES	1978	D	60*	78' 00"	28' 00"	5' 02"
Vista Star	ES	1987	D	95*	91' 00"	24' 09"	7' 08"
(Island Empress '87 - '88)							
V-4 — V. M. SHIPPING L.L.C., BARK RIVER, MI							
Great Lakes Trader	SU	2000	B	38,200	740' 00"	78' 00"	45' 00"
Joyce L. Van Enkevort	TB	1998	D	1,178*	135' 04"	50' 00"	26' 00"
[Great Lakes Trader/Joyce L. Van Enkevort overall dimensions together]					844' 10"	78' 00"	45' 00"
V-5 — VOIGHT'S MARINE SERVICES, ELLISON BAY, WI							
Bounty	ES	1968	D		40' 00"	14' 00"	3' 03"
Island Clipper {2}	ES	1987	D	149*	65' 00"	20' 00"	5' 00"
Yankee Clipper	ES	1971	D		54' 00"	17' 00"	5' 00"
V-6 — VOYAGEUR CRUISES, INC., CHARLEVOIX, MI							
Voyageur	ES	1981	D	72*	105' 00"	21' 06"	6' 00"*
V-7 — VOYAGEURS MARINE CONSTRUCTION CO., VAUDREUIL, PQ							
Glenlivet II	TB	1944	D	111*	76' 08"	20' 09"	10' 02"
(HMCS Glenlivet [W-43] '44 - '75, Glenlivet II '75 - '77, Canadian Franko '77 - '82)							
Soulanges	TB	1905	D	72*	77' 00"	17' 00"	8' 00"
(Dandy '05 - '39)							
W-1 — WAGNER CHARTER CO., INC., CAROL STREAM, IL							
Buccaneer	ES	1925	D	98*	100' 00"	23' 00"	14' 06"
(USCG Dexter '25 - '35, USS Dexter '35 - '46, Kingfisher '46 - '61, Jamica II '61 - '61, Trinidad {1} '61 - '94)							
Jamica	ES	1967	D	88*	105' 00"	25' 00"	10' 06"
Trinidad {2}	ES	1926	D	98*	100' 00"	23' 00"	14' 06"
W-2 — WASHINGTON ISLAND FERRY LINE, INC., WASHINGTON ISLAND, WI							
C. G. Richter	CF	1950	D	82*	70' 06"	25' 00"	9' 05"
Eyrarbakki	CF	1970	D	95*	87' 00"	36' 00"	7' 06"
Robert Noble	CF	1979	D	97*	90' 04"	36' 00"	8' 03"
Voyager	CF	1960	D	98*	65' 00"	35' 00"	8' 00"
Washington {2}	CF	1989	D	93*	100' 00"	37' 00"	9' 00"
W-3 — WATERWAYS TRANSPORTATION SERVICES CORP., TORONTO, ON							
Waterways 1	PC	1988	D	387*	119' 02"	30' 11"	11' 04"
(Condor 8 '88 - '97)							
W-4 — WELLINGTON MARITIME, SAULT STE. MARIE, MI							
Soo River Belle	PB		D				
W-5 — WENDELLA SIGHTSEEING CO., CHICAGO, IL							
Queen of Andersonville	ES	1962	D	23*	40' 00"	15' 00"	3' 05"
Wendella Clipper	ES	1958	D	41*	67' 00"	20' 00"	4' 00"
Wendella Limited	ES	1992	D	66*	68' 00"	20' 00"	4' 09"
Wendella Sunliner	ES	1961	D	35*	68' 00"	17' 00"	6' 05"
W-6 — WISCONSIN & MICHIGAN STEAMSHIP CO., DETROIT, MI							
Highway 16	AC	1942	D	190 cars	328' 00"	50' 00"	25' 00"
(USS LST-393 '42 - '48)							

(Last operated 31 July, 1973 — Currently laid up in Muskegon, MI.)
(During World War II the Highway 16 earned 3 Battle Stars and participated in the Normandy Invasion of 6 June 1944 as the USS LST-393.)

International Fleet Listings

Space does not permit listing every potential saltwater visitor to the Great Lakes and Seaway (at the end of 1997, the world fleet totaled 85,494 vessels over 100 gross tons, according to Lloyd's Register of Shipping). Therefore we have included only those fleets and vessels that make regular transits of the St. Lawrence Seaway and Great Lakes system, according to reports compiled by the St. Lawrence Seaway Authority.

Fleet No. & Name Vessel Name	Type of Vessel	Year Built	Type of Engine	Cargo Cap. or Gross*	Overal Length	Breadth	Depth or Draft*
IA-1 — A. C. OERSSLEFF'S EFTF. A/S, HOLTE, DENMARK							
Emilie K	GC	1982	D	2,150	237' 08"	37' 04"	22' 00"
Greenland Saga	GC	1989	D	3,200	285' 07"	47' 10"	25' 03"
Industrial Faith	GC	1993	D	4,000	290' 00"	49' 03"	24' 07"
Malene	GC	1984	D	922	176' 08"	31' 06"	18' 05"
Sea Flower	GC	1982	D	1,630	237' 09"	36' 11"	22' 06"
Sea Pearl	GC	1973	D	3,615	293' 01"	44' 09"	27' 11"
Sea Rose	GC	1980	D	1,304	229' 00"	34' 03"	19' 09"
Susan K	GC	1982	D	2,158	237' 08"	37' 03"	22' 00"
Vinland Saga	GC	1982	D	932	207' 04"	31' 06"	18' 05"
IA-2 — ACOMARIT (U.K.) LTD., GLASGOW, SCOTLAND							
Repulse Bay	GC	1977	D	6,835	352' 02"	54' 02"	27' 11"
IA-3 — AEGEUS SHIPPING S.A., PIREAUS, GREECE							
Aegean Sea	BC	1983	D	31,431	598' 09"	77' 06"	50' 06"
IA-4 — AG SHIPMANAGEMENT LTD., LONDON, ENGLAND							
Sedoy	BC	1984	D	24,105	605' 08"	75' 00"	46' 05"
Uznadze	TK	1988	D	128,956	496' 05"	73' 07"	39' 10"
Vakhtangov	BC	1984	D	24,105	605' 00"	75' 00"	46' 05"
Vekua	TK	1987	D	126,377	496' 05"	73' 07"	39' 10"
IA-5 — AKMAR SHIPPING & TRADING S.A., ISTANBUL, TURKEY							
Aynur Kalkavan	BC	1974	D	27,299	583' 10"	75' 02"	45' 05"
Ayse Ana	BC	1979	D	25,452	607' 08"	75' 05"	46' 05"
IA-6 — ALBA SHIPPING LTD. A/S, AALBORG, DENMARK							
Kasla	TK	1974	D	8,639	427' 07"	57' 10"	26' 03"
IA-7 — ALL TRUST SHIPPING CO., PIRAEUS, GREECE							
Aghia Marina	BC	1978	D	16,868	481' 03"	75' 02"	40' 01"
IA-8 — AMASUS SHIPPING B.V., FARMSUM, NETHERLANDS							
Aldebaran	GC	1997	D	2,270	270' 06"	37' 05"	13' 02"
Antares	GC	1984	D	1,576	258' 08"	33' 02"	13' 10"
Aquatique	GC	1962	D	580	180' 05"	23' 08"	10' 02"
Auriga	GC	1978	D	1,670	276' 04"	35' 03"	17' 03"
Bolder	GC	1986	D	1,500	266' 06"	34' 03"	15' 02"

Fleet No. & Name Vessel Name	Type of Vessel	Year Built	Type of Engine	Cargo Cap. or Gross*	Overall Length	Breadth	Depth or Draft*
Christiaan	GC	1984	D	2,280	261' 09"	36' 05"	17' 01"
Compaen	GC	1975	D	1,458	262' 09"	29' 07"	14' 05"
Daan	GC	1979	D	1,163	204' 11"	30' 11"	13' 01"
Diamant	GC	1985	D	1,497	255' 09"	32' 08"	13' 10"
Eemshorn	GC	1995	D	4,250	293' 10"	43' 03"	23' 04"
Elisabeth G	GC	1978	D	1,163	204' 11"	32' 06"	13' 01"
Gitana	GC	1970	D	830	219' 10"	26' 08"	12' 03"
Laurina Neeltje	GC	1995	D	2,310	279' 04"	35' 05"	17' 07"
Miska	GC	1963	D	507	182' 03"	23' 11"	8' 10"
Morgenstond	GC	1967	D	530	203' 10"	23' 06"	10' 00"
Njord	GC	1985	D	1,490	258' 06"	34' 09"	13' 10"
Quo-Vadis	GC	1983	D	1,564	259' 03"	32' 08"	14' 10"
Ulmo	GC	1961	D	700	188' 00"	23' 06"	10' 02"
Vega	GC	1992	D	2,880	371' 09"	50' 04"	11' 06"
Vesting	GC	1992	D	2,166	288' 07"	39' 02"	15' 09"
Vikingbank	GC	1978	D	3,040	268' 01"	46' 10"	21' 02"
Vios	GC	1984	D	1,485	255' 09"	33' 00"	13' 10"
Zuiderzee	GC	1985	D	998	208' 00"	32' 08"	12' 06"

IA-9 — ANANGEL SHIPPING ENTERPRISES S.A., PIRAEUS, GREECE

Amilla	BC	1972	D	22,589	539' 02"	75' 02"	44' 06"
Anangel Ares	GC	1980	D	17,154	477' 04"	68' 11"	43' 00"
Anangel Endeavor	GC	1978	D	23,130	539' 02"	75' 00"	44' 06"
Anangel Fidelity	BC	1979	D	22,000	539' 02"	75' 00"	44' 06"
Anangel Honesty	BC	1983	D	31,774	598' 07"	77' 05"	50' 06"
Anangel Honour	BC	1976	D	22,600	539' 02"	75' 00"	44' 06"
Anangel Hope	BC	1974	D	22,670	539' 02"	75' 00"	44' 06"
Anangel Horizon	BC	1977	D	27,090	580' 10"	75' 02"	46' 03"
Anangel Liberty	BC	1976	D	22,668	539' 02"	75' 00"	44' 06"
Anangel Might	BC	1978	D	23,130	539' 02"	75' 00"	46' 06"
Anangel Prosperity	BC	1976	D	22,314	539' 02"	75' 00"	44' 06"
Anangel Sky	GC	1979	D	17,199	477' 04"	68' 11"	43' 00"
Anangel Spirit	GC	1978	D	22,109	539' 02"	75' 00"	44' 06"
Anangel Triumph	BC	1976	D	22,311	539' 02"	75' 00"	44' 06"
Anangel Victory	GC	1979	D	17,188	477' 04"	68' 11"	44' 06"
Anangel Wisdom	BC	1974	D	22,353	539' 02"	75' 02"	44' 05"
Evimeria	BC	1973	D	22,630	539' 02"	75' 02"	44' 06"
Maria Angelicoussi	GC	1978	D	16,934	477' 05"	69' 00"	43' 00"
Pistis	BC	1973	D	22,627	539' 02"	75' 02"	44' 06"

IA-10 — ANGLO-GEORGIAN SHIPPING CO. LTD., LONDON, ENGLAND

Davitaja	BC	1983	D	24,150	605' 00"	75' 05"	46' 06"

IA-11 — ARMADA (GREECE) CO. LTD., PIRAEUS, GREECE

Anthos	GC	1979	D	16,897	477' 05"	69' 00"	43' 00"

IA-12 — ARTEMIS SHIPPING, INC., MONROVIA, LIBERIA

Artaki	BC	1977	D	19,077	508' 10"	74' 11"	41' 06"

IA-13 — ASIAN SHIPPING S.A., PANAMA CITY, PANAMA

Rubin Stork	BC	1996	D	18,315	446' 00"	74' 10"	40' 00"

IA-14 — ASLAN DENIZCILIK A.S., ISTANBUL, TURKEY

Aslan-1	GC	1990	D	8,284	395' 10"	55' 09"	30' 06"

IA-15 — ASTRON MARITIME CO. S.A., PIRAUUS, GREECE

Agamemnon	GC	1983	D	23,443	539' 02"	75' 02"	46' 06"
Arabella	GC	1983	D	23,440	539' 00"	75' 01"	46' 05"

IA-16 — ATLANTIS MANAGEMENT, INC., PIRAEUS, GREECE

Atlantis Joy	BC	1977	D	18,216	511' 11"	73' 10"	39' 05"
Atlantis Spirit	BC	1977	D	19,019	497' 10"	75' 00"	42' 00"
Mentor	BC	1973	D	22,247	539' 02"	75' 02"	44' 06"

IA-17 — ATLANTSKA PLOVIDBA D.D., DUBROVNIK, CROATIA

Cvijeta Zuzoric	BC	1974	D	27,020	599' 05"	73' 09"	46' 07"
Kupari	HL	1979	D	2,720	266' 05"	48' 09"	21' 08"
Lapad	HL	1978	D	1,970	307' 11"	52' 07"	24' 00"
Mljet	BC	1982	D	29,643	622' 01"	74' 11"	49' 10"
Plitvice	HL	1979	D	2,720	266' 05"	48' 09"	21' 08"

Fleet No. & Name Vessel Name	Type of Vessel	Year Built	Type of Engine	Cargo Cap. or Gross*	Overal Length	Breadth	Depth or Draft*
Ruder Boskovic	BC	1974	D	27,020	599' 05"	73' 09"	46' 07"
Slano	HL	1978	D	2,811	289' 04"	51' 02"	24' 10"
IA-18 — AURORA SHIPPING, INC., MANILA, PHILIPPINES							
Aurora Gold	GC	1976	D	10,027	419' 10"	60' 02"	32' 06"
Aurora Jade	BC	1979	D	13,206	436' 04"	67' 08"	37' 09"
Aurora Topaz	BC	1982	D	28,268	639' 09"	75' 10"	46' 11"
IA-19 — AZOV SEA SHIPPING CO., MARIUPOL, UKRAINE							
Avdeevka	BC	1977	D	26,398	570' 11"	75' 03"	47' 07"
Catherine	TK	1989	D	58,641	419' 00"	65' 07"	32' 10"
Dobrush	BC	1982	D	28,160	644' 06"	75' 10"	46' 11"
Fatezh	GC	1981	D	7,805	399' 08"	57' 09"	32' 06"
General Blazhevich	GC	1981	D	7,805	399' 09"	67' 00"	27' 03"
Komsomolets Adzharii	GC	1974	D	8,264	426' 04"	58' 06"	32' 02"
Komsomolets Armenii	GC	1973	D	8,264	426' 04"	58' 06"	32' 02"
Komsomolets Moldavii	GC	1971	D	8,230	426' 06"	58' 06"	32' 02"
Komsomolets Rossii	GC	1974	D	8,254	426' 04"	58' 06"	32' 02"
Kramatorsk	GC	1980	D	7,805	399' 09"	57' 09"	32' 06"
Makeevka	BC	1982	D	28,136	644' 06"	75' 07"	46' 11"
Mekhanik Aniskin	GC	1973	D	8,264	426' 04"	58' 06"	32' 02"
Sumy	BC	1978	D	22,904	540' 00"	75' 00"	45' 00"
IB-1 — B & N SEA PARTNER AB, SKARHAMN, SWEDEN							
Ada Gorthon	RR	1984	D	9,981	512' 07"	73' 00"	46' 09"
Alida Gorthon	GC	1977	D	14,299	463' 09"	71' 04"	38' 08"
Bergon	GC	1978	D	5,449	330' 10"	54' 02"	26' 03"
Bremon	GC	1976	D	8,650	393' 10"	54' 06"	33' 04"
Corner Brook	GC	1976	F	7,173	445' 06"	61' 00"	40' 01"
Humber Arm	GC	1976	D	7,173	426' 07"	61' 00"	40' 01"
Ingrid Gorthon	GC	1977	D	14,298	463' 10"	73' 00"	38' 09"
Ivan Gorthon	RR	1974	D	3,500	387' 08"	51' 02"	37' 03"
Joh. Gorthon	RR	1977	D	7,182	512' 07"	69' 07"	47' 01"
Lovisa Gorthon	RR	1979	D	6,420	440' 07'	69' 01"	37' 09"
Margit Gorthon	GC	1977	D	14,298	463' 10"	73' 00"	38' 09"
Maria Gorthon	RR	1984	D	9,995	512' 07"	73' 00"	48' 09"
Munksund	GC	1968	D	12,497	503' 03"	66' 07"	36' 09"
Norcove	RR	1977	D	6,671	466' 07"	63' 02"	47' 08"
Nordon	GC	1977	D	7,884	370' 09"	63' 00"	28' 07"
Ragna Gorthon	RR	1979	D	7,583	442' 07"	69' 01"	37' 09"
Stig Gorthon	RR	1979	D	6,382	440' 08"	69' 01"	37' 09"
Storon	BC	1975	D	10,880	470' 02"	61' 00"	33' 04"
Tofton	GC	1980	D	14,883	522' 02"	70' 03"	41' 04"
Tor Belgia	RR	1979	D	8,400	558' 07"	69' 00"	42' 00"
Tor Flandria	RR	1979	D	8,400	558' 07"	69' 00"	42' 00"
Tor Scandia	RR	1978	D	8,412	558' 07"	69' 00"	42' 00"
Viola Gorthon	RR	1987	D	10,917	544' 08"	75' 08"	43' 02"
Weston	GC	1979	D	14,938	522' 02"	70' 03"	41' 04"
IB-2 — B & N, BYLOCK & NORDSJOFRAKT AB, SKARHAMN, SWEDEN							
Holmon	GC	1978	D	10,900	442' 11"	59' 06"	32' 10"
IB-3 — B+H EQUIMAR SINGAPORE PTE. LTD., SINGAPORE, MALAYSIA							
Narragansett	BC	1977	D	35,910	729' 11"	76' 00"	47' 00"
IB-4 — BERGEN BULK CARRIERS A/S, BERGEN, NORWAY							
Bergen Bay	BC	1977	D	27,765	579' 11"	75' 02"	48' 03"
Bergen Sea	BC	1977	D	28,218	579' 11"	75' 02"	48' 03"
IB-5 — BIRLIK DENIZCILIK ISLETMECILIGI SANAYI VE TICARET A.S., ISTANBUL, TURKEY							
Haci Hilmi Bey	BC	1977	D	24,354	607' 07"	75' 00"	46' 05"
Haci Hilmi II	GC	1992	D	6,443	367' 04"	50' 06"	27' 11"
Pira	BC	1974	D	26,923	599' 10"	73' 09"	46' 07"
Riza Sonay	GC	1989	D	8,219	380' 07"	56' 06"	32' 02"
IB-6 — BISON SHIPMANAGEMENT & CHARTERING CO. PTE. LTD., SINGAPORE, MALAYASIA							
Ida	BC	1995	D	18,172	486' 01"	74' 10"	40' 00"
Lita	BC	1995	D	18,173	486' 01"	74' 10"	40' 00"
Olga	BC	1996	D	18,173	486' 01"	74' 10"	40' 00"

Fleet No. & Name Vessel Name	Type of Vessel	Year Built	Type of Engine	Cargo Cap. or Gross*	Overal Length	Breadth	Depth or Draft*
IB-7 — BLACK STAR LINE LTD., HAMBURG, GERMANY							
Keta Lagoon	GC	1980	D	16,667	548' 11"	75' 05"	42' 08"
Volta River	GC	1980	D	16,687	548' 11"	75' 03"	42' 08"
IB-8 — BLUE MARINE S.A. LIBERIA, PIRAEUS, GREECE							
Anthony	GC	1981	D	15,883	532' 09"	73' 00"	44' 02"
IB-9 — BOTANY BAY MANAGEMENT SERVICES PTY. LTD., SYDNEY, NEW SOUTH WALES							
Botany Trader	TK	1995	D	89,191	458' 08"	69' 09"	34' 03"
Botany Trojan	TK	1996	D	90,000	454' 09"	71' 06"	39' 08"
Infra	TK	1985	D	87,719	404' 06"	65' 09"	36' 09"
Marinor	TK	1992	D	53,464	368' 01"	59' 02"	31' 02"
Tradewind Express	TK	1986	D	87,719	404' 06"	65' 09"	36' 09"
IB-10 — BULKVANG A/S, GREAKER, NORWAY							
Allvag	GC	1983	D	950	251' 01"	40' 07"	13' 07"
Allvang	GC	1984	D	1,150	251' 01"	40' 07"	22' 04"
Stalvang	GC	1983	D	950	251' 01"	40' 07"	13' 07"
Steinvang	GC	1982	D	950	251' 01"	40' 07"	13' 07"
IB-11 — BURMA NAVIGATION CORP., YANGON, MYANMAR							
Emerald Wave	TK	1992	D	61,560	341' 02"	61' 08"	31' 04"
Great Laker	BC	1987	D	28,358	590' 07"	75' 10"	48' 07"
Sea Eagle	GC	1984	D	17,330	519' 03"	75' 09"	44' 00"
IB-12 — BURSALIOGLU SANAYII VE TICARET LTD. SIRKETI, ISTANBUL, TURKEY							
Gozde-B	GC	1971	D	7,500	410' 02"	56' 07"	33' 02"
Yavuz Sultan Selim	GC	1975	D	8,153	386' 10"	59' 04"	29' 07"
IB-13 — BYZANTINE MARITIME CORP., PIRAEUS, GREECE							
Barbara H	BC	1976	D	30,242	621' 08"	75' 00"	47' 11"
Ellie	BC	1979	D	30,084	622' 00"	75' 00"	49' 10"
Stella	BC	1974	D	22,059	510' 10"	75' 05"	44' 07"
IC-1 — CAPE SHIPPING S.A., PIRAEUS, GREECE							
Cape Kennedy	GC	1971	D	14,934	466' 09"	65' 01"	40' 06"
IC-2 — CAPELLE CHARTERING EN TRADING B.V., IJSSEL, NETHERLANDS							
Alecto	GC	1984	D	5,050	301' 05"	49' 08"	26' 07"
Elina	GC	1975	D	1,559	216' 00"	35' 06"	16' 09"
Irene	GC	1978	D	1,548	216' 00"	36' 05"	16' 09"
IC-3 — CARISBROOKE SHIPPING PLC, COWES, ISLE OF WIGHT							
Anja C	GC	1991	D	3,222	327' 03"	41' 00"	20' 10"
Cheryl C	GC	1983	D	2,367	230' 01"	42' 11"	19' 09"
Elizabeth C	GC	1971	D	2,823	278' 11"	41' 10"	20' 04"
Emily C	GC	1996	D	4,650	294' 07"	43' 02"	23' 05"
Greta C	GC	1974	D	2,628	255' 02"	43' 03"	19' 09"
Heleen C	GC	1974	D	2,159	233' 10"	38' 00"	21' 08"
Klazina C	GC	1983	D	2,554	266' 09"	39' 04"	17' 09"
Mark C	GC	1996	D	4,620	294' 11"	43' 04"	23' 05"
Mary C	GC	1977	D	2,440	216' 10"	42' 11"	20' 05"
Minka C	GC	1975	D	2,657	258' 00"	40' 10"	20' 00"
Natacha C	GC	1982	D	2,467	230' 01"	42' 10"	19' 08"
Nordstrand	GC	1991	D	2,800	289' 08"	41' 00"	21' 04"
Tina C	GC	1974	D	2,591	258' 02"	40' 10"	20' 00"
Vanessa C	GC	1974	D	3,165	262' 11"	44' 08"	22' 01"
Vectis Falcon	GC	1978	D	3,564	285' 06"	45' 01"	22' 04"
Vectis Isle	GC	1990	D	3,222	327' 02"	41' 00"	20' 10"
IC-4 — CARSTEN REHDER (GMBH & CO.), HAMBURG, GERMANY							
Arosette	GC	1971	D	1,968	244' 06"	35' 06"	19' 09"
Astra Lift	GC	1977	D	3,861	307' 00"	54' 06"	26' 06"
Industrial Advantage	GC	1984	D	17,330	519' 03"	75' 08"	44' 00"
Vento Del Golfo	GC	1983	D	9,300	416' 11"	65' 03"	35' 02"
IC-5 — CEBI METAL SANAYI VE TICARET A.S., ISTANBUL, TURKEY							
Mina Cebi	BC	1980	D	27,311	627' 07"	75' 03"	44' 03"
IC-6 — CERES HELLENIC SHIPPING ENTERPRISES LTD., PIRAEUS, GREECE							
Agios Georgios	BC	1970	D	3,062	214' 10"	50' 02"	21' 08"
George L.	BC	1975	D	27,419	597' 01"	75' 02"	48' 03"

Fleet No. & Name Vessel Name	Type of Vessel	Year Built	Type of Engine	Cargo Cap. or Gross*	Overall Length	Breadth	Depth or Draft*
Kalliopi L.	BC	1974	D	26,998	585' 08"	75' 01"	47' 06"
Maria G. L.	BC	1974	D	26,998	585' 07"	75' 04"	47' 06"
Marka L.	BC	1975	D	27,418	597' 01"	75' 02"	48' 03"
Mini Lace	GC	1969	D/W	3,217	214' 11"	50' 03"	21' 08"
Pantazis L.	BC	1974	D	27,434	597' 02"	75' 02"	48' 03"
Tatiana L.	GC	1978	D	16,251	482' 00"	72' 04"	39' 05"

IC-7 — CHARTWORLD SHIPPING CORP., PIRAEUS, GREECE

Akebono Star	GC	1980	D	8,071	475' 07"	61' 04"	38' 09"
Ariake Star	GC	1980	D	8,076	475' 07"	61' 06"	38' 10"
Capricorn	GC	1973	D	12,180	575' 03"	75' 00"	44' 04"
Fuji Star	GC	1979	D	8,084	475' 07"	61' 06"	38' 09"
Golden Sky	BC	1975	D	30,449	625' 06"	75' 00"	47' 11"
Golden Sun	BC	1977	D	22,647	539' 03"	75' 01"	44' 06"
Pelagos	GC	1973	D	10,973	511' 02"	70' 01"	41' 08"
Perseus	GC	1972	D	10,974	511' 02"	70' 01"	41' 08"
Tokachi Star	GC	1985	D	3,621	367' 04"	53' 11"	31' 06"

IC-8 — CHELLARAM SHIPPING LTD., HONG KONG

Darya Kamal	BC	1981	D	30,900	617' 04"	76' 00"	47' 07"
Darya Ma	BC	1983	D	30,750	617' 04"	76' 00"	47' 07"

IC-9 — COMMERCIAL TRADING & DISCOUNT CO. LTD., ATHENS, GREECE

Ira	BC	1979	D	26,697	591' 02"	75' 10"	45' 08"
Ivi	BC	1979	D	26,697	591' 04"	75' 10"	45' 08"

IC-10 — COMPAGNIE TUNISIENNE DE NAVIGATION S.A., TUNIS, TUNISIA

Bizerte	GC	1979	D	8,312	450' 06"	64' 01"	34' 05"
El Jem	GC	1977	D	8,626	417' 07"	59' 02"	34' 05"
El Kef	BC	1982	D	26,355	599' 10"	75' 08"	46' 00"
Habib	RR	1978	D	3,372	478' 01"	77' 02"	27' 05"
Kairouan	GC	1979	D	8,345	450' 06"	64' 01"	34' 05"
Moulares	BC	1976	D	16,114	465' 11"	71' 07"	40' 01"
Nebhana	RR	1976	D	2,499	386' 08"	51' 10"	33' 00"
S' Hib	BC	1977	D	16,104	465' 11"	71' 07"	40' 01"
Tabarka	GC	1952	D	1,651	272' 04"	39' 02"	15' 04"
Tozeur	GC	1977	D	8,628	417' 07"	59' 02"	34' 05"

IC-11 — COSCO SHIPPING CO. LTD., HONG KONG

An Qing Jiang	GC	1985	D	14,913	491' 02"	71' 06"	41' 00"
An Ze Jiang	GC	1987	D	14,913	491' 02"	71' 06"	41' 00"
Aptmariner	BC	1979	D	31,000	619' 03"	75' 11"	47' 07"
Handymariner	BC	1978	D	31,200	619' 03"	75' 11"	47' 07"
Hui Fu	BC	1978	D	35,887	734' 02"	76' 08"	47' 05"
Hun Jiang	GC	1981	D	15,265	474' 11"	67' 01"	38' 07"
Jing Hong Hai	BC	1976	D	28,863	594' 01"	76' 01"	47' 07"
Jollity	BC	1975	D	22,623	539' 03"	75' 02"	44' 06"
Ocean Priti	BC	1982	D	27,019	599' 05"	75' 04"	46' 08"
Rong Cheng	GC	1977	D	18,687	484' 07"	75' 00"	42' 08"
Rong Jiang	GC	1978	D	15,189	462' 07"	67' 05"	38' 06"
Seadaniel	BC	1976	D	27,000	580' 10"	75' 00"	46' 04"
Yick Hua	BC	1984	D	28,086	584' 08"	75' 11"	48' 05"

IC-12 — CROATIA LINE, RIJEKA, CROATIA

Bribir	RR	1979	D	7,478	482' 03"	71' 04"	43' 11"
Buzet	GC	1979	D	12,430	474' 10"	75' 07"	35' 02"
Grobnik	GC	1981	D	14,425	514' 07"	71' 08"	39' 01"
Hreljin	CO	1977	D	11,031	504' 10"	70' 09"	36' 09"
Karlobag	GC	1980	D	24,432	634' 04"	75' 04"	46' 05"
Krk	GC	1977	D	13,694	514' 07"	71' 08"	39' 01"
Kupa	BC	1973	D	30,832	645' 00"	75' 05"	47' 06"
Ledenice	RR	1979	D	7,478	473' 09"	71' 04"	43' 11"
Losinj	GC	1972	D	15,169	485' 07"	67' 09"	41' 01"
Moscenice	GC	1976	D	13,914	514' 07"	71' 08"	39' 01"
Motovun	GC	1977	D	13,914	514' 07"	71' 08"	39' 01"
Opatija	GC	1973	D	15,142	485' 07"	67' 09"	41' 01"
Pionir	CO	1973	D	5,580	390' 00"	53' 03"	27' 03"
Rab	GC	1972	D	14,956	482' 10"	67' 09"	41' 00"
Rijeka	GC	1981	D	16,728	525' 00"	77' 02"	46' 00"

Fleet No. & Name Vessel Name	Type of Vessel	Year Built	Type of Engine	Cargo Cap. or Gross*	Overall Length	Breadth	Depth or Draft*
Sava	BC	1973	D	30,832	645' 00"	75' 05"	47' 06"
Slavonija	GC	1980	D	24,432	634' 04"	75' 04"	46' 05"
Slovenija	GC	1980	D	14,425	514' 07"	71' 08"	39' 01"
Susak	CO	1977	D	11,031	504' 09"	70' 09"	36' 09"
Triglav	GC	1981	D	15,642	500' 04"	74' 04"	41' 11"
Tuhobic	GC	1983	D	16,648	524' 11"	77' 02"	46' 00"
Velebit	GC	1981	D	15,709	500' 04"	74' 04"	41' 11"

IC-13 — CYGNUS STEAMSHIP S.A., PANAMA CITY, PANAMA

Manila Angus	BC	1985	D	28,019	584' 08"	75' 11"	48' 05"

IC-14 — CZECH OCEAN SHIPPING JOINT-STOCK CO., PRAQUE, CZECH REPUBLIC

Slapy	GC	1981	D	15,236	477' 06"	71' 00"	41' 00"

ID-1 — DALEX SHIPPING CO. S.A., PIRAEUS, GREECE

Arabian Express	GC	1977	D	17,089	483' 05"	72' 04"	39' 01"
Caribbean Express I	GC	1977	D	17,057	483' 05"	72' 04"	39' 01"
Iberian Express	GC	1982	D	17,279	509' 03"	74' 10"	43' 04"
Indian Express	GC	1982	D	17,279	509' 03"	74' 10"	43' 04"
Ionian Express	GC	1982	D	16,467	509' 03"	74' 10"	43' 04"
Istrian Express	GC	1983	D	16,439	509' 03"	74' 10"	43' 04"
Italian Express	GC	1984	D	17,279	509' 03"	74' 10"	43' 04"
Philippine Express	GC	1970	D	26,502	572' 09"	75' 00"	47' 00"

ID-2 — DENHOLM SHIP MANAGEMENT (OVERSEAS) LTD., HONG KONG

Broompark	BC	1982	D	30,670	617' 04"	76' 00"	47' 07"

ID-3 — DENSAN SHIPPING CO. LTD., ISTANBUL, TURKEY

Gunay-A	BC	1981	D	30,900	617' 04"	76' 00"	47' 07"
Necat A	BC	1981	D	28,645	655' 06"	75' 00"	45' 11"

ID-4 — DET NORDENFJELDSKE D/S AS, TRONDHEIM, NORWAY

Consensus Manitou	BC	1983	D	28,192	584' 08"	75' 11"	48' 05"

ID-5 — DIANA SHIPPING AGENCIES S.A., PIRAEUS, GREECE

CMBT Ensign	CO	1979	D	18,002	534' 10"	75' 03"	41' 10"
Elm	BC	1984	D	21,978	509' 02"	75' 01"	44' 07"
Maple	BC	1977	D	19,020	497' 10"	75' 00"	42' 00"
Oak	BC	1981	D	21,951	509' 02"	75' 02"	44' 07"

ID-6 — DILMUN SHIPPING CO. LTD., MANAMA, BAHRAIN

Dilmun Fulmar	TK	1980	D	10,150	361' 04"	60' 02"	32' 10"
Dilmuan Shearwater	TK	1983	D	19,217	486' 06"	69' 00"	38' 03"
Dilmun Tern	TK	1980	D				

ID-7 — DOBSON FLEET MANAGEMENT LTD., LIMASSOL, CYPRUS

Evangeline	GC	1975	D	4,250	316' 07"	52' 07"	28' 11"
Fetish	GC	1977	D	4,240	309' 09"	50' 08"	27' 03"
Jenny D	BC	1972	D	19,306	508' 11"	74' 11"	41' 06"
Jodie D	BC	1972	D	16,999	480' 04"	74' 02"	39' 08"
Karen D	BC	1976	D	8,186	385' 10"	59' 02"	29' 07"
Kirby D	BC	1976	D	8,197	385' 10"	59' 02"	29' 07"
Nicola D	BC	1977	D	9,267	439' 01"	59' 03"	29' 06"
Norman Star	GC	1979	D	9,996	551' 04"	74' 03"	41' 01"
Saxon Star	GC	1979	D	9,996	551' 04"	74' 03"	41' 01"
Scarab	GC	1983	D	4,240	309' 01"	50' 07"	27' 03"

ID-8 — DOCKENDALE SHIPPING CO. LTD., NASSAU, BAHAMAS

Clipper Majestic	GC	1979	D	17,154	477' 04"	68' 11"	43' 00"

ID-9 — DONNELLY SHIPMANAGEMENT LTD., LIMASSOL, CYPRUS

Altnes	BC	1978	D	5,995	352' 04"	49' 04"	28' 09"
Finnsnes	BC	1978	D	12,394	441' 04"	67' 11"	37' 09"
Fonnes	BC	1978	D	5,753	346' 09"	50' 07"	26' 03"
Frines	BC	1978	D	12,358	441' 04"	67' 11"	37' 09"
Fullnes	BC	1979	D	12,274	441' 04"	67' 11"	37' 09"
Garnes	GC	1980	D	5,995	351' 01"	49' 04"	28' 09"
Kianda	GC	1973	D	9,637	402' 11"	62' 06"	36' 01"
Rafnes	BC	1976	D	6,351	339' 09"	52' 06"	28' 11"
Risnes	BC	1976	D	5,699	339' 09"	52' 10"	28' 11"
Rollnes	BC	1976	D	5,789	334' 09"	52' 00"	28' 09"

Nassau-registered *Clipper Falcon* (top), bound for Lake Superior 11 October, 1998.

Spar Opal downbound for an overseas port. The vessel is owned by Spar Shipping and chartered to Canada's Fednav fleet.

(Roger LeLievre)

Fleet No. & Name Vessel Name	Type of Vessel	Year Built	Type of Engine	Cargo Cap. or Gross*	Overal Length	Breadth	Depth or Draft*
Vigsnes	BC	1979	D	6,105	352' 04"	49' 03"	28' 09"

ID-10 — DORVAL KAIUN K.K., TOKYO, JAPAN
Golden Fumi	TK	1996	D	78,895	383' 10"	65' 07"	36' 09"
Golden Georgia	TK	1996	D		452' 09"	72' 02"	38' 03"
Tenyu	GC	1985	D	4,240	277' 09"	47' 07"	28' 07"

ID-11 — DYNASTY SHIPPING CO. LTD., ATHENS, GREECE
Seaglory	BC	1978	D	29,212	593' 03"	75' 11"	47' 07"

IE-1 — EGON OLDENDORFF LTD., LUEBECK, GERMANY
Anna Oldendorff	BC	1994	D	18,355	486' 05"	74' 10"	40' 00"
Erna Oldendorff	BC	1994	D	18,355	486' 05"	74' 10"	40' 00"
Helena Oldendorff	BC	1984	D	28,354	644' 06"	75' 10"	46' 11"
Regina Oldendorff	BC	1986	D	28,031	639' 09"	75' 10"	46' 11"
Rixta Oldendorff	BC	1986	D	28,031	639' 09"	75' 10"	46' 11"
T. A. Adventurer	GC	1988	D	20,586	595' 06"	77' 01"	44' 00"
T. A. Discoverer	GC	1989	D	28,386	595' 06"	75' 08"	44' 00"
T. A. Explorer	GC	1987	D	22,500	614' 10"	75' 11"	42' 08"
T. A. Voyager	GC	1987	D	22,800	614' 10"	75' 11"	42' 08"

IE-2 — ELITE-SHIPPING A/S, COPENHAGEN, DENMARK
Arktis Atlantic	GC	1992	D	4,110	290' 01"	49' 08"	24' 07"
Arktis Blue	GC	1992	D	4,110	290' 01"	49' 08"	24' 07"
Arktis Breeze	GC	1987	D	2,671	261' 01"	44' 02"	21' 00"
Arktis Carrier	GC	1988	D	2,671	261' 01"	44' 02"	21' 00"
Arktis Crystal	GC	1994	D	5,401	319' 07"	53' 08"	27' 11"
Arktis Dream	GC	1993	D	4,110	290' 01"	49' 08"	24' 07"
Arktis Fantasy	GC	1994	D	7,120	331' 08"	63' 00"	30' 06"
Arktis Fighter	GC	1994	D	7,120	331' 08"	63' 00"	30' 06"
Arktis Future	GC	1994	D	7,120	331' 08"	63' 00"	30' 06"
Arktis Grace	GC	1988	D	2,671	261' 01"	44' 02"	21' 00"
Arktis Hope	GC	1994	D	5,401	319' 07"	53' 08"	27' 11"
Arktis Hunter	GC	1995	D	5,401	319' 07"	53' 08"	27' 11"
Arktis Light	GC	1993	D	5,401	319' 07"	53' 08"	27' 11"
Arktis Meridian	GC	1996	D	8,900	330' 08"	67' 01"	36' 01"
Arktis Morning	GC	1996	D	8,947	330' 08"	67' 01"	36' 01"
Arktis Ocean	GC	1987	D	2,433	249' 07"	38' 03"	21' 00"
Arktis Orion	GC	1978	D	1,360	236' 11"	34' 02"	19' 09"
Arktis Pearl	GC	1984	D	2,298	243' 10"	37' 03"	22' 01"
Arktis Pioneer	GC	1993	D	4,110	290' 01"	49' 08"	24' 07"
Arktis Pride	GC	1991	D	4,110	290' 01"	49' 08"	24' 07"
Arktis River	GC	1986	D	2,433	249' 07"	38' 03"	21' 00"
Arktis Sea	GC	1984	D	2,298	243' 10"	37' 03"	22' 01"
Arktis Sirius	GC	1989	D	2,671	261' 01"	44' 02"	21' 00"
Arktis Sky	GC	1987	D	2,671	261' 01"	44' 02"	21' 00"
Arktis Spring	GC	1993	D	4,110	290' 01"	49' 08"	24' 07"
Arktis Star	CO	1993	D	12,200	488' 10"	75' 11"	37' 01"
Arktis Sun	CO	1993	D	12,216	488' 10"	75' 11"	37' 01"
Arktis Trader	GC	1987	D	2,433	249' 07"	38' 03"	21' 00"
Arktis Venture	GC	1992	D	4,110	290' 01"	49' 08"	24' 07"
Arktis Vision	GC	1994	D	5,401	319' 07"	53' 08"	27' 11"
Ratana Sopa	CO	1993	D	12,216	487' 10"	75' 05"	37' 01"

IE-3 — EPIDAURUS S.A., PIRAEUS, GREECE
Phoenix M	BC	1976	D	26,874	580' 08"	75' 04"	47' 07"

IE-4 — ER DENIZCILIK SANAYI NAKLIYAT VE TICARET A.S., ISTANBUL, TURKEY
Balaban 1	BC	1979	D	24,747	562' 06"	75' 00"	46' 00"

IE-5 — ERSHIP S.A., MADRID, SPAIN
La Rabida	BC	1988	D	11,901	468' 10"	65' 10"	33' 04"
Manjoya	BC	1974	D	11,848	445' 02"	63' 05"	35' 09"
Milanos	BC	1975	D	11,849	445' 02"	63' 05"	35' 09"
Sac Flix	BC	1982	D	15,855	479' 09"	70' 03"	40' 00"
Sac Huelva	BC	1972	D	5,645	379' 02"	50' 07"	28' 08"
Sac Malaga	BC	1976	D	30,499	625' 06"	75' 00"	47' 10"

IE-6 — ESTONIAN SHIPPING CO., TALLINN, ESTONIA
Gustav Sule	BC	1986	D	24,150	605' 00"	75' 00"	46' 06"

Fleet No. & Name Vessel Name	Type of Vessel	Year Built	Type of Engine	Cargo Cap. or Gross*	Overal Length	Breadth	Depth or Draft*
Valga	RR	1979	D	4,600	458' 01"	63' 01"	43' 00"
Viljandi	RR	1978	D	4,600	458' 01"	63' 01"	43' 00"
IE-7 — EURASIA SHIPPING & MANAGEMENT CO. LTD., HONG KONG							
Ming Talent	CO	1986	D	18,155	539' 07"	75' 08"	44' 04"
IE-8 — EUROCARRIERS S.A., ATHENS, GREECE							
Anastasia	BC	1974	D	17,567	502' 04"	73' 00"	39' 04"
Golden Venture	BC	1971	D	16,887	486' 11"	74' 00"	35' 00"
Mitsa	BC	1973	D	20,815	514' 08"	74' 11"	44' 03"
Queen	BC	1968	D	19,297	512' 04"	74' 04"	42' 04"
IF-1 — FABRICIUS & CO. A/S, MARSTAL, DENMARK							
Laola	GC	1980	D	2,920	327' 06"	37' 05"	14' 02"
Sea Maid	GC	1984	D/W	1,632	237' 08"	36' 09"	22' 00"
IF-2 — FAFALIOS SHIPPING S.A., PIRAEUS, GREECE							
Irene	BC	1993	D	65,671	738' 02"	72' 02"	59' 01"
Nea Doxa	BC	1984	D	30,900	617' 03"	76' 00"	47' 07"
Nea Elpis	BC	1978	D	29,300	593' 03"	76' 00"	47' 07"
Nea Tyhi	BC	1978	D	29,300	593' 03"	76' 00"	47' 07"
IF-3 — FAIRMONT SHIPPING (CANADA) LTD., VANCOUVER, BRITISH COLUMBIA							
Ophelia	GC	1986	D	12,359	399' 07"	65' 08"	36' 02"
IF-4 — FAR-EASTERN SHIPPING CO., VLADIVOSTOK, RUSSIA							
Argut	BC	1990	D	3,600	311' 08"	51' 10"	25' 07"
Kapitan Milovzorov	BC	1975	D	14,204	497' 10"	69' 01"	38' 00"
IF-5 — FG-SHIPPING OY AB, HELSINKI, FINLAND							
Astrea	RR	1990	D	6,672	423' 07"	70' 01"	43' 06"
Finnfighter	GC	1978	D	14,931	522' 02"	70' 03"	41' 05"
Finnmaster	RR	1973	D	5,710	451' 02"	73' 04"	52' 10"
Finnpine	RR	1984	D	7,669	394' 05"	69' 00"	47' 07"
Kemira	BK	1981	D	8,250/19,323	369' 09"	57' 05"	34' 06"
Railship I	RR	1975	D	8,970	581' 04"	71' 00"	43' 00"
IF-6 —FRANCO COMPANIA NAVIERA S.A., ATHENS, GREECE							
Rhea	BC	1978	D	29,300	593' 10"	76' 00"	47' 07"
IF-7 — FREJA TANKERS A/S, COPENHAGEN, DENMARK							
Freja Nordic	TK	1980	D	85,178	406' 10"	60' 00"	35' 00"
Freja Scandic	TK	1981	D	77,442	405' 07"	59' 09"	32' 02"
IG-1 — GODBY SHIPPING A/B, GODBY, FINLAND							
Jenolin	GC	1992	D	5,314	345' 04"	55' 11"	27' 01"
Julia	GC	1993	D	5,314	345' 04"	55' 11"	27' 01"
Link Star	RR	1989	D	4,453	349' 05"	56' 05"	32' 06"
Mimer	RR	1990	D	4,232	355' 06"	57' 04"	42' 00"
Mini Star	RR	1988	D	4,452	352' 06"	56' 05"	32' 06"
Miniforest	GC	1972	D	2,545	290' 04"	42' 01"	26' 02"
IG-2 — GOOD FAITH SHIPPING CO. S.A., PIRAEUS, GREECE							
Amitie	AC	1970	D	20,139	485' 07"	74' 10"	44' 03"
Encouragement	GC	1974	D	19,920	537' 01"	75' 02"	47' 03"
Enterprise I	GC	1974	D	19,920	537' 01"	75' 02"	47' 03"
Epos	BC	1975	D	24,482	608' 04"	74' 10"	46' 04"
Euroreefer	GC	1982	D	3,945	302' 06"	53' 02"	22' 06"
Krissa	BC	1979	D	20,698	521' 00"	74' 03"	43' 08"
Mana	GC	1978	D	17,089	505' 03"	72' 11"	41' 03"
Ocean Grace	GC	1976	D	1,381	212' 01"	31' 06"	16' 01"
Ocean Lake	GC	1976	D	20,950	521' 08"	75' 06"	44' 03"
IG-3 — GOURDOMICHALIS MARITIME S.A., PIRAEUS, GREECE							
Kavo Alexandros	BC	1977	D	26,414	567' 09"	74' 10"	48' 05"
Kavo Flora	BC	1976	D	24,854	607' 07"	75' 00"	46' 05"
Kavo Mangalia	BC	1976	D	24,850	607' 07"	75' 00"	46' 05"
Kavo Sidero	BC	1976	D	26,671	592' 11"	75' 04"	47' 07"
Kavo Yerakas	BC	1981	D	25,854	585' 00"	75' 08"	45' 11"

Fleet No. & Name / Vessel Name	Type of Vessel	Year Built	Type of Engine	Cargo Cap. or Gross*	Overall Length	Breadth	Depth or Draft*
IG-4 — GREAT CIRCLE SHIPPING AGENCY LTD., BANGKOK, THAILAND							
Chada Naree	BC	1981	D	18,668	479' 03"	75' 01"	41' 04"
Fujisan Maru	BC	1976	D	16,883	481' 03"	75' 02"	40' 00"
Wana Naree	BC	1980	D	26,977	566' 00"	75' 11"	48' 05"
IG-5 — GRECOMAR SHIPPING AGENCY LTD., PIRAEUS, GREECE							
Anezina	BC	1977	D	12,010	422' 06"	64' 05"	34' 06"
Lamda	BC	1978	D	16,644	465' 08"	71' 07"	40' 00"
Sentosa	BC	1975	D	26,620	600' 06"	75' 00"	47' 01"
IG-6 — GREEN MANAGEMENT AS, MINDE, NORWAY							
Carmencita	GC	1992	D	6,000	357' 07"	59' 01"	32' 02"
Green Flake	GC	1976	D	1,284	277' 03"	54' 06"	23' 07"
Green Winter	GC	1989	D	6,526	409' 01"	58' 05"	32' 04"
Nomadic Patria	GC	1978	D	17,160	511' 09"	73' 11"	45' 10"
Nomadic Pollux	GC	1977	D	17,161	511' 10"	73' 11"	46' 00"
Nomadic Princess	GC	1977	D	26,991	564' 04"	75' 02"	47' 03"
IG-7 — GUNES TANKERCILIK A.S., ISTANBUL, TURKEY							
Sadan Kaptanoglu	BC	1977	D	26,854	568' 02"	74' 10"	48' 05"
IH-1 — H.C. GRUBE I/S, MARSTAL, DENMARK							
Jenclipper	GC	1976	D	710	163' 00"	27' 02"	18' 01"
IH-2 — H.S.S. HOLLAND SHIP SERVICE B.V., ROTTERDAM, NETHERLANDS							
Alidon	GC	1978	D	6,110	274' 07"	56' 01"	33' 03"
Alsydon	GC	1979	D	6,110	274' 07"	56' 01"	33' 03"
Andrealon	GC	1978	D	6,110	274' 07"	56' 01"	33' 03"
Anita I	GC	1979	D	7,800	321' 10"	56' 01"	33' 03"
Blue Topaz	GC	1975	D	1,473	214' 07"	35' 05"	16' 01"
Carola I	GC	1983	D	9,620	372' 04"	56' 02"	37' 01"
Claudia I	GC	1981	D	5,900	276' 03"	56' 01"	33' 04"
IH-3 — HANSEATIC SHIPPING CO. LTD., LIMASSOL, CYPRUS							
Jo Hassel	TK	1986	D	8,139	356' 00"	58' 05"	32' 02"
IH-4 — HAPAG-LLOYD A.G., HAMBURG, GERMANY							
c. Columbus	PA	1997	D	14,000*	472' 06"	70' 06"	18' 06"*
IH-5 — HARBOR SHIPPING & TRADING CO. S.A.							
Chios Harmony	BC	1977	D	29,337	594' 01"	75' 11"	47' 07"
IH-6 — HELIKON SHIPPING ENTERPRISES LTD., LONDON, ENGLAND							
Elikon	BC	1980	D	16,106	582' 00"	75' 02"	44' 04"
IH-7 — HELLENIC STAR SHIPPING CO. S.A., ATHENS, GREECE							
Faith Star	BC	1972	D	16,914	486' 11"	74' 00"	39' 00"
Glory Star	GC	1977	D	16,543	483' 05"	72' 07"	39' 01"
Winter Star	BC	1978	D	28,660	655' 06"	75' 09"	45' 11"
World Star	GC	1980	D	16,640	548' 11"	75' 02"	42' 08"
IH-8 — HERMAN BUSS GMBH & CIE., LEER, GERMANY							
Baltic Trader	CO	1995	D	6,928	381' 11"	64' 00"	30' 02"
Edda	GC	1985	D	2,812	322' 07"	44' 04"	23' 00"
IH-9 — HERMANN C. BOYE & CO., MARSTAL, DENMARK							
Andreas Boye	GC	1979	D	1,304	229' 00"	34' 03"	19' 09"
Anne Boye	GC	1985	D	1,680	251' 02"	36' 09"	22' 00"
Birthe Boye	GC	1983	D/W	1,630	237' 08"	36' 11"	22' 00"
Camilla Weber	GC	1967	D	715	163' 01"	27' 04"	18' 01"
Elisabeth Boye	GC	1990	D	2,650	251' 06"	36' 09"	17' 03"
Hermann C. Boye	GC	1980	D	1,525	229' 00"	34' 03"	19' 09"
Lette Lill	GC	1966	D	1,296	217' 00"	35' 00"	21' 00"
Lis Weber	GC	1978	D	1,050	196' 11"	34' 02"	19' 09"
IH-10 — HILAL SHIPPING TRADING & INDUSTRY CO., ISTANBUL, TURKEY							
Hilal II	BC	1981	D	25,845	585' 00"	75' 09"	45' 11"
IH-11 — HOLBUD SHIP MANAGEMENT LTD., LONDON, ENGLAND							
A. Alamdar	BC	1974	D	27,212	577' 05"	75' 02"	46' 03"
Al Aliyu	BC	1975	D	27,226	577' 05"	75' 02"	46' 03"
Al Baky	GC	1973	D	15,057	470' 06"	65' 00"	40' 06"

Fleet No. & Name Vessel Name	Type of Vessel	Year Built	Type of Engine	Cargo Cap. or Gross*	Overal Length	Breadth	Depth or Draft*
Al Hafizu	GC	1970	D	15,241	462' 09"	67' 06"	38' 06"
Ya Latif	BC	1977	D	27,751	579' 10"	75' 00"	48' 03"
Ya Rab	BC	1971	D	19,469	512' 06"	74' 04"	42' 04"
Ya Samadu	GC	1977	D	14,960	470' 06"	65' 01"	40' 06"
Zulfikar	GC	1970	D	15,177	466' 09"	65' 01"	40' 06"
Zuljenah	GC	1972	D	15,108	470' 06"	65' 01"	40' 06"

II-1 — INTERSCAN SCHIFFAHRTSGESELLSCHAFT MBH, HAMBURG, GERMANY

Jan Meeder	GC	1986	D	1,920	270' 07"	37' 02"	17' 09"
Paloma I	GC	1984	D	1,735	270' 06"	37' 01"	17' 09"
Pamela	GC	1985	D	1,738	273' 07"	37' 01"	17' 09"
Patria	GC	1995	D	3,519	270' 03"	41' 02"	23' 07"
Pia	GC	1987	D	2,850	270' 00"	41' 03"	23' 07"
Pinta	GC	1993	D	2,795	270' 00"	41' 02"	21' 08"
Pionier	GC	1989	D	2,801	270' 00"	41' 00"	23' 07"
Pirat	GC	1984	D	1,720	270' 06"	37' 01"	18' 01"
Pirol	GC	1981	D	1,540	270' 07"	37' 02"	17' 09"
Poseidon	GC	1984	D	1,717	270' 07"	37' 04"	17' 09"
Premiere	GC	1985	D	1,631	270' 06"	37' 02"	17' 09"
Provence	GC	1985	D	1,890	270' 06"	37' 01"	17' 09"
Sooneck	GC	1986	D	2,019	270' 07"	37' 01"	17' 09"

II-2 — IONIA MANAGEMENT S.A., PIRAEUS, GREECE

Albatros	TK	1972	D	42,526	339' 00"	53' 07"	26' 03"
Alkyon	TK	1981	D	126,610	487' 06"	73' 06"	38' 05"
Ostria I	TK	1974	D	15,857	290' 05"	42' 02"	21' 04"
Patriot	TK	1975	D				

IJ-1 — J. BEKKERS CO. B.V., ROTTERDAM, NETHERLANDS

Falcon Carrier	GC	1975	D	21,367	531' 08"	75' 02"	45' 11"

IJ-2 — J. G. GOUMAS (SHIPPING) CO. S.A., PIRAEUS, GREECE

Washington Rainbow II	BC	1984	D	22,828	515' 11"	75' 07"	44' 08"

IJ-3 — J. G. ROUSSOS SHIPPING S.A., ATHENS, GREECE

Pany R	BC	1978	D	22,174	528' 00"	75' 02"	44' 04"

IJ-4 — J. POULSEN SHIPPING A/S, KORSOR, DENMARK

Ocean Bird	GC	1991	D	4,222	309' 09"	50' 10"	25' 11"

IJ-5 — JAN WIND SHIPPING, NANSUM, NETHERLANDS

Lida	GC	1974	D	1,448	214' 03"	35' 05"	16' 01"

IJ-6 — JARDINE SHIP MANAGEMENT LTD., LONDON, ENGLAND

Golden Laker	BC	1996	D	30,838	607' 01"	77' 05"	48' 11"

IJ-7 — JAYSHIP LTD., LONDON, ENGLAND

Gur Maiden	GC	1976	D	16,251	491' 06"	69' 01"	40' 03"
Gur Master	GC	1978	D	15,767	492' 00"	69' 00"	40' 03"
M. Melody	GC	1978	D	15,765	491' 06"	69' 00"	40' 03"

IJ-8 — JEBSENS SHIP MANAGEMENT (BERGEN) LTD., BERGEN, NORWAY

Brunto	BC	1977	D	12,100	478' 07"	64' 04"	35' 00"
Fossnes	BC	1995	D	16,880	490' 03"	76' 00"	39' 08"
Furunes	BC	1979	D	12,274	441' 04"	68' 00"	37' 09"
General Cabal	BC	1976	D	12,100	477' 04"	64' 03"	34' 11"
Menominee	GC	1967	D	12,497	503' 03"	66' 07"	36' 09"

IJ-9 — JO TANKERS AS, BERGEN, NORWAY

Jo Adler	TK	1992	D	89,632	456' 00"	69' 09"	34' 03"
Jo Aspen	TK	1991	D	87,839	456' 00"	69' 09"	34' 03"
Jo Calluna	TK	1986	D	93,865	448' 02"	68' 00"	35' 02"
Jo Ebony	TK	1986	D	88,443	422' 11"	66' 04"	36' 01"
Jo Elm	TK	1981	D	202,026	569' 00"	75' 01"	46' 08"
Jo Hegg	TK	1985	D	51,200	356' 00"	58' 07"	32' 02"
Jo Maple	TK	1991	D	60,968	377' 11"	59' 05"	31' 02"
Jo Palm	TK	1991	D	60,968	377' 11"	59' 05"	31' 02"
Proof Gallant	TK	1980	D	23,763	293' 08"	46' 00"	27' 11"

IJ-10 — JOHN CHRISTENSEN JESPERGAARD, AEROSKOBING, DENMARK

Finlith	GC	1977	D	1,510	236' 01"	43' 00"	20' 08"

Fleet No. & Name Vessel Name	Type of Vessel	Year Built	Type of Engine	Cargo Cap. or Gross*	Overal Length	Breadth	Depth or Draft*
IJ-11 — JOINT-STOCK NORTHERN SHIPPING CO., ARKHANGELSK, RUSSIA							
Vladimir Timofeyev	BC	1973	D	14,204	493' 00"	69' 01"	38' 00"
IJ-12 — JUMBO SHIPPING CO. S.A., GENEVA, SWITZERLAND							
Daniella	HL	1989	D	7,600	322' 09"	68' 06"	37' 02"
Fairlift	HL	1990	D	7,780	329' 02"	68' 10"	43' 08"
Fairload	HL	1995	D	7,500	313' 11"	60' 03"	37' 02"
Fairmast	HL	1983	D	6,833	360' 07"	63' 07"	34' 05"
Gajah Borneo	HL	1978	D	5,076	327' 05"	59' 02"	32' 00"
Jumbo Challenger	HL	1983	D	6,375	360' 11"	63' 00"	34' 05"
Jumbo Spirit	HL	1995	D	5,200	313' 11"	60' 03"	37' 02"
Stellamare	HL	1982	D	2,850	289' 04"	51' 02"	24' 00"
Stellanova	HL	1996	D	5,198	313' 08"	60' 03"	37' 02"
Stellaprima	GC	1991	D	7,600	329' 02"	68' 10"	43' 08"
IK-1 — KNUTSEN O.A.S. SHIPPING A/S, HAUGESUND, NORWAY							
Ellen Knutsen	TK	1992	D	105,193	464' 03"	75' 07"	38' 09"
Helene Knutsen	TK	1992	D	114,577	464' 08"	75' 07"	39' 10"
Hilda Knutsen	TK	1989	D	112,275	464' 08"	75' 07"	39' 10"
Pascale Knutsen	TK	1993	D	112,275	464' 08"	75' 07"	38' 09"
Sidsel Knutsen	TK	1993	D	163,463	533' 02"	75' 05"	48' 07"
Synnove Knutsen	TK	1992	D	105,193	464' 03"	75' 07"	38' 09"
Torill Knutsen	TK	1990	D	112,275	464' 08"	75' 07"	38' 09"
Turid Knutsen	TK	1993	D	163,463	533' 03"	75' 07"	48' 07"
IL-1 — LATVIAN SHIPPING CO., RIGA, LATVIA							
Juris Avots	RR	1983	D	5,500	501' 00"	63' 01"	43' 00"
IL-2 — LINEAS ECOA S.A., MADRID, SPAIN							
Misty	GC	1983	D	8,150	392' 01"	60' 10"	31' 03"
IL-3 — LINK LINE LTD., PIRAEUS, GREECE							
Aktis	GC	1976	D	18,627	532' 02"	75' 02"	44' 00"
Beluga	BC	1977	D	23,725	585' 02"	74' 04"	44' 02"
Ochimos	GC	1976	D	17,000	521' 11"	75' 00"	43' 04"
Phaethon	GC	1977	D	24,300	567' 07"	75' 00"	47' 11"
IL-4 — LITHUANIAN SHIPPING CO., KLAIPEDA, LITHUANIA							
Kapitonas A. Lucka	BC	1980	D	14,550	479' 08"	67' 09"	42' 04"
Kapitonas Andzejauskas	BC	1978	D	14,550	479' 08"	67' 09"	42' 04"
Kapitonas Chromcov	BC	1976	D	14,550	479' 08"	67' 09"	42' 04"
Kapitonas Daugela	BC	1975	D	14,631	479' 08"	67' 09"	42' 04"
Kapitonas Daugirdas	BC	1976	D	14,631	479' 08"	67' 09"	42' 04"
Kapitonas Domeika	BC	1979	D	14,550	479' 08"	67' 09"	42' 04"
Kapitonas Kaminskas	BC	1978	D	14,550	479' 08"	67' 09"	42' 04"
Kapitonas Marcinkus	BC	1977	D	14,550	479' 08"	67' 09"	42' 04"
Kapitonas Serafinas	BC	1980	D	14,550	479' 08"	67' 09"	42' 04"
Kapitonas Sevcenko	BC	1977	D	14,550	479' 08"	67' 09"	42' 04"
Kapitonas Stulpinas	BC	1981	D	14,550	479' 08"	67' 09"	42' 04"
IM-1 — M. ODYSSEOS SHIPMANAGEMENT LTD., NICOSIA, CYPRUS							
Hellenic Confidence	BC	1977	D	17,616	479' 00"	73' 04"	40' 10"
Tropic Confidence	BC	1986	D	17,832	473' 03"	75' 06"	40' 00"
IM-2 — M. T. M. SHIP MANAGEMENT PTE. LTD., SINGAPORE, MALAYSIA							
Chembulk Fortitude	TK	1989	D	104,036	432' 01"	66' 11"	36' 09"
Chembulk Singapore	TK	1989	D	104,036	433' 01"	66' 11"	36' 09"
Encounter	TK	1983	D	89,386	413' 05"	65' 09"	36' 09"
Entity	TK	1985	D	89,474	404' 06"	65' 09"	36' 09"
Equity	TK	1985	D	89,386	404' 06"	65' 08"	36' 09"
Espoir	TK	1979	D	105,193	438' 00"	72' 03"	39' 01"
Kwan Siu	TK	1976	D	16,203	264' 10"	40' 01"	21' 02"
Pacific Star	TK	1984	D	38,922	351' 01"	52' 07"	26' 11"
Po Siu	TK	1982	D	85,191	416' 08"	65' 09"	36' 09"
IM-3 — MARINE MANAGEMENT SERVICES M.C., PIRAEUS, GREECE							
Gonio	TK	1984	D	126,377	496' 05"	73' 07"	39' 10"
Kobuleti	TK	1985	D	126,377	496' 05"	73' 07"	39' 11"
IM-4 — MARINE MANAGERS LTD., PIRAEUS, GREECE							
Trident Mariner	BC	1984	D	28,503	590' 03"	75' 04"	47' 07"

Federal Agno upbound in the St. Clair River near St. Clair, MI, 11 December, 1998. *(John C. Meyland)*

Fleet No. & Name Vessel Name	Type of Vessel	Year Built	Type of Engine	Cargo Cap. or Gross*	Overal Length	Breadth	Depth or Draft*
IM-5 — MARMARAS NAVIGATION LTD., PIRAEUS, GREECE							
Kydonia	BC	1977	D	18,737	479' 03"	75' 00"	41' 04"
Kyzikos	BC	1978	D	19,374	496' 01"	75' 01"	42' 08"
Proussa	BC	1979	D	18,750	504' 07"	75' 00"	41' 01"
Redestos	GC	1977	D	15,180	462' 07"	67' 01"	38' 06"
IM-6 — MARTI SHIPPING & TRADING CO., INC., ISTANBUL, TURKEY							
Tevfik Kaptan I	GC	1977	D	1,036	212' 05"	28' 03"	13' 02"
Zafer Tomba	GC	1970	D	979	189' 01"	31' 00"	13' 05"
IM-7 — MEDITERRANEA DI NAVIGAZIONE S.R.L., RAVENNA, ITALY							
Barbarossa	TK	1982	D	163,538	517' 01"	75' 04"	43' 00"
Caterina Tomacelli	TK	1967	D	18,115	274' 00"	43' 11"	16' 05"
Fradiavolo	TK	1973	D	31,324	333' 10"	41' 11"	21' 04"
Longobarda	TK	1992	D		411' 01"	62' 04"	30' 00"
Metauro	TK	1991	D	29,972	323' 06"	49' 03"	23' 00"
IM-8 — MEDSTAR SHIPMANAGEMENT LTD., LIMASSOL, CYPRUS							
Serenade	BC	1972	D	6,341	332' 07"	52' 07"	30' 03"
IM-9 — METRON SHIPPING & AGENCIES S.A., PIRAEUS, GREECE							
Pontokratis	BC	1981	D	28,738	590' 02"	75' 11"	47' 07"
Pontoporos	BC	1984	D	29,155	590' 02"	75' 11"	47' 07"
IM-10 — METZ CONTAINER LINE S.A.L., BEIRUT, LEBANON							
Carl Metz	GC	1980	D	7,796	417' 05"	58' 11"	32' 00"
Celine M	GC	1970	D	1,521	257' 05"	38' 11"	20' 05"
Metz Beirut	GC	1967	D	10,150	492' 07"	66' 05"	38' 05"
Metz Belgica	GC	1967	D	10,080	493' 01"	66' 05"	38' 06"
Metz Italia	GC	1967	D	10,080	493' 01"	66' 05"	38' 06"
Old Fox	GC	1959	D	1,262	235' 11"	32' 07"	17' 03"
Pablo Metz	CO	1970	D	4,250	375' 08"	68' 03"	26' 11"
Pauline Metz	GC	1970	D	3,030	313' 08"	52' 10"	25' 07"
Peter Metz	CO	1979	D	7,285	414' 03"	59' 03"	24' 06"
IM-11 — MIDMED SHIPPING LTD., BIRKIRKARA, MALTA							
Anna John	GC	1972	D	15,000	470' 06"	65' 01"	40' 06"
IM-12 — MILBROS SHIPPING AS, LYSAKER, NORWAY							
Jakov Sverdlov	TK	1989	D	20,502	496' 01"	73' 05"	39' 10"
Kapitan Rudnev	TK	1988	D	20,502	496' 01"	73' 05"	41' 01"
IM-13 — MURMANSK SHIPPING CO., MURMANSK, RUSSIA							
Admiral Ushakov	BC	1979	D	19,885	531' 07"	75' 01"	44' 05"
Aleksandr Nevskiy	BC	1978	D	19,590	532' 02"	75' 02"	44' 05"
Dmitriy Donskoy	BC	1977	D	19,885	531' 10"	75' 02"	44' 05"
Dmitriy Pozharskiy	BC	1977	D	19,885	531' 10"	75' 02"	44' 05"
Fastov	GC	1979	D	7,810	399' 08"	57' 08"	32' 06"
Ivan Bogun	BC	1981	D	19,885	531' 10"	75' 02"	44' 05"
Ivan Susanin	BC	1981	D	19,885	531' 10"	75' 02"	44' 05"
Kapitan Bochek	BC	1982	D	19,253	531' 10"	75' 02"	44' 05"
Kapitan Chukhchin	BC	1981	D	19,240	531' 10"	75' 02"	44' 05"
Kapitan Kudley	BC	1983	D	19,252	531' 10"	75' 02"	44' 05"
Mikhail Kutuzov	BC	1979	D	19,590	531' 10"	75' 01"	44' 05"
Pyotr Velikiy	BC	1978	D	19,885	531' 10"	75' 02"	44' 05"
Stepan Razin	BC	1980	D	19,590	531' 09"	75' 01"	44' 05"
Tonya Bondarchuk	GC	1972	D	4,687	346' 07"	51' 04"	26' 03"
Yuriy Dolgorukiy	BC	1980	D	19,885	532' 02"	75' 02"	44' 05"
IN-1 — N. MICHALOS & SONS CO. LTD., PIRAEUS, GREECE							
Akmi	BC	1977	D	26,874	580' 09"	75' 04"	47' 07"
Evmar	BC	1976	D	29,212	593' 02"	76' 00"	47' 07"
IN-2 — NARVAL SHIPPING CORP., PIRAEUS, GREECE							
Cay	BC	1976	D	18,726	507' 09"	73' 11"	41' 01"
Lyra	BC	1976	D	27,140	579' 10"	75' 00"	46' 04"
IN-3 — NAUTILUS CHARTERING N.V., KALMTHOUT, BELGIUM							
Dennis Danielson	GC	1978	D	2,537	261' 10"	43' 00"	24' 08"
Ulla Danielsen	GC	1978	D	2,534			

Fleet No. & Name Vessel Name	Type of Vessel	Year Built	Type of Engine	Cargo Cap. or Gross*	Overal Length	Breadth	Depth or Draft*
IN-4 — NAVARONE S.A., PIRAEUS, GREECE							
Mallard	GC	1977	D	18,791	479' 03"	75' 01"	41' 05"
Seapearl II	BC	1974	D	26,641	580' 09"	75' 03"	47' 06"
Tim Buck	BC	1983	D	19,240	531' 10"	75' 02"	44' 04"
IN-6 — NAVIERA POSEIDON, HAVANA, CUBA							
South Islands	GC	1986	D	15,147	472' 05"	67' 02"	38' 07"
IN-6 — NAVIGATION MARITIME BULGARE LTD., VARNA, BULGARIA							
Balkan	BC	1975	D	25,714	607' 08"	74' 10"	46' 05"
Kamenitza	BC	1980	D	24,150	605' 08"	75' 00"	46' 05"
Kapitan Georgi Georgiev	BC	1980	D	24,150	605' 08"	75' 00"	46' 05"
Malyovitza	BC	1983	D	24,456	605' 00"	75' 05"	46' 06"
Milin Kamak	BC	1979	D	24,285	607' 07"	75' 00"	46' 05"
Okoltchitza	BC	1982	D	24,148	605' 08"	75' 05"	46' 06"
Perelik	BC	1998	D	13,971	437' 10"		
Shipka	BC	1979	D	24,285	607' 07"	75' 00"	46' 05"
IN-7 — NAVROM S.A., CONSTANTZA, ROMANIA							
Hagieni	GC	1982	D	8,750	428' 10"	58' 11"	33' 06"
Razboieni	GC	1982	D	15,555	520' 08"	74' 10"	43' 04"
Zarnesti	GC	1983	D	4,620	347' 10"	48' 08"	27' 11"
IN-8 — NESTE OY, ESPOO, FINLAND							
Kihu	TK	1984	D	160,507	527' 11"	76' 00"	46' 08"
Lunni	TK	1976	D	108,231	539' 06"	72' 09"	39' 04"
Melkki	TK	1982	D	82,417	461' 11"	69' 08"	32' 04"
Rankki	TK	1982	D	82,417	461' 11"	69' 08"	32' 04"
Sirri	TK	1981	D	47,502	351' 01"	59' 00"	30' 01"
Sotka	TK	1976	D	101,991	539' 07"	73' 00"	39' 05"
Tavi	TK	1985	D	160,507	527' 11"	76' 00"	58' 05"
Tiira	TK	1977	D	108,231	539' 07"	72' 10"	39' 05"
Uikku	TK	1977	D	108,231	539' 07"	73' 00"	39' 05"
Vikla	TK	1982	D	53,490	437' 04"	63' 02"	31' 03"
IN-9 — NISSEN KAIUN K.K., EHIME, JAPAN							
Rubin Eagle	BC	1995	D	18,315	447' 10"	74' 10"	40' 00"
Rubin Falcon	BC	1996	D	18,000	486' 01"	74' 10"	40' 00"
Rubin Hawk	BC	1995	D	18,233	486' 01"	74' 10"	40' 00"
IN-10 — NOMADIC MANAGEMENT AS, MINDE, NORWAY							
Green Freesia	GC	1978	D	4,348	353' 03"	48' 04"	25' 08"
Green Frost	GC	1985	D	2,979	281' 11"	52' 06"	35' 01"
Green Ice	GC	1985	D	2,900	281' 11"	52' 06"	35' 01"
Green Lily	GC	1978	D	4,348	353' 03"	48' 04"	25' 08"
Green Rose	GC	1979	D	4,348	353' 03"	48' 04"	25' 08"
Green Tulip	GC	1977	D	4,352	353' 03"	48' 04"	25' 08"
Green Violet	GC	1978	D	4,348	353' 03"	48' 04"	25' 08"
Nomadic Princess	BC	1978	D	26,991	564' 04"	75' 02"	47' 03"
IN-11 — NORDANE SHIPPING A/S, SVENDBORG, DENMARK							
Ardal	GC	1978	D	1,050	196' 11"	34' 02"	19' 09"
Gerda Vesta	GC	1983	D	2,610	243' 03"	36' 10"	22' 00"
Hanne Mette	GC	1978	D	850	176' 07"	31' 06"	18' 05"
Helle Stevns	GC	1980	D	7,909	349' 08"	54' 03"	29' 06"
Latania	GC	1966	D	3,300	270' 08"	42' 09"	25' 05"
Stevns Bulk	GC	1975	D	3,320	246' 01"	43' 08"	25' 04"
Stevns Pearl	GC	1984	D	5,900	327' 09"	58' 06"	29' 07"
Stevns Sea	GC	1972	D	3,610	290' 04"	45' 04"	26' 03"
Stevns Trader	GC	1970	D	2,245	290' 04"	45' 05"	26' 03"
IN-12 — NORTHERN SHIPPING CO., ARKHANGELSK, RUSSIA							
Kapitan Alekseyev	GC	1971	D	16,618	556' 05"	71' 07"	43' 05"
Kapitan Glazachev	BC	1976	D	14,200	497' 10"	69' 01"	38' 00"
Kapitan Zamyatin	BC	1976	D	14,200	497' 10"	69' 01"	38' 00"
Nikolay Novikov	BC	1973	D	13,955	492' 11"	69' 01"	38' 00"
Petr Strelkov	BC	1977	D	14,200	497' 10"	69' 01"	38' 00"
Vasiliy Musinskiy	BC	1974	D	14,200	497' 10"	69' 01"	38' 00"

Fleet No. & Name Vessel Name	Type of Vessel	Year Built	Type of Engine	Cargo Cap. or Gross*	Overal Length	Breadth	Depth or Draft*
IN-13 — NOVOROSSIYSK SHIPPING CO., NOVOROSSIYSK, RUSSIA							
Boris Livanov	BC	1986	D	23,920	605' 09"	75' 00"	46' 05"
Sergey Lemeshev	BC	1983	D	24,110	605' 08"	74' 10"	46' 05"
Vladimir Vysotskiy	TK	1988	D	128,315	497' 01"	73' 07"	39' 10"
IN-14 — NST CHALLENGE MARITIME S.A., PANAMA CITY, PANAMA							
NST Challenge	BC	1984	D	29,192	593' 03"	75' 10"	47' 07"
IO-1 — O. T. TONNEVOLD AS, GRIMSTAD, NORWAY							
Thorhild	GC	1983	D	6,666	452' 02"	61' 02"	33' 08"
Thornburg	GC	1981	D	4,447	332' 04"	56' 02"	29' 07"
Thorndale	GC	1981	D	4,380	332' 04"	55' 11"	29' 06"
Thorunn	GC	1982	D	6,370	477' 06"	58' 06"	34' 05"
IO-2 — OCEANBULK MARITIME S.A., ATHENS, GREECE							
Aurora	GC	1976	D	15,513	491' 05"	69' 00"	40' 03"
Etoile	GC	1990	D	17,430	520' 10"	75' 00"	44' 00"
Strange Attractor	BC	1978	D	28,873	593' 02"	76' 00"	47' 07"
IO-3 — OLYMPIC SHIPPING AND MANAGEMENT S.A., MONTE CARLO, MONACO							
Calliroe Patronicola	BC	1985	D	29,608	599' 09"	75' 11"	48' 07"
Olympic Melody	BC	1984	D	29,640	599' 09"	75' 11"	48' 07"
Olympic Mentor	BC	1984	D	29,693	599' 09"	75' 11"	48' 07"
Olympic Merit	BC	1985	D	29,611	599' 09"	75' 11"	48' 07"
Olympic Miracle	BC	1984	D	29,670	599' 09"	75' 11"	48' 07"
IO-4 — ORION SCHIFFAHRTS-GESELLSCHAFT , HAMBURG, GERMANY							
Baltia	BC	1986	D	12,337	399' 07"	65' 07"	36' 01"
Caro	BC	1984	D	19,429	485' 07"	75' 09"	41' 08"
Concordia	GC	1985	D	8,881	378' 00"	61' 01"	32' 02"
Crio	BC	1984	D	19,483	485' 07"	75' 09"	41' 08"
Fortuna	GC	1984	D	8,875	378' 00"	61' 01"	32' 02"
Gotia	GC	1985	D	12,349	399' 07"	65' 07"	36' 01"
Hero	BC	1984	D	19,505	485' 11"	75' 10"	41' 08"
Meta	BC	1987	D	18,612	477' 04"	75' 11"	40' 08"
Patria	GC	1985	D	8,880	377' 11"	61' 01"	32' 02"
Rugia	BC	1986	D	12,342	399' 07"	65' 08"	36' 02"
IP-1 — PACC SHIP MANAGERS PTE. LTD., SINGAPORE, MALAYSIA							
Alam Jaya	GC	1996	D	2,500	226' 04"	59' 00"	15' 08"
Alam Karang	TK	1985	D	51,621	377' 04"	58' 05"	28' 11"
Alam Kembong	TK	1985	D	63,736	383' 06"	59' 09"	32' 02"
Alam Kerisi	TK	1982	D	57,867	372' 08"	57' 05"	31' 06"
Alam Pari	TK	1981	D	27,191	308' 06"	47' 04"	24' 08"
Alam Sejahtera	BC	1985	D	29,692	599' 09"	75' 10"	48' 07"
Alam Sempurna	BC	1984	D	28,094	584' 08"	75' 11"	48' 05"
Alam Senang	BC	1984	D	28,098	584' 08"	75' 11"	48' 05"
Alam Tabah	GC	1977	D	15,098	470' 06"	65' 02"	40' 06"
Alam Talang	GC	1985	D	17,322	477' 05"	69' 00"	43' 01"
Alam Tangkas	GC	1979	D	15,097	470' 06"	65' 01"	40' 06"
Alam Tegas	GC	1979	D	17,187	477' 05"	69' 00"	43' 00"
Alam Teguh	GC	1980	D	17,169	477' 06"	69' 00"	43' 00"
Alam Teladan	GC	1979	D	17,168	477' 04"	69' 01"	43' 00"
Alam Tenega	GC	1977	D	15,097	470' 06"	65' 01"	40' 06"
Alam Tenggiri	GC	1985	D	17,322	477' 05"	69' 00"	43' 01"
Alam Tenteram	BC	1979	D	16,902	477' 04"	69' 00"	43' 00"
Ikan Selar	BC	1978	D	21,652	539' 02"	75' 02"	44' 06"
Ikan Selayang	BC	1981	D	29,514	590' 01"	76' 00"	47' 07"
Ikan Sepat	BC	1984	D	28,503	590' 03"	75' 04"	47' 07"
Ikan Tamban	GC	1980	D	17,159	477' 05"	69' 00"	43' 00"
Ikan Tanda	GC	1979	D	16,916	477' 05"	69' 00"	43' 00"
Ulloa	BC	1983	D	28,126	584' 08"	75' 11"	48' 05"
Union	BC	1984	D	28,166	584' 08"	75' 11"	48' 05"
United	BC	1984	D	27,223	584' 08"	75' 11"	48' 05"
IP-2 — PACIFIC BASIN AGENCIES LTD., HONG KONG							
Nordic Moor	BC	1981	D	29,002	589' 11"	76' 01"	47' 07"
IP-3 — PAN OCEAN SHIPPING CO. LTD., SEOUL, SOUTH KOREA							
Pan Hope	BC	1977	D	22,289	539' 02"	75' 03"	44' 06"

Fleet No. & Name Vessel Name	Type of Vessel	Year Built	Type of Engine	Cargo Cap. or Gross*	Overal Length	Breadth	Depth or Draft*
Pan Noble	BC	1977	D	27,307	580' 10"	75' 02"	46' 03"
Pan Voyager	BC	1985	D	29,432	589' 11"	75' 09"	47' 07"
Sammi Aurora	BC	1978	D	23,101	559' 08"	75' 00"	45' 00"
Sammi Herald	BC	1978	D	24,231	559' 05"	75' 00"	45' 11"

IP-4 — PERGAMOS SHIPPING CO. S.A., PIRAEUS, GREECE

Adventure	GC	1971	D	15,178	466' 09"	65' 00"	40' 06"
Astron	GC	1976	D	14,800	462' 06"	67' 04"	38' 06"

IP-5 — PETER DOHLE SCHIFFAHRTS-KG (GMBH & CO.), HAMBURG, GERMANY

Alexandria	GC	1994	D	6,918	351' 04"	59' 11"	26' 03"

IP-6 — PINAT GIDA SANAYI VE TICARET A.S., ISTANBUL, TURKEY

Ihsan	GC	1993	D	10,560	420' 05"	59' 01"	34' 05"
Kevser Gunes	GC	1994	D	11,307	441' 01"	59' 01"	34' 09"
Maersk Manila	CO	1996	D	12,630	460' 11"	68' 03"	38' 05"
Nimet	GC	1991	D	7,416	376' 04"	54' 02"	30' 06"
Suat Ulusoy	GC	1995	D	11,366	441' 01"	59' 01"	34' 09"

IP-7 — POLCLIP (LUXEMBOURG) S.A., LUXEMBOURG, LUXEMBOURG

Clipper Eagle	BC	1994	D	16,900	490' 04"	76' 00"	39' 08"
Clipper Falcon	BC	1994	D	16,900	490' 04"	76' 00"	39' 08"

IP-8 — POLISH STEAMSHIP CO., SZCZECIN, POLAND

Odranes	BC	1992	D	13,790	471' 05"	68' 08"	37' 02"
Pomorze Zachodnie	BC	1985	D	26,696	591' 04"	75' 11"	45' 08"
Wartanes	BC	1992	D	13,790	471' 05"	68' 08"	37' 02"
Wislanes	BC	1992	D	13,770	471' 05"	68' 08"	37' 02"
Ziemia Chelminska	BC	1984	D	26,700	591' 04"	75' 11"	45' 08"
Ziemia Gnieznienska	BC	1985	D	26,696	591' 04"	75' 11"	45' 08"
Ziemia Suwalska	BC	1984	D	26,706	591' 04"	75' 11"	45' 08"
Ziemia Tarnowska	BC	1985	D	26,700	591' 04"	75' 11"	45' 08"
Ziemia Zamojska	BC	1984	D	26,600	591' 04"	75' 11"	45' 08"

IP-9 — PREKOOKEANSKA PLOVIDBA, BAR, YUGOSLAVIA

Obod	GC	1988	D	18,235	543' 00"	75' 07"	44' 00"

IP-10 — PRIMAVERA MONTANA S.A., EHIME, JAPAN

Spring Laker	BC	1996	D	30,855	577' 05"	77' 05"	48' 11"
Spring Ocean	BC	1986	D	11,769	382' 00"	75' 05"	44' 00"

IP-11 — PRIME ORIENT SHIPPING S.A., PANAMA CITY, PANAMA

Luna Verde	BC	1986	D	26,706	591' 06"	75' 10"	48' 07"

IP-12 — PROJECT SHIPPING, INC., PIRAEUS, GREECE

Elena G	GC	1978	D	16,436	475' 10"	71' 03"	29' 06"
Kathrin	GC	1981	D	11,301	392' 01"	65' 09"	34' 09"
Marinik G	BC	1972	D	25,635	591' 06"	75' 02"	45' 01"
Silvia	GC	1981	D	11,274	392' 01"	65' 09"	33' 00"

IP-13 — PROSPERITY BAY SHIPPING CO. LTD., PIRAEUS, GREECE

Anna	BC	1976	D	26,702	600' 06"	74' 08"	47' 01"

IP-14 — PYRSOS MANAGING CO., PIRAEUS, GREECE

Anax	BC	1979	D	30,084	622' 00"	74' 10"	49' 10"
Anemi	BC	1978	D	14,840	469' 02"	65' 00"	40' 06"
Anemone	GC	1979	D	17,179	477' 04"	68' 11"	43' 00"
Audacious	BC	1977	D	27,560	600' 06"	74' 08"	43' 09"
Clipper Amaryllis	GC	1983	D	23,000	539' 02"	75' 02"	46' 05"
Clipper Amethyst	GC	1978	D	23,536	539' 02"	75' 00"	46' 05"
Clipper Antares	BC	1986	D	17,777	481' 05"	74' 10"	40' 01"
Eagle Quick	GC	1990	D	3,168	299' 03"	49' 05'	24' 11"
Industrial Hope	GC	1990	D	3,194	299' 04"	49' 03"	25' 00"
Industrial Spirit	GC	1991	D	3,194	299' 01"	49' 07"	24' 11"

IR-1 — REDERI DONSOTANK A/B, DONSO, SWEDEN

Credo	GC	1978	D	10,620	449' 02"	56' 00"	36' 01"
Madzy	BC	1976	D	11,065	470' 02"	61' 00"	33' 04"
Navigo	TK	1992	D	123,471	466' 10"	72' 06"	42' 00"

IR-2 — REEDEREI "NORD" KLAUS E. OLDENDORFF LTD., LIMASSOL, CYPRUS

San Marino	TK	1988	D	71,189	414' 10"	68' 07"	32' 04"

Fleet No. & Name Vessel Name	Type of Vessel	Year Built	Type of Engine	Cargo Cap. or Gross*	Overall Length	Breadth	Depth or Draft*
IR-3 — REEDEREI HANS-PETER ECKHOFF GMBH CO. HG, HOLLENSTEDT, GERMANY							
Kamilla	GC	1985	D	2,785	322' 06"	44' 07"	23' 00"
IR-4 — REGAL AGENCIES CORP., PIRAEUS, GREECE							
Dali	GC	1977	D	18,784	479' 03"	75' 00"	41' 04"
Kent Forest	BC	1978	D	14,931	522' 02"	69' 02"	41' 04"
IR-5 — RIGEL SCHIFFAHRTS GMBH, BREMEN, GERMANY							
Alsterstern	TK	1994	D	125,327	529' 05"	75' 05"	38' 05"
Donaustern	TK	1995	D	123,371	529' 05"	75' 05"	38' 05"
Havelstern	TK	1994	D	126,264	529' 05"	75' 05"	38' 05"
Isarstern	TK	1995	D	123,830	529' 05"	75' 05"	38' 05"
Ledastern	TK	1993	D	76,737	405' 11"	58' 01"	34' 09"
Oderstern	TK	1992	D	65,415	360' 00"	58' 02"	34' 09"
Rheinstern	TK	1993	D	127,937	529' 05"	75' 05"	38' 05"
Travestern	TK	1993	D	123,346	529' 05"	75' 05"	38' 05"
Weserstern	TK	1992	D	65,415	360' 00"	58' 02"	34' 09"
IS-1 — S. FRANGOULIS (SHIP MANAGEMENT) LTD., PIRAEUS, GREECE							
Stamon	BC	1977	D	17,509	485' 11"	71' 04"	40' 00"
IS-2 — SAMRAT ASIA MARITIME LTD., MUMBAI, INDIA							
Samrat Ajaya	GC	1995	D	2,873	269' 00"	46' 07"	16' 05"
Samrat Rucaka	BC	1982	D	28,076	646' 10"	75' 10"	46' 11"
Samrat Vijaya	GC	1995	D	2,873	269' 00"	46' 07"	16' 05"
IS-3 — SANDFORD SHIP MANAGEMENT LTD., VENTNOR, ISLE OF WIGHT							
Clipper Aquamarine	BC	1978	D	23,573	539' 02"	75' 00"	46' 06"
IS-4 — SARK VENUS DENIZCILIK A/S, ISTANBUL, TURKEY							
Snowrose	BC	1979	D	24,326	565' 03"	75' 03"	44' 08"
IS-5 — SCANSCOT SHIPPING SERVICES (DEUTSCHLAND) GMBH, HAMBURG, GERMANY							
Scan Polaris	HL	1996	D	4,800	331' 00"	61' 00"	31' 10"
IS-6 — SEAARLAND SHIPPING MANAGEMENT GMBH, VILLACH, AUSTRIA							
Allegra	TK	1986	D	179,112	536' 07"	75' 06"	37' 09"
Conny	TK	1984	D	176,879	536' 07"	75' 06"	37' 09"
Giacinta	TK	1984	D	176,879	536' 07"	75' 06"	37' 09"
Grazia	TK	1987	D	176,879	536' 07"	75' 06"	37' 09"
Peonia	BC	1983	D	27,995	647' 08"	75' 10"	46' 11"
IS-7 — SEAGER CORP., ATHENS, GREECE							
Ithaki	BC	1977	D	27,540	600' 06"	74' 08"	47' 01"
IS-8 — SEA-PRAXIS MARITIME CO. LTD., NICOSIA, CYPRUS							
Apollo C	GC	1983	D	12,665	492' 08"	69' 01"	33' 00"
IS-9 — SEASCOT SHIPTRADING LTD., GLASGOW, SCOTLAND							
Nyanza	GC	1978	D	16,923	497' 10"	71' 08"	40' 09"
IS-10 — SEASTAR NAVIGATION CO. LTD., ATHENS, GREECE							
Periandros	BC	1974	D	26,784	579' 10"	75' 01"	46' 03"
Polydefkis	BC	1976	D	30,244	621' 06"	75' 00"	47' 11"
Polykratis	BC	1976	D	21,148	520' 00"	75' 02"	44' 08"
Praxitelis	BC	1976	D	30,242	621' 06"	75' 00"	47' 11"
IS-11 — SEAWAYS SHIPPING ENTERPRISES LTD., PIRAEUS, GREECE							
Triena	GC	1991	D	16,979	520' 10"	75' 00"	44' 00"
IS-12 — SHERIMAR MANAGEMENT CO. LTD., ATHENS, GREECE							
A. M. Spiridon	GC	1968	D	3,780	309' 02"	47' 11"	26' 00"
Blue Bay	BC	1972	D	22,302	522' 04"	75' 02"	42' 11"
Blue Breeze	BC	1975	D	16,549	465' 09"	71' 07"	40' 00"
Blue Lagoon	GC	1979	D	5,500	417' 11"	59' 00"	33' 09"
Blue Marine	GC	1974	D	15,107	454' 02"	70' 04"	39' 05"
Blue Moon	GC	1975	D	11,612	404' 06"	67' 05"	34' 09"
Noor	GC	1967	D	5,912	353' 05"	50' 09"	27' 07"
S. M. Spiridon	GC	1967	D	2,730	287' 05"	42' 10"	23' 00"
IS-13 — SHUNZAN KAIUN CO. LTD., EHIME, JAPAN							
Spring Ocean	BC	1986	D	11,769	382' 00"	75' 06"	44' 00"
Spring Trader	RR	1989	D	8,242	377' 04"	63' 00"	26' 03"

Fleet No. & Name Vessel Name	Type of Vessel	Year Built	Type of Engine	Cargo Cap. or Gross*	Overall Length	Breadth	Depth or Draft*
IS-14 — SIDEMAR SERVIZI ACCESSORI S.P.A., GENOA, ITALY							
Cygnus	BC	1987	D	28,500	610' 03"	75' 11"	46' 11"
Galassia	BC	1987	D	29,369	610' 03"	75' 11"	46' 11"
Gemini	BC	1986	D	28,500	610' 03"	75' 11"	46' 11"
Sagittarius	BC	1987	D	29,365	610' 03"	75' 10"	46' 11"
Sideracrux	GC	1983	D	7,988	328' 09"	57' 10"	29' 07"
Sidercastor	GC	1982	D	7,988	328' 09"	57' 10"	29' 07"
Siderpollux	GC	1982	D	8,010	328' 09"	57' 10"	29' 07"
IS-15 — SILVER SHIPPING LTD., KINGSTON, ST. VINCENT & THE GRENADINES							
Concorde	TK	1975	D	24,518	319' 11"	52' 06"	24' 11"
IS-16 — SLOBODNA PLOVIDBA, SIBENIK, CROATIA							
Bilice	BC	1976	D	19,056	319' 11"	74' 11"	41' 01"
Biograd	GC	1988	D	8,490	392' 01"	60' 10"	31' 03"
Dinara	BC	1974	D	26,962	599' 04"	73' 09"	46' 07"
Drnis	GC	1972	D	7,702	404' 08"	55' 10"	29' 06"
Humbolt Current	GC	1981	D	24,432	634' 04"	75' 04"	46' 05"
Primosten	BC	1972	D	7,580	404' 05"	56' 00"	29' 07"
Prvic	GC	1973	D	6,450	370' 02"	54' 00"	27' 07"
Rossel Current	GC	1981	D	24,432	634' 04"	75' 04"	46' 05"
Skradin	BC	1976	D	19,055	506' 03"	74' 10"	41' 01"
Zlarin	GC	1985	D	9,246	392' 01"	60' 10"	31' 03"
IS-17 — SOCIETE ANONYME MONEGASQUE D' ADMINISTRATION MARITIME ET AERIENNE, MONTE CARLO, MONACO							
Alpha	BC	1976	D	28,193	580' 00"	75' 02"	47' 11"
Gemini	BC	1977	D	27,106	585' 11"	75' 00"	47' 04"
Haight	BC	1977	D	26,779	580' 10"	75' 04"	47' 07"
Hydra	BC	1977	D	26,715	567' 08"	74' 10"	48' 05"
IS-18 — SOCIETE NATIONALE DE TRANSPORT MARITIME & COMPAGNIE NATIONALE ALGERIENNE DE NAVIGATION MARITIME, ALGIERS, ALGERIA							
Nememcha	BC	1978	D	26,145	565' 02"	75' 11"	47' 01"
IS-19 — SOENDERBORG REDERIAKTIESELSKAB, EGERNSUND, DENMARK							
Bison	GC	1977	D	1,370	238' 02"	43' 00"	22' 02"
IS-20 — SOHTORIK DENIZCILIK SANAYI VE TICARET A.S., ISTANBUL, TURKEY							
Duden	BC	1981	D	26,975	567' 07"	74' 11"	48' 05"
Eber	BC	1978	D	18,739	504' 07"	75' 01"	41' 00"
Med Transporter	BC	1973	D	21,570	510' 03"	75' 02"	44' 00"
Sapanca	BC	1975	D	19,030	506' 04"	75' 00"	41' 00"
IS-21 — SOLAR SCHIFFAHRTSGES MBH & CO. KG							
Argonaut	GC	1978	D	2,384	283' 10"	42' 09"	24' 11"
IS-22 — SPLIETHOFF'S BEVRACHTINGSKANTOOR LTD., AMSTERDAM, NETHERLANDS							
Bataafgracht	GC	1981	D	3,444	263' 02"	52' 10"	34' 06"
Bickersgracht	GC	1981	D	3,488	263' 02"	52' 10"	34' 06"
Bontegracht	BC	1981	D	3,437	263' 02"	52' 10"	34' 06"
Looiersgracht	GC	1987	D	9,606	371' 02"	63' 07"	37' 01"
Parkgracht	GC	1986	D	9,656	371' 02"	62' 03"	37' 01"
Poolgracht	GC	1986	D	9,672	371' 02"	62' 03"	37' 01"
MAMMOET SHIPPING B.V. - A DIVISION OF SPLIETHOFF'S BEVRACHTINGSKANTOOR LTD.							
Enchanter	HL	1998	D	16,069	452' 09"		
Happy Rover	HL	1997	D	13,000	418' 09"	74' 07"	42' 06"
Project Americas	HL	1979	D	12,811	455' 10"	70' 08"	42' 08"
Project Arabia	HL	1982	D	12,800	455' 11"	70' 08"	42' 08"
Project Europa	HL	1983	D	13,493	456' 02"	75' 02"	42' 08"
Project Orient	HL	1981	D	10,434	454' 07"	70' 08"	42' 08"
Thor Scan	HL	1982	D	9,800	404' 08"	67' 09"	33' 10"
Titan Scan	HL	1982	D	9,864	404' 08"	67' 11"	33' 10"
IS-23 — SPLIT SHIP MANAGEMENT LTD., SPLIT, CROATIA							
Alka	GC	1979	D	14,930	532' 07"	73' 00"	43' 11"
Bol	GC	1980	D	14,930	532' 07"	73' 00"	43' 11"
Hope I	BC	1982	D	30,900	617' 03"	76' 00"	47' 07"
Jelsa	GC	1977	D	13,450	532' 07"	73' 00"	43' 11"

Fleet No. & Name Vessel Name	Type of Vessel	Year Built	Type of Engine	Cargo Cap. or Gross*	Overal Length	Breadth	Depth or Draft*
Kairos	GC	1977	D	8,538	424' 03"	63' 02"	33' 08"
Kraljica Mira	RR	1965	D	752	283' 04"	53' 10"	17' 05"
Marjan I	GC	1978	D	13,450	532' 07"	73' 00"	43' 11"
Omis	GC	1977	D	13,450	532' 07"	73' 00"	43' 11"
Pharos	GC	1977	D	8,512	424' 03"	63' 02"	33' 08"
Solin	GC	1985	D	23,240	579' 05"	75' 00"	45' 11"
Solta	BC	1984	D	29,785	622' 00"	74' 11"	49' 10"
Split	GC	1981	D	22,042	585' 08"	75' 02"	46' 00"

IS-24 — SPRANTE SCHIFFAHRTS-VERWALTUNGS GMBH, BRUNSBUTTEL, GERMANY

St. George	GC	1979	D	7,309	395' 03"	57' 10"	32' 06"
St. Martin	GC	1980	D	7,250	395' 04"	57' 10"	32' 06"
St. Thomas	GC	1976	D	7,496	395' 07"	57' 10"	32' 06"
Topaz	GC	1975	D	4,798	288' 09"	42' 08"	25' 07"

IS-25 — STARLADY MARINE LTD., PIRAEUS, GREECE

Coral	BC	1981	D	24,482	605' 08"	75' 00"	46' 04"
Sunrise	BC	1971	D	20,930	550' 00"	74' 02"	41' 06"

IS-26 — STEPHENSON CLARKE SHIPPING LTD., NEWCASTLE ON TYNE, ENGLAND

Durrington	GC	1981	D	11,990	451' 05"	61' 03"	35' 01"

IS-27 — STEVNS LINE APS, SVENDBORG, DENMARK

Stevnsland	GC	1972	D	2,510	290' 04"	45' 05"	26' 03"

IS-28 — STFA MARITIME INDUSTRY & TRADING CO., ISTANBUL, TURKEY

Danis Koper	BC	1978	D	22,174	528' 00"	75' 02"	44' 04"

IS-29 — SUNLIGHT COMPANIA NAVIERA S.A., PIRAEUS, GREECE

Mariana	BC	1977	D	23,151	570' 07"	75' 02"	46' 00"
Stefanos	GC	1978	D	15,767	488' 03"	69' 00"	40' 03"

IS-30 — SUNNY SHORE SHIPPING FINANCE, HONG KONG

Lady Emily	GC	1988	D	17,506	520' 11"	74' 11"	44' 00"

IS-31 — SURRENDRA OVERSEAS LTD., CALCUTTA, INDIA

APJ Anand	BC	1977	D	16,882	459' 04"	73' 04"	41' 00"
APJ Angad	BC	1977	D	27,305	581' 08"	75' 02"	47' 11"
APJ Anjli	BC	1982	D	27,192	577' 05"	75' 11"	47' 11"
APJ Karan	BC	1977	D	27,305	581' 08"	75' 02"	47' 11"
APJ Priti	BC	1976	D	16,745	470' 05"	71' 10"	40' 01"
APJ Sushma	BC	1983	D	27,213	577' 05"	75' 11"	47' 11"

IT-1 — TARGET MARINE S.A., PIRAEUS, GREECE

Corithian Trader	BC	1973	D	27,398	599' 10"	73' 06"	46' 07"

IT-2 — TEO SHIPPING CORP., PIRAEUS, GREECE

Antalina	BC	1984	D	28,082	584' 08"	75' 11"	48' 05"
Erikousa Wave	BC	1986	D	26,858	600' 08"	73' 08"	46' 08"
Marilis T.	BC	1984	D	28,097	584' 08"	75' 11"	47' 10"
Sevilla Wave	BC	1986	D	26,858	600' 08"	73' 08"	46' 08"
Vamand Wave	BC	1985	D	28,303	580' 08"	75' 11"	47' 07"

IT-3 — THE SHIPPING CORP. OF INDIA LTD., BOMBAY, INDIA

Jhulelal	TK	1981	D		505' 03"	74' 07"	45' 04"
Lok Maheshwari	BC	1986	D	26,728	605' 03"	75' 03"	47' 03"
Lok Pragati	BC	1984	D	26,928	564' 11"	75' 00"	48' 03"
Lok Prakash	BC	1989	D	26,790	606' 11"	75' 04"	47' 03"
Lok Pratap	BC	1993	D	26,718	605' 09"	75' 04"	47' 04"
Lok Pratima	BC	1989	D	26,925	565' 00"	74' 11"	48' 03"
Lok Prem	BC	1990	D	26,714	605' 08"	75' 04"	47' 03"
Lok Rajeshwari	BC	1988	D	26,639	605' 08"	75' 04"	47' 03"
State of Haryana	GC	1983	D	16,799	465' 07"	75' 02"	47' 04"

IT-4 — THENAMARIS (SHIPS MANAGEMENT), INC., ATHENS, GREECE

Searanger II	BC	1976	D	29,300	594' 01"	76' 00"	47' 07"

IT-5 — THIEN & HEYENGA BEREEDERUNGS-UND BREFRACHTUNGSGESELLSCHAFT MBH, HAMBURG, GERMANY

Rantum	TK	1978	D	39,312	346' 00"	46' 09"	28' 03"

IT-6 — TOKUMARU KAIUN K.K., TOKYO, JAPAN

Golden Shield	TK	1982	D	88,594	416' 08"	65' 08"	36' 09"

Fleet No. & Name / Vessel Name	Type of Vessel	Year Built	Type of Engine	Cargo Cap. or Gross*	Overall Length	Breadth	Depth or Draft*
IT-7 — TOLANI SHIPPING CO. LTD., MUMBAI, INDIA							
Prabhu Daya	BC	1987	D	26,716	608' 11"	75' 04"	47' 03"
IT-8 — TOMASOS BROTHERS, INC., PIRAEUS, GREECE							
Alexis	BC	1984	D	27,048	599' 10"	75' 04"	42' 04"
IT-9 — TOMAZOS SHIPPING CO. LTD., PIRAEUS, GREECE							
Jeannie	BC	1977	D	27,541	600' 06"	74' 08"	47' 01"
Kalisti	BC	1977	D	27,540	600' 06"	74' 08"	47' 01"
Trias	BC	1977	D	38,568	729' 11"	76' 00"	47' 00"
IT-10 — TORKEL ALENDAL REDERI AS, KARMSUND, NORWAY							
Moon Trader	TK	1969	D	33,878	324' 10"	41' 04"	24' 11"
South Trader	TK	1974	D	41,262	339' 02"	52' 00"	27' 03"
Spirit Trader	TK	1975	D	18,819	317' 08"	39' 06"	23' 11"
IT-11 — TRANSMAN SHIPPING ENTERPRISES S.A., ATHENS, GREECE							
Luckyman	BC	1980	D	27,000	584' 08"	75' 10"	48' 05"
IU-1 — UNIMAR SHIP MANAGEMENT SERVICES S.A., ATHENS, GREECE							
Ocean Leader	BC	1981	D	27,125	627' 07"	75' 03"	44' 04"
IU-2 — UNION MARINE ENTERPRISES S.A. OF PANAMA, PIRAEUS, GREECE							
Capetan Michalis	BC	1981	D	28,600	593' 03"	75' 11"	47' 07"
IU-3 — UNIVAN SHIP MANAGEMENT LTD., HONG KONG							
Pathum Navee	GC	1972	D	20,814	515' 00"	75' 00"	44' 03"
IV-1 — V. SHIPS (CYPRUS) LTD., LIMASSOL, CYPRUS							
Cheetah	BC	1977	D	27,535	584' 08"	75' 02"	48' 03"
Lynx	BC	1978	D	29,536	584' 07"	75' 00"	48' 03"
IV-2 — V. SHIPS MARINE LTD., MINEOLA, NEW YORK							
Spear	GC	1983	D	5,233	379' 00"	57' 07"	29' 07"
IV-3 — V. SHIPS SHIPPING MANAGEMENT S.A.M., MONTE CARLO, MONACO							
Docegulf	BC	1979	D	30,689	674' 03"	75' 08"	47' 07"
IV-4 — VANGUARD ENTERPRISE CO. LTD., HIROSHIMA, JAPAN							
Moor Laker	BC	1984	D	27,915	584' 08"	69' 03"	48' 05"
IV-5 — VENTURE SHIPPING (MANAGERS) LTD., HONG KONG							
Rose Islands	BC	1984	D	15,175	472' 05"	67' 01"	38' 07"
IV-6 — VENUS SHIPPING CORP., MANILA, PHILIPPINES							
Baltic Confidence	BC	1979	D	17,686	481' 03"	75' 01"	40' 01"
IW-1 — WAGENBORG SHIPPING B.V., DELFZIJL, NETHERLANDS							
Arion	GC	1997	D	9,100	441' 04"	54' 02"	32' 02"
Egbert Wagenborg	GC	1998	D	9,100	441' 04"	54' 02"	32' 02"
Kasteelborg	GC	1998	D	9,025	428' 08"	52' 01"	33' 06"
Keizerborg	GC	1996	D	9,025	428' 08"	52' 01"	33' 06"
Koningsborg	GC	1999	D	9,025	428' 08"	52' 01"	33' 06"
Kroonborg	GC	1995	D	9,025	428' 08"	52' 01"	33' 06"
Markborg	GC	1997	D	9,100	441' 04"	54' 02"	32' 02"
Merweborg	GC	1998	D	9,100	441' 04"	54' 02"	32' 02"
Moezelborg	GC	1999	D	9,100	441' 04"	54' 02"	32' 02"
Morraborg	GC	1999	D	9,100	441' 04"	54' 02"	32' 02"
Munteborg	GC	1998	D	9,100	441' 04"	54' 02"	32' 02"
Musselborg	GC	1999	D	9,100	441' 04"	54' 02"	32' 02"
Vechtborg	GC	1998	D	8,300	434' 00"	52' 01"	31' 07"
Veerseborg	GC	1998	D	8,300	433' 09"	52' 01"	31' 07"
Vlieborg	GC	1999	D	8,300	434' 00"	52' 01"	31' 07"
Vlistborg	GC	1999	D	8,300	434' 00"	52' 01"	31' 07"
Voorneborg	GC	1999	D	8,300	434' 00"	52' 01"	31' 07"
IZ-1 — Z. & G. HALCOUSSIS CO. LTD., PIRAEUS, GREECE							
Agiodektini	BC	1977	D	18,611	500' 05"	75' 01"	41' 00"
Akti	BC	1977	D	28,935	593' 10"	76' 00"	47' 07"
Alexandria	BC	1981	D	29,372	589' 11"	76' 00"	47' 00"

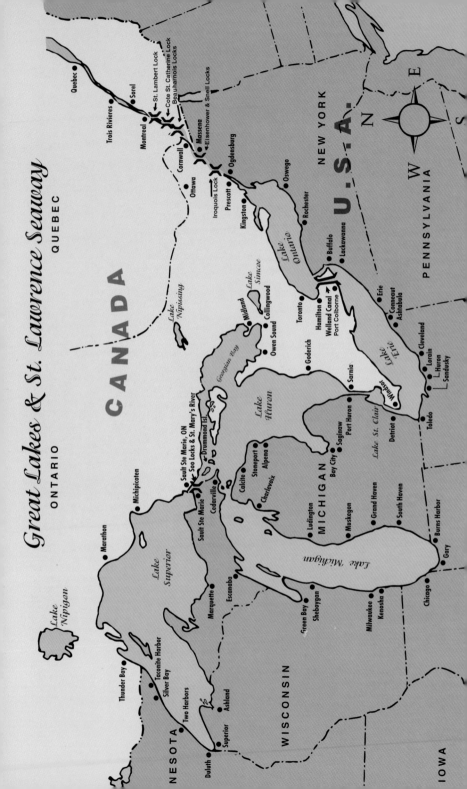

GREAT LAKES LOADING PORTS

Iron Ore	Limestone	Coal	Grain	Cement
Duluth	Port Inland	Superior	Thunder Bay	Charlevoix
Superior	Cedarville	Thunder Bay	Duluth	Alpena
Two Harbors	Drummond	Chicago	Milwaukee	
Taconite	Island	Toledo	Chicago	**Gypsum**
Harbor	Calcite	Sandusky	Saginaw	Port Gypsum
Marquette	Stoneport	Ashtabula	Sarnia	Alabaster
Escanaba	Marblehead	Conneaut	Toledo	

Petroleum

Sarnia
East Chicago

UNLOADING PORTS

The primary iron ore and limestone receiving ports are Cleveland, Lorain, Chicago, Gary, Burns and Indiana Harbors, Detroit, Toledo, Ashtabula and Conneaut. Coal is carried to Milwaukee, Green Bay and a host of smaller ports in the U.S. and Canada. Most grain loaded on the lakes is destined for export via the St. Lawrence Seaway. Cement is delivered to terminals stretching from Duluth to Buffalo. Tankers bring petroleum products to cities as diverse in size as Cleveland and Detroit or Escanaba and Muskegon.

Algogulf unloads at Indiana Harbor 10 October 1998.
(Gary R. Clark)

MEANINGS OF BOAT WHISTLES

1 SHORT: I am directing my course to starboard (right) for a port to port passing.

2 SHORT: I am directing my course to port (left) for a starboard to starboard passing.

5 OR MORE SHORT BLASTS SOUNDED RAPIDLY: Danger.

1 PROLONGED: Vessel leaving dock.

3 SHORT: Vessel moving astern.

1 PROLONGED, SOUNDED ONCE PER MINUTE: Vessel moving in fog.

1 SHORT, 1 PROLONGED, 1 SHORT: Vessel at anchor in fog.

3 PROLONGED and 2 SHORT: Salute.

1 PROLONGED and 2 SHORT: Master's salute.

BOOKING PASSAGE

Can the public book a trip on a laker? The answer is no. Great Lakes cargo vessels are not certified to carry passengers for hire. Some vessels do have guest quarters, but these are reserved for industry-related customers, technicians and others who have business on board. Occasionally, a charitable group may sell raffle tickets for a laker trip (see our home page for details), but that's about the only chance the public has for getting a ride.

Vessel in the Iroquois Lock shortly after the Seaway opened for traffic.
(St. Lawrence Seaway Authority)

ST. LAWRENCE SEAWAY

The St. Lawrence Seaway, celebrating its 40th anniversary in 1999, is a deep waterway extending some 2,038 miles (3,701.4 km) from the Atlantic Ocean to the head of the Great Lakes at Duluth, including Montreal harbor and the Welland Canal.

More specifically, it is the system of locks and canals (both U.S. and Canadian), opened in 1959, that allow vessels to pass from Montreal to the Welland Canal at the western end of Lake Ontario. The vessel size limit within this system is 740 feet (225.6 meters) long, 78 feet (23.8 meters) wide and 26 feet (7.9 meters) draft.

Closest to the ocean is the **St. Lambert Lock,** which lifts ships some 15 feet (4.6 meters) from Montreal harbor to the level of the Laprairie Basin, through which the channel sweeps in a great arc 8.5 miles (13.7 km) long to the second lock. The **Cote St. Catherine Lock,** like the other six St. Lawrence Seaway locks, is built to the following standard dimensions:

> **Length** .... 766 feet (233.5 meters)
> **Width** .... 80 feet (24.4 meters)
> **Depth** .... 30 feet (9.1 meters)

The Cote St. Catherine requires 24 million gallons (90.9 million liters) to fill and can be filled or emptied in less than 10 minutes. It lifts ships from the level of the Laprairie Basin 30 feet (9.1 meters) to the level of Lake St. Louis, bypassing the Lachine Rapids. Beyond it, the channel runs 7.5 miles (12.1 km) before reaching Lake St. Louis.

The **Lower Beauharnois Lock,** bypassing the Beauharnois Power House, lifts ships 41 feet (12.5 meters) and sends them through a short canal to the **Upper Beauharnois Lock**, where they are again lifted 41 feet (12.5 meters) to reach the level of the Beauharnois Canal. After a 13-mile (20.9 km) trip in the canal, and a 30 mile (48.3 km) voyage through Lake St. Francis, vessels reach the U.S. border and the **Snell Lock,** which has a lift of 45 feet (13.7 meters) and empties into the 10-mile (16.1 km) long Wiley-Dondero Canal. After passing through Wiley-Dondero, ships are raised another 38 feet (11.6 meters) by the **Dwight D. Eisenhower Lock,** after which they enter Lake St. Lawrence, the pool upon which nearby HEPCO and PASNY generating stations draw for their turbines located a mile to the north.

At the Western end of Lake St. Lawrence, the **Iroquois Lock** allows ships to bypass the Iroquois Control Dam. The lift here is only about one foot (.3 meters).

Once in the waters west of Iroquois, the channel meanders through the scenic Thousand Islands to Lake Ontario, the Welland Canal and eventually, to Lake Erie.

WELLAND CANAL

The 26-mile long (42 km) **Welland Canal,** built to bypass nearby Niagara Falls, overcomes a difference in water level of 326.5 feet (99.5 meters) between lakes Erie and Ontario.

The first Welland Canal opened in 1829; the present canal opened officially in 1932 with the passage of the steamer **Lemoyne**.

Each of the seven Welland Canal locks has an average lift of 46.5 feet (14.2 meters). Locks 1-7 are lift locks, while Lock 8 is a regulating lock making the final adjustment to Lake Erie's level. Locks 4, 5 and 6 are twinned and placed end to end, looking like giant stair-steps. All locks (except Lock 8) are 829 feet (261.8 meters) in length, 80 feet (24.4 meters) wide and 30 feet (9.1 meters) deep. All locks (except Lock 8) are 829 feet (261.8 meters) in length, 80 feet (24.4 meters) wide and 30 feet (9.1 meters) deep. The maximum sized vessel that may transit the canal is 740 feet (225.6 meters) in length, 78 feet (24.4 meters) wide and 26 feet (7.9 meters) in draft. Connecting channels are kept at a minimum of 27 feet (8.2 meters), allowing vessels drawing 26 feet (7.9 meters) fresh water draft to transit the canal. The average transit time for the Welland Canal is about 12 hours. Vessels transiting the Welland Canal and St. Lawrence Seaway must carry a qualified pilot; pilot boats are a familiar sight at either end of the Welland Canal.

Locks 1, 2 and **3** are at St. Catharines. At Lock 3, the Welland Canal Viewing Center and Museum houses an information desk (with a list of vessels expected at the lock), a gift shop and a restaurant.

At Thorold, the twinned **locks 4, 5** and **6**, are controlled with an elaborate interlocking system for safety. The flight locks have an aggregate lift of 139.5 feet (42.5 meters) and are similar to the Gatun Locks on the Panama Canal. Just south of the flight locks is **Lock 7**, while **Lock 8** at Port Colborne completes the process, making the final adjustment to Lake Erie's level. A park and visitor information center adjoin Lock 8.

In 1973, a new channel was constructed to replace the section of the canal which bisected the city Welland. The bypass eliminated delays to ship navigation, road and rail traffic.

Vessels transiting the Welland Canal and St. Lawrence Seaway locks pay tolls based on registered tonnage and cargo on-board.

There are also 11 railway and highway bridges crossing the Welland Canal. The most significant are the landmark vertical lift bridges which provide clearance above the water of 126 feet (36.6 meters) for vessels passing underneath. Tunnels at Thorold and South Welland allow automobile traffic to pass beneath the waterway.

All vessel traffic though the Welland Canal is regulated by a control center. Upbound vessels must call Seaway Welland off Port Weller on VHF Ch. 14 (156.700 Mhz), while downbound vessels are required to make contact off Port Colborne.

Manitoulin in the Welland Canal. (John C. Knecht)

SOO LOCKS & St. Mary's River

Soo Locks

MacArthur Lock

Named after World War II Gen. Douglas MacArthur, the MacArthur lock measures 800 feet (243.8 meters) long between inner gates, 80 feet (24.4 meters) wide and 31 feet (9.4 meters) deep over the sills. The lock was built by the U.S in the years 1942-43 and opened to traffic 11 July 1943. The maximum sized vessel that can transit the MacArthur Lock is 730 feet (222.5 meters) long by 75 feet (22.9 meters) wide. In emergencies, this limit may be exceeded for vessels up to 767 feet (233.8 meters) in length.

Poe Lock

The Poe Lock is 1,200 feet (365.8 meters) long, 110 feet (33.5 meters) wide and has a depth over the sills of 32 feet (9.8 meters). Named after Col. Orlando M. Poe, it was built by the U.S. in the years 1961-68. The lock's vessel limit is 1,100 feet (335.3 meters) long by 105 feet (32 meters) wide, and it is the only lock now capable of handling vessels of that size. There are currently 30 vessels sailing the lakes restricted by size to the Poe Lock.

Davis Lock

Named after Col. Charles E.L.B. Davis, the Davis Lock measures 1,350 feet (411.5 meters) long between inner gates, 80 feet (24.4 meters) wide and 23 feet (7 meters) deep over the sills. It was built by the U.S. in the years 1908-14 and now sees very limited use due to its shallow depth.

Sabin Lock

Measuring the same as the Davis Lock, the Sabin Lock was built from 1913-19. Named after L.C. Sabin, the lock is currently inactive.

St. Mary's River

Connecting Lake Superior with Lake Huron, the 80-mile (128.7 km) long St. Mary's River is a beautiful waterway that includes breathtaking scenery, picturesque islands and more than its share of hazardous twists and turns.

Remote Isle Parisienne marks its beginning; the equally-lonely DeTour Reef Light marks its end. In between, are two marvels of engineering, the West Neebish Cut, a channel literally dynamited out of solid rock, and the Soo Canal, which stands where Native Americans in dugout canoes once challenged the St. Mary's Rapids. Vessels in the St. Mary's River system are under control of the U.S. Coast Guard at Sault Ste. Marie, and are required to check in with Soo Traffic on VHF Ch.12 (156.600 Mhz) at various locations in the river. In the vicinity of the locks, they fall under jurisdiction of the Lockmaster, who must be contacted on VHF Ch. 14 (156.700 Mhz) for transit reports, lock assignments and other instructions.

The first lock was built on the Canadian side of the river by the Northwest Fur Co. in 1797-98. That lock was 38 feet (11.6 meters) long and barely 9 feet (2.7 meters) wide.

The first ship canal on the American side, known as the State Canal, was built from 1853-55 by engineer Charles T. Harvey. There were two tandem locks on masonry, each 350 feet (106.7 meters) long by 70 feet (21.3 meters) wide, with a lift of about 9 feet (2.7 meters). ▶

Middletown is at the upper pool (Lake Superior) level, while Algocape locks downbound to the level of Lake Huron.

(Roger LeLievre)

The locks were destroyed in 1888 by workers making way for the larger canals of the future.

Discussion continues about building a new lock in the space now occupied by the inactive Davis and Sabin locks. It would relieve the pressure on the Poe, the only lock which is able to handle vessels more than 730 feet long.

The Canadian Canal

The present Canadian lock was constructed in 1887-95 through St. Mary's Island on the north side of the St. Mary's Rapids. It is the most westerly canal on the Seaway route. It was cut through red sandstone and is 7,294 feet (2,223.4 meters), or about 1.4 miles (2.2 km) long, from end to end of upper and lower piers.

The lock itself is 900 feet (274.3 meters) long, 60 feet (18.3 meters) wide and 21 feet (6.4 meters) deep. The approaches above and below the lock were dredged through boulder shoals.

Collapse of a lock wall in 1987 closed the historic Canadian canal, however repairs enabled the lock to reopen for pleasure craft traffic in 1998.

All traffic through the Soo Locks is passed toll-free. Locks in the Seaway system operate on gravity - no pumps are needed. Maintenance on the locks is done during the winter, when the chambers are then pumped dry.

Roger Blough moves downbound through the Poe Lock at the Soo. The view is from the Lockmaster's tower. *(Roger LeLievre)*

FOLLOWING THE FLEET

Prerecorded messages help track vessel arrivals and departures.

Algoma Central Marine	**905-708-3873**	ACM vessel movements
Boatwatcher's Hotline	**218-722-6489**	Superior,WI, Duluth, Two Harbors, Taconite Harbor and Silver Bay, MN
CSX Coal Docks/Torco Dock	**419-697-2304**	Toledo, OH, arrivals
DMIR Ore Dock	**218-628-4590**	Duluth, MN, arrivals
DMIR Ore Dock	**218-834-8190**	Two Harbors, MN, arrivals
Eisenhower Lock	**315-769-2422**	Eisenhower Lock vessel movements
Inland Lakes Management	**517-354-4400**	ILM fleet movements
Lorain Pellet Terminal	**440-244-2054**	Vessel arrivals at the LTV dock
Michigan Limestone Docks	**517-734-2117**	Rogers City / Cedarville, MI arrivals
Oglebay Norton Co.	**800-861-8760**	O-N Vessel movements
Presque Isle Corp.	**517-595-6611**	Stoneport, MI, arrivals
Soo Control	**906-635-3224**	Previous day's traffic - St. Mary's River
Superior Midwest Energy Terminal	**715-395-3559**	Superior, WI, arrivals
Thunder Bay Port Authority	**807-345-1256**	Thunder Bay, ON, arrivals
USS Great Lakes Fleet	**218-628-4389**	USS fleet movements
ULS Group	**905-688-5878**	ULS vessel movements
Welland Canal	**905-688-6462**	Welland Canal vessel movements

With a VHF scanner, boatwatchers can tune to ship-to-ship and ship-to-shore traffic, using the following guide.

Commercial vessels only	**Ch. 13** (156.650 Mhz)	**Bridge to Bridge Communications**
Calling / Distress ONLY	**Ch. 16** (156.800 Mhz)	**Calling / Distress ONLY**
Commercial vessels only	**Ch. 06** (156.300 Mhz)	**Working Channel**
Commercial vessels only	**Ch. 08** (156.400 Mhz)	**Working Channel**
Supply boat at Soo	**Ch. 08** (156.400 Mhz)	**Soo Supply Warehouse**
Detour Reef to Lake St. Clair Light	**Ch. 11** (156.550 Mhz)	**Sarnia Traffic - Sector 1**
Long Point Light to Lake St. Clair Light	**Ch. 12** (156.600 Mhz)	**Sarnia Traffic - Sector 2**
Montreal to about mid-Lake St. Francis	**Ch. 14** (156.700 Mhz)	**Seaway Beauharnois - Sector 1**
Mid-Lake St. Francis to Bradford Island	**Ch. 12** (156.600 Mhz)	**Seaway Eisenhower - Sector 2**
Bradford Island to Crossover Island	**Ch. 11** (156.550 Mhz)	**Seaway Iroquois - Sector 3**
Crossover Island to Cape Vincent	**Ch. 13** (156.650 Mhz)	**Seaway Clayton - Sector 4** *St. Lawrence River portion*
Cape Vincent to mid-Lake Ontario	**Ch. 13** (156.650 Mhz)	**Seaway Sodus - Sector 4** *Lake Ontario portion*
Mid-Lake Ontario to Welland Canal	**Ch. 11** (156.550 Mhz)	**Seaway Newcastle - Sector 5**
Welland Canal	**Ch. 14** (156.700 Mhz)	**Seaway Welland - Sector 6**
Welland Canal to Long Point Light Lake Erie	**Ch. 11** (156.550 Mhz)	**Seaway Long Point - Sector 7**
St. Mary's River Traffic Service	**Ch. 12** (156.600 Mhz)	**Soo Traffic**
Lockmaster, Soo Locks	**Ch. 14** (156.700 Mhz)	**Soo Lockmaster (call WUE-21)**
Coast Guard traffic	**Ch. 21** (157.050 Mhz)	**United States Coast Guard**
Coast Guard traffic	**Ch. 22** (157.100 Mhz)	**United States Coast Guard**
U.S. Mailboat, Detroit, MI	**Ch. 10** (156.500 Mhz)	**J. W. Westcott II**

Lakes and Seaway on the Web

A virtual treasure trove of maritime web sites are now available on the Internet, connecting to just about everything imaginable concerning ships and shipping on the lakes and Seaway. To start, visit **www.boatnerd.com**, the Great Lakes' shipping home page. In addition to maintaining its own sites for vessel news and rumors, vessel passages, winter lay-up ports, upcoming Great Lakes events and photos of Great Lakes vessels, Boatnerd links to hundreds of shipping-related addresses on the Web. Among them are links to marine museums and historic vessels, Great Lakes shipwrecks (the **Edmund Fitzgerald** has nearly a dozen sites), lighthouses, port cities, Great Lakes area newspapers, the mailboat **J.W. Westcott II**, Great Lakes carferries, the Soo Locks and Welland Canal, and the home pages of various Great Lakes and Seaway shipping companies.

While on the Web, we invite you to visit this book's home page at **www.knowyourships.com** and click on the Update button (use the password "BOATNEWS" to enter) for vessel changes announced after "Know Your Ships" went to press. Marine Publishing Co. also sells a wide range of Great Lakes shipping-related books, videos, photographs and other items. Included is a complete list, information about how to order and links to dozens of other Great Lakes and Seaway sites.

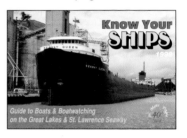

Newsgroups

There are two newsgroups of Great Lakes interest on line where visitors may exchange information, ask questions or post opinions on a variety of related (and sometimes unrelated) topics. These are **alt.great-lakes** and **misc.transport.marine**.

In Print

To track vessel news, information and rumors in more traditional ways, join one or more of the marine societies around the lakes (send a stamped, self-addressed envelope to **Marine Publishing Co.** for a free list including addresses and subscription rates). In particular, the Great Lakes Maritime Institute, the Marine Historical Society of Detroit, the Toronto Marine Historical Society and the Great Lakes Historical Society offer long-standing and informative publications.

WELCOME
ABOARD . . .

The Museum Ship
VALLEY CAMP

2 blocks from the locks
Sault Ste. Marie, MI

906-632-3658 or 1-888-744-7867
Open for Tours ~ See page 140 for details

VESSEL MUSEUMS

A-Admission fee; **T**-Tours; **G**-Gift Shop

(Information subject to change; museum hours and days open can be irregular. Please phone ahead.)

Vessel Name	Year Built	Type of Engine	Cargo Cap. or Gross*	Length	Beam	Depth or Draft*
Willis B. Boyer	1911	T	15,000	617' 00"	64' 00"	33' 01"

Willis B. Boyer

(Col. James M. Schoonmaker '11 - '69)
Built for the now-defunct Shenango Furnace fleet, this former Cleveland Cliffs Steamship Co. bulk carrier last operated 17 December 1980 and opened as a museum at Toledo, OH, in 1987. ***419-936-3070 - A,T,G** - open all year; call for winter hours.*

City of Milwaukee
1931   R   26 cars 360' 00"   56' 03"   21' 06"

Owned by the nonprofit Society for the Preservation of the S.S. City of Milwaukee, this former Lake Michigan rail and passenger ferry is under conversion to a museum at Elberta, MI. She is open to members by special arrangement for work activities, fireworks and other events. *To join, write to S.P.C.M., P.O. Box 506, Beulah, MI 49617.*

Cobia
1943   D   1,500*   312' 00"   27' 00"   15' 00"

Former U.S.Navy Emergency Program (Gato) class submarine (SS / AGSS-245) is currently a museum vessel in Manitowoc, WI, operated by the Wisconsin Maritime Museum. ***920-684-0218 - A,G,T** - open all year.*

Cod
1943   D   1,500*   312' 00"   27' 00"   15' 00"

Former U.S. Navy Albacore (Gato) class submarine (SS / AGSS / IXSS-224 is currently a museum vessel in Cleveland, OH, operated by the Great Lakes Historical Society. ***216-566-8770 - A,T,G** - May 1-Labor Day (tour restrictions may apply).*

Croaker
1942   D   1,526*   311' 09"   27' 00"   15' 03"

Former U.S. Navy Emergency Program (Gato) class submarine (SS / SSK / AGSS / IXSS-246) is open to the public at the Naval and Serviceman's Park Museum in Buffalo, NY. ***716-847-1773 - A,T,G -** April-Nov.*

Edna G.
1896   R   154*   102' 00"   23' 00"   14' 06"

Steam tug served the Duluth, Missabe & Iron Range Railway for almost 100 years. Refurbished in 1994, and opened to the public at Two Harbors, MN, in 1996 by the Lake County Historical Society. ***218-834-4898 -A-** seasonal.*

Fraser
1957   T   2,585*   366' 00"   42' 00"   19' 08"

Former Royal Canadian Navy St. Laurent (Rover) class helicopter-carrying frigate (DDE/DDH-233) was decommissioned in 1994. She is open to the public at Bridgewater, NS. ***902-624-1557.***

Haida
1943   T   2,000*   377' 00"   37' 06"   11' 02"

Former Royal Canadian Navy Tribal class destroyer (G63 / 215) is now a museum at Ontario Place in Toronto, ON. ***416-314-9900 -A,T,G-** late May-mid-Oct.*

Alexander Henry
1959   D   1,674*   210' 00"   44' 00"   17' 09"

Ex-Canadian Coast Guard icebreaker, retired from service in 1985 and now owned by the Marine Museum of the Great Lakes at Kingston, ON, is open for tours and as a bed and breakfast from May-September. The adjacent marine museum is open year-'round. ***613-542-2261 - A,T,G***

Huron
1921   D   392*   97' 00"   27' 00"   10' 00"

The lightship **Huron,** built in 1921 and the last of its kind on the Great Lakes, guided mariners into lower Lake Huron for 50 years. Owned by the City of Port Huron Museum ▶

of Arts & History, the vessel is docked at Pine Grove Park in Port Huron. *810-985-7101 - A,T - mid-May-Sept.*

William A. Irvin   1938   T   14,050   610' 09"   60' 00"   32' 06"

Former United States Steel Corp. flagship, which last operated 16 December 1978, became a museum in Duluth, MN, in 1986, operated by the Duluth and Area Convention Center. Also on display is the former Corps of Engineers' tug **Lake Superior** *(Major Emil H. Block '43 - '47, US Army LT-18 '47 - '50). 218-722-7876 - A,T,G - late spring-fall.*

Keewatin   1907   Q   3,856*   346' 00"   43' 08"   26' 06"

Passenger steamer sailed for the Canadian Pacific Railway from 1907 until 1965, and opened as a museum at Douglas, MI, in 1968. Also on display is the steam tug **Reiss** *(Q. A. Gillmore '13 - '32). 616-857-2464 or 616-857-2107 - A,T,G - Memorial Day-Labor Day.*

Ernest Lapointe   1940   R   1,675*   185' 00"   36' 00"   22' 06"

Retired icebreaker is the centerpiece of the Bernier Maritime Museum at L'Islet-Sur-Mer, PQ. The retired tug **Daniel McAllister** is also on display. *418-247-5001 - A - open all year.*

Maj. Elisha K. Henson   1943   D   249*   114' 00"   26' 00"   14' 00"

The former U.S. Army Corps of Engineers tug *Nash,* operated by the H. Lee White Marine Museum in Oswego, NY, is the only known surviving such vessel associated with D-Day. **Derrick Barge No. 8** is also on display. *315-342-0480 - A,G- May-Sept.*

Little Rock   1945   T   10,000*   610' 01"   66' 04"   25' 00"

Former US Navy Cleveland class cruiser (CL-92 / CLG-4) is open to the public at the Naval and Serviceman's Park Museum in Buffalo, NY. *716-847-1773 - A,T,G - April-Nov.*

Maple   1939   D   350*   122' 03"   27' 00"   7' 06"

Former U.S. Coast Guard lighthouse tender, which served as the EPA research vessel *Roger R. Simons* from 1973-1991, is now open as a museum in St. Ignace, MI., owned by the Great Lakes Center for Marine History. *517-321-3590 - Seasonal.*

William G. Mather   1925   T   13,950   618' 00"   62' 00"   32' 00"

Former flagship of the Cleveland-Cliffs Iron Co. fleet last sailed in 1980, and was donated to the city of Cleveland for use as a marine museum in 1987. Operated by Harbor Heritage Society, she is moored adjacent to the Rock and Roll Hall of Fame. *216-574-6262 - A,T,G - May-Oct.*

Meteor   1896   R   4,635   380' 00"   45' 00"   26' 00"

(Frank Rockefeller 1896 - '28, South Park '28 - '43)

The **Meteor**, built in 1896 as a bulk carrier, was converted in 1927 for use in the sand and gravel trade. In 1936, she was altered to carry autos and grain. Rebuilt as a tanker and given her present name in 1943, she was retired in 1969, and brought to Superior's Barker's Island for use as a museum by Head of the Lakes Maritime Society in 1973. The Meteor is the last surviving example of the "whaleback" vessel design popular on the lakes a century ago. The dipper dredge **Col. D.D. Gaillard** is also on display. *715-392-1083. - A,T,G - May-mid-Oct.*

Milwaukee Clipper   1904   Q   4,272   361' 00"   45' 00"   28' 00"

(Juniata '04 - '41, Milwaukee Clipper '41 - '70, Clipper '70-'93)

Former Wisconsin & Michigan Steamship Co. passenger and auto ferry last operated in 1970. Now owned by the Great Lakes Clipper Preservation Association, she is awaiting conversion to a visitor attraction at Muskegon, MI. *Donations needed; write to P.O. Box 1370, Muskegon, MI 49443, or call (616) 744-5101.*

Niagara   SAIL   493*   119' 00"   30' 00"   9' 00"

Former U.S. Navy brigantine, Commodore Oliver Hazard Perry's flagship in the War of 1812's Battle of Lake Erie, is rebuilt and open to the public at Erie, PA, courtesy of the Pennsylvania Historical and Museum Commission. From the Niagara's decks, Perry proclaimed "We have met the enemy and they are ours." *814-452-2744 - A,T - (phone ahead to make sure ship is in port).*

▶

Norgoma   1950   D   1,477*   188' 00"   37' 06"   22' 06"

Built in 1950 for the Owen Sound Transportation Co., **Norgoma** served the Georgian Bay-Sault Ste. Marie area in freight and passenger service until its retirement in 1974. She is open to the public at the St. Mary's River Marine Centre, Roberta Bondar Park, on the Sault Ste. Marie, ON, waterfront. *705-256-7447 - A,T,G - mid-April - Oct.*

Norisle   1946   R   1,668*   215' 09"   36' 03"   16' 00"

Former Georgian Bay-area passenger and freight carrier, operated by the Owen Sound Transportation Co., was retired from service in 1974. Owned by the Township of Assiginak, ON, the Norisle is now open to the public at Manitowaning, ON, on Manitoulin Island. *No phone number available. - A,T - June 1-Labor Day.*

Sackville   1941   T   1,170*   208' 00"   33' 00"   17' 06"

Former Royal Canadian Navy Flower Class corvette (K-181) was decommissioned in 1982. She is operated as a museum by the Canadian Naval Memorial Trust at Halifax, NS. *902-429-2132.*

Silversides   1941   D   1,525*   312' 00"   27' 00"   33' 09"

Former U.S. Navy submarine is open for public viewing at Muskegon, MI. Also on display is the **McLane,** a 125', former U.S. Coast Guard Buck & A Quarter class medium endurance cutter. *616-755-1230 - A,T- April-October.*

The Sullivans   1943   T   2,050*   376' 05"   39' 07"   33' 09"

Former U.S. Navy Fletcher class destroyer (DD-537) is a museum at Buffalo, NY. *716-847-1773 - A,T,G - April-Nov.*

U-505   1941   D   1,178*   252' 00"   22' 00"   15' 06"

Chicago's Museum of Science and Industry (57th Street at Lakeshore Drive) houses this former German Type IX C submarine, captured by the U.S. Navy in the Atlantic Ocean off Africa in 1944. *773-684-1414 - T - open all year.*

Valley Camp {2}   1917   R   12,000   550' 00"   58' 00"   31' 00"
(Louis W. Hill '17 - '55)

The 1917-built steamer, which last sailed in 1966 for the Republic Steel Co., is home to an extensive museum at Sault Ste. Marie, MI (Johnston at Water streets). Dedicated in 1968 by Le Sault de Sainte Marie Historic Sites, her vast cargo holds house artifacts, ship models, aquariums, photos and other memorabilia, as well as a tribute to the **Edmund Fitzgerald** that includes the ill-fated vessel's lifeboats. *906-632-3658 or 1-888-744-7867 - A,T,G - May 15-Oct.15.*

MARINE MUSEUMS

Antique Boat Museum *(750 Mary St., Clayton, NY)*
An impressive collection of historic freshwater boats and engines. Annual boat show is the first weekend of August. *315-686-4104 - A-G - May 15-Oct. 15.*

Canal Park Marine Museum *(On the waterfront, Duluth, MN)*
Operating steam engine, full-size replicas of cabins as found on Great Lakes ships, and hands-on exhibits. Also on display: the retired U.S. Army Corps of Engineers harbor tug **Bayfield.** *Operated by the U.S. Army Corps of Engineers - 218-722-6489 - open all year.*

Collingwood Museum *(Memorial Park - St. Paul Street), Collingwood, ON)*
More than 100 years of shipbuilding, illustrated with models, photos and videos. *705-445-4811 - A,G - Open all year.*

Door County Maritime Museum *(120 N. Madison St., Sturgeon Bay, WI)*
Located in the former offices of the Roen Steamship Co., exhibits portray the role shipbuilding has played in the Door Peninsula. Refurbished pilothouse on display. *920-743-5958 - A - Open all year.* ▶

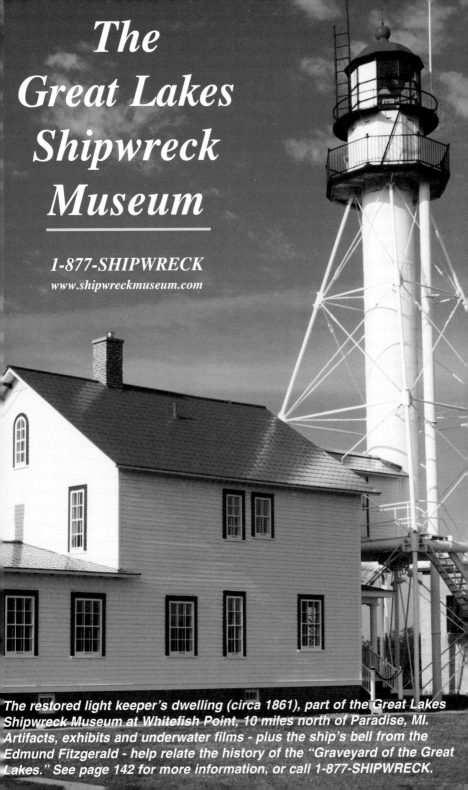

The Great Lakes Shipwreck Museum

1-877-SHIPWRECK

www.shipwreckmuseum.com

The restored light keeper's dwelling (circa 1861), part of the Great Lakes Shipwreck Museum at Whitefish Point, 10 miles north of Paradise, MI. Artifacts, exhibits and underwater films - plus the ship's bell from the Edmund Fitzgerald - help relate the history of the "Graveyard of the Great Lakes." See page 142 for more information, or call 1-877-SHIPWRECK.

Dossin Great Lakes Museum *(100 The Strand, Belle Isle, Detroit, MI)*
Ship models, photographs, interpretive displays, the smoking room from the 1912 passenger steamer
City of Detroit III, an anchor from the **Edmund Fitzgerald** and the working pilothouse from the steamer
William Clay Ford are just a few of the museum's attractions. *313-852-4051 - A (donations), G - open all year.*

Fairport Harbor Marine Museum *(129 Second St., Fairport, OH)*
Located in the Fairport Lighthouse and established in 1945, this museum's displays include the pilothouse
from the lake carrier **Frontenac,** the mainmast of the first **U.S.S. Michigan** and items pertaining to the
history of Fairport Harbor. *440-354-4825 - late May-Labor Day.*

Fathom Five National Marine Park *(On the waterfront, Tobermory, ON)*
Underwater maritime park encompasses 19 of the area's 26 shipwrecks, two of which can be seen from a
glass-bottom boat. *519-596-2233 - A - April-mid-Nov.*

Great Lakes Historical Society *(480 Main St., Vermilion, OH)*
Museum tells the story of the Great Lakes through ship models, paintings, exhibits and artifacts, including
engines and other machinery. Pilothouse of retired laker **Canopus** and a replica of the Vermilion lighthouse are on display. *216-967-3467 - A,G - museum open year 'round.* An affiliated operation is the **USS
Cod** (see vessel above).

Great Lakes Marine & U.S. Coast Guard Memorial Museum *(1071-73 Walnut Blvd.,
Ashtabula, OH)*
Housed in the 1898-built former lighthouse keepers' residence, the museum includes models, paintings,
artifacts, photos, the world's only working scale model of a Hulett ore unloading machine and the pilothouse from the steamer **Thomas Walters**. *216-964-6847 - A (donations) - T,G - Memorial Day-Oct. 31.*

Great Lakes Shipwreck Museum *(Whitefish Point, MI)*
Located next to the Whitefish Point lighthouse, the museum houses lighthouse and shipwreck artifacts, a
shipwreck video theater and an **Edmund Fitzgerald** display that includes the ship's bell. *906-635-1742 or
800-635-1742 -A,G - May 15-Oct. 15.*

Marquette Maritime Museum *(East Ridge & Lakeshore Dr., Marquette, MI)*
Contained in an 1890s waterworks building, the museum recreates the offices of the first commercial
fishing and passenger freight companies. Displays also include charts, photos, models and maritime
artifacts. *906-226-2006 - A - May 31-Sept. 30.*

Michigan Maritime Museum *(off I-196 at Dyckman Ave., South Haven, MI)*
Exhibits are dedicated to the U.S. Lifesaving Service and U.S. Coast Guard. Displays tell the story of
various kinds of boats and their uses on the Great Lakes. *616-637-8078 - A,G - open all year.*

Owen Sound Marine-Rail Museum *(1165 First Ave., Owen Sound, ON)*
Museum depicts the history of each industry (but leans more toward the marine end) through displays,
models and photos. *519-371-3333 - A - seasonal*

The Pier *(245 Queens Quay W, Toronto, ON)*
Exhibits detail the development of the shipping industry from sail to steam on the Great Lakes and St.
Lawrence Seaway, with a special focus on Toronto. The 79-foot steam tug **Ned Hanlan,** built in 1932, is
also on display. *1-888-675-7437 - A,T,G - open all year.*

Port Colborne Historical & Marine Museum *(280 King St., Port Colborne, ON)*
Wheelhouse from the steam tug **Yvonne Dupre Jr.,** anchor from the propeller ship **Raleigh,** and a
lifeboat from the steamer **Hochelaga** are among the museum's displays. *905-834-7604 - free - May-Dec.*

Sunken Treasures Maritime Museum *(off Hwy, 32, Port Washington, WI)*
Many artifacts recovered from Lake Michigan shipwrecks are on display. *May 1-Sept. 30*

U.S. Army Corps of Engineers Museum *(inside the Soo Locks Visitor
Center, E. Portage Avenue, Sault Ste. Marie, MI)*
Exhibits include a working model of the Soo Locks, photos and a 25-minute film. Also, three observation
decks adjacent to the MacArthur Lock provide an up-close view of ships locking through. *906-632-3311-
free - May-Nov. Check at the information desk for a list of vessels expected at the locks.*

Welland Canal Visitor Center *(At Lock 3, Welland Canal, Thorold, ON)*
Museum traces the development of the Welland Canal. *905-984-8880 - G - museum open year 'round.
Observation deck open during the navigation season. Check at the information desk for vessels expected
at Lock 3.*

Wisconsin Maritime Museum *(75 Maritime Dr., Manitowoc, WI)*
Displays explore the history of area shipbuilding, and also honor submariners and submarines built in
Manitowoc during World War 2. See **Cobia** (above). *920-684-0218 - A,G,T - open all year.*

City of Milwaukee at Elberta, MI. (Andy Laborde)